CW00894163

A SCRIBBLER IN SOHO

*A Celebration
of Auberon Waugh*

A SCRIBBLER IN SOHO

A Celebration of Auberon Waugh

AN ANTHOLOGY,
WITH COMMENTARY BY NAIM ATTALLAH

QUARTET BOOKS

First published in 2019 by Quartet Books Limited
A member of the Namara Group
27 Goodge Street, London, W1T 2LD

A catalogue record for this book is available from the British Library

ISBN 9780704374577

Typeset by Tetragon, London
Printed and bound in Great Britain by TJ International Ltd, Padstow, Cornwall

To David Elliott

For his friendship and support over the years and for his part in making publishing and writing for me more pleasurable and enriching pastimes than I ever thought possible.

NAIM ATTALLAH

Contents

Another damned, thick, square book!
Always scribble, scribble, scribble! Eh! Mr Gibbon?
WILLIAM HENRY, 1ST DUKE OF GLOUCESTER
(also attributed to the
Duke of Cumberland and King George III)

'Scribble, scribble, scribble, Mr Waugh.'
JEREMY THORPE,
outside the Minehead Magistrate's Court,
Autumn 1978

Foreword

THE DEATH OF AUBERON WAUGH IN JANUARY 2001 RADICALLY changed my life. Over the years we had known each other, he had become my cherished friend, my mentor in many ways and, above all, my hero. I admired him for his wit, his charming contrariness and his vision of the world, which to him was an amalgam of insanity and impertinence.

From the sublime to the ridiculous, he used words as an art form, weaving them into masterpieces of comedy and satire. When affronted by some outrage, his criticism could be deadly but his judgements were delivered with style. Fiercely loyal to his friends, his rancour towards his foes was legendary. Yet kindness was to be found lurking behind the comically harsh way he often expressed himself, even making light of the hypocrisy he so abhorred.

I miss him, especially when I see the mediocrity we are surrounded by in today's world. What a field day Bron would have had pronouncing on the current state of affairs in his unique way. When I look around, I see no one who comes close to possessing his gift with the pen.

This book about Bron is but a small testimony to what a giant he was. His memory will never leave me and I rejoice that I had the privilege of enjoying his company and knowing him so well. I can still hear outpourings of his priceless wisdom being swallowed up in explosions of hilarity.

Bron was my idol and I shall always owe him a great deal.

NAIM ATTALLAH

Overture

The Bohemian Condition

'Here, at all events, are to be found some true bohemians. For bohemia is not the name of a country, or a place, or even of "a quarter", but is that of a condition, a state of mind and heart, the outward expression of a temperament that revels in the joy of life.'

ROBERT MACHRAY,
The Night Side of London (1902)

I T WAS AUBERON WAUGH'S GRANDFATHER, ARTHUR WAUGH, WHO started off the Waugh/Soho connection when, as chairman of Chapman & Hall, he commissioned and published Arthur Ransome's *Bohemia in London* (1907). Though, to be strictly accurate, establishing such a link was not part of his grandfather's initial plan.

According to Ransome, he was having tea with G. K. Chesterton's brother, Cecil, also a journalist, at the St George's Café in St Martin's Lane, when a literary agent, one Stefana Stevens, a 'clever young woman' who worked for Curtis Brown, a brash American-style literary agency only seven years established, leant across his table and said: 'There's a book to be written, and you are the one to write it, a book on bohemia in London, an essayistical sort of book, putting bohemia of today against a background of the past. Think it over ... I've got a publisher waiting for it.'

Ransome produced a synopsis the next day and two days later signed the contract Curtis Brown had negotiated with Chapman & Hall. A deal with the American publisher Dodd, Mead sold for 'respectable royalties' and Ransome, plus crates of books from the London Library, went off to his beloved Westmorland and 'settled down at Wall Nook to be Hazlitt, Lamb and Leigh Hunt all rolled into one'. The book that came of this was to be his first literary success. What follows is an amalgamation of extracts from two of its chapters, 'Old and New Soho' and 'Coffee Houses about Soho'.

Soho has always been a merry place. Even at the time when Keats wrote scornfully of it in a letter to Haydon: 'Then who would go / Into dark Soho, / To chatter with dank-haired critics, / When he might stay in the new-mown hay / And startle the dappled prickets?' – even then there were plenty of fellows, more merry than critical, who sported as playfully in its narrow streets as ever poets did in hayfields. A street out of Soho Square, now so heavily odorous of preserved fruit, from the factory at the corner, was for a time the home of so redoubtable a merrymaker, so sturdy a bohemian, as Pierce Egan, the author of *Life in London, or the Day and Night Scenes of Jerry Hawthorn, Esq., and his elegant friend Corinthian Tom, accompanied by Bob Logic the Oxonian, in their Rambles and Sprees through the Metropolis.* A jolly book indeed … I can never see this giddy, rampant book without thinking of a paragraph in it that shows us, through the Venetian-coloured glass of Mr Egan's slang:

> Mr Hazlitt, in the evening, lolling at his ease upon one of Ben Medley's elegant couches, enjoying the reviving comforts of a good tinney (which is a fire), smacking his chaffer (which is his tongue) over a glass of old hock, and topping his glim (which is a candle) to a classic nicety, in order to throw a new light upon the elegant leaves of Roscoe's *Life of Lorenzo de Medici*, as a composition for a New Lecture at the Surrey Institution. This is also Life in London.

Pierce Egan knew well the bohemian life of his day. There is a story that is a better compliment to his spirit than his head. Some of his friends lifted him, dead drunk after a masquerade, into a cab, put some money in his pocket, gave the cabby his address, and announced that he was a foreign nobleman.

Off drives the cabby, and finds the house, with ten bell-pulls ringing to the rooms belonging to the different tenants. Cheerfully, as one with nobility in his cab, he tugs the whole ten. From every window indignant night-capped heads deny relationship with any foreign nobleman.

'But I've brought him from the masquerade, and he's got money in his pocket.' Instantly everybody in the house runs downstairs and out into the street. Egan's wife recognized her errant husband, and, with the help of the other lodgers, carried him to his room. He was out on the spree again the following day...

But Soho has known more lettered men than Egan.

De Quincey, young and new to London, before he had lost the poor woman of the streets who, out of her own penury, bought port wine for him when he was likely to die on a doorstep in Soho Square, found lodging in an unfurnished house in Greek Street. The ground floor of the house was occupied by a rascally lawyer, whose best quality was a devotion to literature that led him to shelter the boy scholar, or at least to allow him to sleep on the floor of nights with waste papers for a pillow, and an old horse-blanket for a covering, that he shared with a hunger-bitten child.

Hazlitt rests in the graveyard of St Anne's, Wardour Street, having put off the wild, nervous tangle of joys and miseries, hopes and disappointments, and violent hates, that he summarized on his death-bed as a happy life. He died in Frith Street. In Gerrard Street, Dryden lived at No. 43, and doubtless found it very convenient for walking down of an afternoon to the coffee-houses about Covent Garden. Burke lived for a time at No. 37, and the greatest of all clubs, The Club, of Johnson, Goldsmith, and Reynolds, met at the Turk's Head Tavern in the same street.

There were clubs here in the early nineteenth century, and Thackeray described one of them in his novel *The Newcomes*:

We tap at a door in an old street in Soho: an old maid with a kind, comical face opens the door, and nods friendly, and says, 'How do, sir? ain't seen you this ever so long. How do, Mr Noocom?'

'Who's here?'

'Most everybody's here.'

We pass by a little snug bar, in which a trim elderly lady is seated by a great fire, on which boils an enormous kettle; while two gentlemen are attacking a cold saddle of mutton and West Indian pickles: hard by Mrs Nokes, the landlady's elbow – with mutual bows – we recognize Hickson the sculptor, and Morgan, intrepid Irish chieftain, chief of the reporters of the *Morning Press* newspaper. We pass through a passage into a back room, and are received with a roar of welcome from a crowd of men, almost invisible in the smoke.

All the districts of London that have once made themselves a special atmosphere, keep it with extraordinary tenacity … The Turk's Head has disappeared, Thackeray's club is not to be found; but every Tuesday a dozen, more or less, of the writers of the day meet at a little restaurant in the very street where Goldsmith and Johnson walked to meet their friends. This is the Mont Blanc, a very old house, whose walls have once been panelled. In the rooms upstairs the mouldings of the panels can be felt plainly through the canvas that has been stretched across them and papered to save the cost of painting. And all over Soho are similar small meeting places, where irregulars of all sorts flock to lunch and dine. Still, in some of the upper rooms of the streets where De Quincey walked to warm himself before sleeping on the floor, the student life goes on. Still in some of the upper windows may be seen the glitter of a candle-light where a scholar, probably foreign, pores over a book in the hours when the British Museum is closed to him. And in a hundred of the small rooms in the piles of Soho flats, small rooms furnished with a bed, a chair, and a table that also serves for a washing-stand, are there young actors and actresses, studying great parts and playing small ones, eager to be Macduff and content meanwhile to represent the third witch on the boards of a suburban theatre, copying the mannerisms of Miss Edna May, and keeping alive by smiling at the pit from the medley of the ballet. It is odd to think of the days when a shilling dinner was beyond achievement, when a sandwich and a couple of bananas seemed a supper for a Shakespeare.

Yet those were happy days, and had their luxuries. There are sandwiches and sandwiches. In one of the narrower streets that run up from Shaftesbury Avenue towards Oxford Street, there is a shop whose proprietor is an enthusiast, a facile virtuoso in their manufacture. He is an amateur in the best sense, and no selfish, arrogant fellow who will allow none but himself to be men of taste. You stand in the middle of his shop, with all kinds of meats arranged on the shelves about you, a knife on every dish. Veal, potted liver, chicken artfully prepared, pâté de foie gras or a substitute, tongue spiced and garnished, tongue potted and pressed, lobster paste, shrimp paste, cockle paste, and half a hundred other luscious delicacies, wait in a great circle about you, like paints on a palette; while you stand hesitating in the middle, and compose your sandwich, a touch of this, a taste of that, a suspicion of this, a sprinkling of that again, while he, at once a skilful craftsman and a great genius, does the rough handiwork, and executes your design, often, like the great man of the art school, contributing some little detail of his own that is needed for perfection, and presents you finally with the complete work of art, cut in four for convenient eating, for sixpence only, an epicurean triumph, and enough of it to sustain you till the morning.

After your sandwich, you will find, in Little Pulteney Street [now Brewer Street], if I am not mistaken in the name, a man with bananas on a hand barrow, and likely enough an Italian woman with a red or green shawl about her head, turning the handle of a barrel-organ. With these things it is easy to be happy. How happy I used to be, walking along that street peeling and eating my bananas, while my heart throbbed bravely to the music of the organ. Sometimes a couple of children would be dancing in the street, as nautch girls might enliven the supper of an Indian potentate; and often someone would be singing the words to the barrel-organ's melodies. What were the favourite tunes?

9

Ah yes: 'Dsrsy, Dysy, give mc yer awnser, do;/Im arf cryzy all fur the love of you,' and: 'As you walk along The Bar de Bullong with a independent air,/You 'ear the girls declare/There goes the millyonaire,/The man wot broke the benk at Monte Carlo.'

Yes; those were very happy days, and you, O reader, lose much if the fullness of your purse, or the delicacy of your ear, deprives you of such an enjoyment. When your income rises beyond the contentment of bananas and sandwich for dinner, or earlier, when the sale of a picture, or a longer article than usual, entitles you to a tremulous extravagance, you have an adventurous choice to make among the Soho restaurants. Every evening after half-past six or seven Soho takes on itself a new atmosphere. It is grubby and full of romantic memory by day. At night it is suddenly a successful place, where the proprietors of little restaurants are able to retire upon the fortunes they have made there. The streets, always crowded with foreigners, now suffer odder costumes than in daylight. Artists, poets, writers, actors, music-hall performers, crowd to the special restaurants that custom reserves for their use. I do not know how many small eating-houses there are in Soho; though I set out once, in a flush of recklessness at the sale of a book, to eat my way through the lot of them; the plan was to dine at a different restaurant every night, taking street by street, until I had exhausted them all, and could retire with unrivalled experience. The scheme fell through, partly because I fell in love with one or two places, so that my feet insisted on carrying me through their doors, when my conscience announced that duty to the programme demanded a supper elsewhere, and partly because of a relapse into impecuniosity that compelled a return to the diet of bananas and sandwiches.

Alas, that this should be a record of fact! What mansions of the stomach could I not describe, what sumptuous palaces, where wine and Munich lager flow from taps on every table, where food is as good in the mouth as in prospect, where landlords and proprietors stand upon their dignity, and refuse money as an insult to their calling. How perfectly could I reconstruct Soho in a gastronomic dream. Unfortunately I am bound as tight to fact as to penury.

The first Soho restaurant I knew was Roche's, now Béguinot's, in Old Compton Street. A lean painter took me; it was a foggy night, and we crossed Cambridge Circus with difficulty, and then, almost groping our way along the pavement, found the door, and stepped into the glamour and noise of the long room that you enter from the street. The painter wished to show me the whole place. We went right through to the inner room where we so often dined in later years, and downstairs to the hot little inferno, where a few brave spirits descend to feed and talk. The painter nodded to men in both rooms, and then turned to me. 'This is bohemia,' he said, 'what do you think of it?' We went back into the front room and sat down behind the long table, so that I could see the whole place, and observe the people who came in.

Opposite our long table were half a dozen small ones placed along the wall, and at one of these sat a very splendid old man. His long white hair fell down over the collar of his velvet coat, and now and again he flung back his head, so that his hair all rippled in the light, and then he would bang his hand carefully upon the table, so as not to hurt it, and yet to be impressive, as he declaimed continually to a bored girl who sat opposite him, dressed in an odd mixture of fashion and bohemianism. They seemed a queer couple to be together, until the painter told me that the man was one of the old set, who had come to the place for years, and remembered the old mad days when everyone dressed in a luxuriously unconventional manner, like so many Théophile Gautiers. The painter, who was a realist, referred scornfully to the old fellow as 'a piece of jetsam left by the Romantic Movement'. There have been such a number of romantic movements in the last thirty years that it was impossible to know what he meant.

But the tradition is still current at the Soho dinner tables that there were a few grand years in which we rivalled the Quartier in costume, and outdid Montmartre in extravagant conversation. It was pathetic to think of the old Romantic as a relic of that glorious time, alone in his old age, still living the life of his youth.

All down our long table there were not two faces that did not seem to me then to bear the imprint of some peculiar genius. Some were assuredly painters, others journalists, some very obviously poets, and there were several, too, of those amateur irregulars, who are always either exasperating or charming. The painter pointed out man after man by name. There was So-and-So, the musical critic; there was somebody else, who painted like Watteau: 'ridiculous ass', commented my realistic friend; there was So-and-So, the editor of an art magazine; there was a fellow who had given up art for a place in his father's business, but yet kept up his old acquaintanceships with the men more faithful to their ideals.

These Soho dinners are excellently cooked and very cheap. Only the wine is dearer in England than in France. There you can get a *carafon* for a few pence and good it is. But here the cheapest half-bottle is ten pence and often disappointing. The wise drink beer. It is Charles Godfrey Leland who, in his jovial scrap of autobiography, ascribes all the vigour and jolly energy of his life to the strengthening effects of Brobdingnagian draughts of lager beer drunk under the tuition of the German student. It is good, companionable stuff, and a tankard of it costs only sixpence, or less.

In the same street with Béguinot's, a little nearer Piccadilly Circus, there is the Dieppe, a cheaper place, but very amusing. We used to feed there not for the sake of the food so much as for the pictures. Round the walls are several enormous paintings, some of which suggest Botticelli's *Primavera* in the most ridiculous manner, only that all the figures are decently clothed in Early Victorian costume. It is a real joy to dine there, and observe them. They are the dearest funny pictures that I know.

On the other side of the street is a white-fronted restaurant kept by a Monsieur Brice, to whom, through several years, I have been faithful. Night after night I have walked through the glitter and the dusk of the Soho streets, past the little tobacco shop where they sell real Caporal tobacco, one whiff of which transports you as if in an enchanted cloud to the Boul' Mich', where the chansonniers sing their own ballads, to the Bal Bullier and the students' balls, and make you a Parisian in a moment. I have walked along there night after night, and turned in at the small side door, and through into the little white back room, where the best of waiters kept a corner table. What suppers have vanished in that inner room, how many bottles of dark Munich beer have flowed to their appointed havens. Here the Benns, that little painter and his wife, used to join us, and sit and talk and smoke, planning new pictures that were to be better than all that had been done before, talking over stories as yet unwritten, and enjoying great fame in obscurity. Here, too, used other friends to come, so that we often sat down a merry half-dozen at the table, and enjoyed ourselves hugely, and also other people.

That is one of the chief merits of Soho dinners – the company is always entertaining. Sometimes there would be an old philosopher at the table opposite, who would solemnly drink his half-bottle, and then smoke a cigarette over some modern book. One day he leaned across towards our table with Haeckel's *Riddle of the Universe* in his hand. 'Read this book, young people,' he said, 'but you should read it as you read *Punch*.' That was his introduction to our party, and thenceforward, when he had finished his meal, he would always smoke his cigarette with us, and, smoothing his white beard with a pensive hand, employ himself upon our instruction in philosophy.

On other evenings, strangers would come in, and we would guess their ideals from their manners of unfolding their napkins – the gay flourish meant the artist, the deliberate disentanglement the man of prose, the careless fling the poet, and so on – or perhaps one of our enigmas would join in our talk, and puzzle us the more. So many of the faces were far from ordinary, so many had the inexpressible something in their lines that suggests an interesting mind. We were content to let them remain enigmas, and construed them each one of us to please himself.

Once there was a wedding party at a longer table, made by joining the three small ones at one side of the room. The bride was a pretty model, the man a tousled artist; probably, we agreed, a very inferior craftsman, but certainly an excellent fellow, since he insisted on our joining his company, which was made up of others like himself, with their attendant ladies. He and his bride were off to Dieppe for an inexpensive honeymoon, so the feast could not be prolonged. At half-past eight the supper was done, and in a procession of hansom cabs we drove to Victoria, and cheered them off by the evening boat train, the two of them leaning out of the window and tearfully shouting of their devotion to art, to each other, and to us, an excited heterogeneous crowd, who sang *Auld Lang Syne*, *God Save the King*, The *Marseillaise*, and the Faust *Soldiers' Chorus*, according to nationality, in an inextricable tangle of discord. That was a great night.

The Boulogne, the Mont Blanc, Pinoli's, the France, and many another little restaurants knew us in those days; there was scarcely one, from Brice's and the Gourmet's in the south, to the Venice, at the Oxford Street end of Soho Street, that had not suffered our merry dinner parties. There was not one that was not in some way or other linked with a memory of delight. The waiters, Auguste, Alphonse, Jean, le gros Paul, le grand Renard, all were our friends, and joked with us over our evil dialect and our innumerable acquaintance. It was le grand Renard, that great man, who elaborated the jest of greeting us every time, as soon as we entered, with, 'Ah, bon soir, Messieurs. Your friend M'sieur So-and-So has not been here today, nor M'sieur So-and-So, nor M'sieur So-and-So, nor M'sieur So-and-So, nor M'sieur So-and-So, nor M'sieur So-and-So,' as far as his breath would carry him in an incoherent string of fantastic names, real and invented, that delighted us every time.

The day that Casanova, travelling as the Chevalier de Seingalt, arrived in London, he strolled some little way from his lodging through the old streets of Soho, then, as now, the Italian quarter. Presently he says, 'I saw a lot of people in a coffee-house, and I went in. It was the most ill-famed coffee-house in London, and the meeting place of the scum of the Italian population. I had been told of it at Lyons, and had made up my mind never to go there; but chance often makes us turn to the left when we want to go to the right. I ordered some lemonade, and was drinking it, when a stranger who was seated near me took a news-sheet from his pocket, printed in Italian. He began to make corrections in pencil on the margin, which led me to suppose he was an author. I watched him out of curiosity, and noticed that he scratched out the word *ancora*, and wrote it at the side, *anchora*. This barbarism irritated me.

'I told him that for four centuries it had been written without an *h*. "I agree with you," he answered, "but I am quoting Boccaccio, and in quotations one must be exact."

'"I humbly beg your pardon; I see you are a man of letters."

'"A very modest one; my name is Martinelli."

'"I know you by reputation; you are a cousin of Casabigi's, who has spoken of you; I have read some of your satires."

'"May I ask to whom I have the honour of speaking?"

'"My name is Seingalt. Have you finished your edition of the *Decameron*?"

'"I am still working at it, and trying to get more subscribers."

'"Will you allow me to be of the number?"

'He put me down for four copies, at a guinea a copy, and was surprised to hear I had only been in London an hour.

'"Let me see you home," he said, "you will lose your way else."

'When we were outside he told me I had been in the Orange Coffee-House, the most disreputable in all London.

'"But you go."

'"I go because I know the company, and am on my guard against it."

'"Do you know many people here?"

'"Yes, but I only pay court to Lord Spencer. I work at literature, am all alone, earn enough for my wants. I live in furnished lodgings, I own twelve shirts and the clothes I stand up in, and I am perfectly contented."'

That dialogue might serve well enough for an exaggerated description of our own day. For the people of this book are willing to drink anywhere but in the more tame and expensive places of the West End. They 'know the company and are on their guard against it' and go cheerfully where they may get most amusement at the smallest cost.

The coffee-houses best loved by the bohemians are not so disreputable as the Orange; I doubt if their reputations can have gone far beyond Soho. But they have atmospheres of their own; and they are not places where you are likely to meet anyone oppressively more respectable or better dressed than yourself. I am thinking of two small houses in particular – The Moorish Café and The Algerian. Besides these there are many others, and a few neater, more luxurious, more expensive, that help to wean the bohemian from bohemia; and then there are the big drinking palaces by Leicester Square and Piccadilly Circus, where he goes when he needs the inspiration of a string band, or the interest of a crowd of men and women.

Near the Oxford Street end of Soho Street, on the left-hand side as you walk towards Soho Square, is a small green-painted shop, with a window full of coffee cups, and pots, and strainers of a dozen different designs. Looking through the window that is dimmed, likely enough with steam, you may see a girl busied with a big coffee-grinding machine, and watch the hesitant blue flames of the stove on which the coffee is stewed. Opening the door, you step into a babble of voices, and find yourself in a tiny Moorish café. The room is twisted and narrow, so that you must have a care, as you walk, for other people's coffee cups upon the small round tables. At every table men will be sitting, blowing through their half-closed lips long jets of scented smoke that disturb continually the smoke-filled atmosphere.

Some will be playing at cards, some at backgammon, some talking eagerly among themselves. Dark hair, dark eyes, sallow-skinned faces everywhere, here and there a low-caste Englishman, and sometimes, if you are lucky, a bohemian in emerald corduroy, lolling broadly on his chair and puffing at a porcelain pipe. Sit down near him, and it is ten to one that you will be engaged in a wordy battle of acting, of poetry, or of pictures before the sediment has had time to settle in your coffee.

The coffee is thick and dark and sweet; to drink it alone, and to smoke with it an Eastern cigarette, is to hear strange Moorish melodies, to dream of white buildings with green-painted porticoes, to see the card-players as gambling dragomans, to snatch at a coloured memory from the *Arabian Nights*. The material for the dream is all about you; gaudy pictures in bright blues and oranges hang on the walls; there is Stamboul in deliciously impossible perspective, there the tomb of the Prophet, there an Ottoman warship, there Noah's Ark, with a peacock on the topmast, a serpent peering anxiously from a porthole, and Noah and his family flaunting it in caftans and turbans on the poop; from the brackets of the flickering incandescent lamps are hung old Moorish instruments, *tarboukas*, and gambas, dusty, with slackened strings, and yet sufficient, in the dream, to send the tunes of the desert cities filtering through the thick air of the room.

The Algerian is in Dean Street, close by the Royalty Theatre, where Coquelin played Cyrano de Bergerac and kept a whole party, French painters and English writers, quavering between laughter and tears, uplifted with pride that there could be such men as Cyrano, and joy that there was yet such an actor as Coquelin. It is on the same side of the street, a plain, square window, thoroughly orthodox, with 'The Algerian Restaurant' written over the top. Behind a small counter sits Madame, knitting, smiling to all her acquaintance that come in, and selling neat brown packages of wonderful coffee. Beyond is an inner room, whose walls are covered with cocoanut matting, and decorated with tiny mirrors, and advertisements of special drinks. If you can get a corner seat in that crowded little room, you may be happy for an evening, with a succession of coffees and a dozen cigarettes. Sometimes there will be a few women watching the fun, but more often there will be none but men, mostly French or Italian, who play strange card games and laugh and curse at each other. There used to be a charming notice on the wall, which I cannot remember accurately.

ANYONE CAUGHT GAMBLING OR PLAYING FOR MONEY
will be kicked into the gutter and not picked up again.

PROPRIETOR

It ran something like that, but it has now been replaced by a less suggestive placard.

Also there used to be another room downstairs, a gay companionable place, where I have played a penny whistle and seen some dancing to my music. Here we used to come after supper, to drink coffee, smoke cigarettes, and argue according to custom. Here would young Frenchmen bring their ladies, and talk freely in their own tongue. Here would we, too, bring our young women. It used to amuse me to notice the sudden hush that fell on the talk of all the couples and argumentative people when the grim police inspector and his important bodyguard stumped heavily down the stairs, stood solemnly for a moment in the middle of the room, and then went slowly up the stairs again – and the flood of excited chatter in several languages that followed their disappearance.

It is impossible to leave the Algerian without remembering the wonderful big dog who used to be a visitor in the room below. He was a very large ruddy collie. Left to himself he was an easy-going fellow who would accept the hospitality of anybody who had anything to spare; but his master had only to say one word, and he would not dip his nose in the daintiest, prettiest dish of coffee in the world. He was a gentleman of nice manners; if his master directed his attention to any lady who happened to be there, and whispered in his silky ear, 'Toujours la politesse,' immediately, with the gravity of an ambassador, he would walk across and lift a ceremonial paw. It is sad that the room is now filled with lumber that was once so gay with humanity. But perhaps it will be opened again.

Close round the corner opposite the Algerian is a pretty white café, with a big window of a thousand little leaded panes, through which it is impossible to see. The whole suggestion of the outside is comfort and secluded luxury. And indeed so it is; you go there when you are a success; or, not being one of the famous or opulent, when, having just sold a book or a picture, you feel as if you were. Its air is very different from the friendly untidiness of the other two places. White cloths are on the tables, a little cut-glass is scattered about, and there are red and white flowers in silver vases – it is all so neat that I would not describe it, if it were not a favourite place of the more fortunate of the bohemians, and if it had not been so sweet a suggestion of what might sometime be.

I came here in the pride of my first twenty-guinea cheque, and was introduced with due ceremony to Jeanne downstairs – pretty little Jeanne, who says most mournfully that someone has told her from the lines of her hand that she will not be married till she is two-and-thirty – eleven whole years to wait. My companion was a literary agent, who showed me three successes, two novelists and a critic, out of the half-dozen people who were sitting at the other tables. I almost wished he had not brought me, until Jeanne came back with black coffee in tall straight glasses, and some excellent cigarettes, when I changed my mind, and thought how often I would come here, if the world should turn good critic, and recognize in solid wealth the merit of my masterpieces.

Across Shaftesbury Avenue, past the stage doors of Daly's and the Hippodrome, through the narrow asphalt passage that is often crowded with ballet girls and supers, walking up and down before the times of their performances at one or other theatre, you find your way into the brilliance of Leicester Square. The Alhambra and the Empire fill two sides of it with light, and Shakespeare stands on a pedestal between them, resting his chin on his hand in melancholy amazement.

Downstairs at the corner of the Square there is the drinking-hall of the Provence, a long L-shaped room, with a band playing in a corner, and smaller rooms opening out of the first, and seeming a very multitude of little caverns from the repetition of the mirrors with which they are lined. There are frescoes on the walls of the larger room, of gnomes swilling beer, and tumbling headfirst into vats, and waving defiance at the world with all the bravado of a mug of ale. Fat, pot-bellied little brutes they are, and so cheerfully conceived that you would almost swear their artist had been a merry fellow, and kept a tankard on the steps of his ladder where he sat to paint them.

There is always a strange crowd at this place – dancers and singers from the music-halls, sad women pretending to be merry, coarse women pretending to be refined, and men of all types grimacing and clinking glasses with the women. And then there are the small groups indifferent to everything but the jollity and swing of the place, thumping their beer mugs on the table over some mighty point of philosophy or criticism, and ready to crack each other's heads for joy in the arguments of Socialism or Universal Peace.

I was seated at a table here one night, admiring the picture in which a gnome pours some hot liquid on another gnome who lies shrieking in a vat, when I noticed a party of four men sitting at a table opposite. Three were obviously hangers-on of one or other of the arts, the sort of men who are proud of knowing an actor or two to speak to, and are ready to talk with importance of their editorial duties on the *Draper's Compendium* or the *Toyshop Times*. The fourth was different. A huge felt hat banged freely down over a wealth of thick black hair, bright blue eyes, an enormous black beard, a magnificent manner (now and again he would rise and bow profoundly, with his hat upon his heart, to some girls on the other side of the room), a way of throwing his head back when he drank, of thrusting it forward when he spoke, an air of complete abandon to the moment and the moment's thought; he took me tremendously.

He seemed to be delighting his friends with impromptu poetry. I did a mean but justifiable thing, and carried my pot of beer to a table just beside him, where I could see him better, and also hear his conversation. It was twaddle, but such downright, spirited, splendid twaddle, flung out from the heart of him in a grand, careless way that made me think of largesse royally scattered on a mob. His blue, twinkling eyes decided me. When, a minute or two later, he went out, I followed, and found him vociferating to his gang upon the pavement. I pushed in, so as to exclude them, and asked him: 'Are you prose or verse?'

'I write verse, but I dabble in the other thing.' It was the answer I had expected.

'Very good. Will you come to my place tomorrow night at eight? Tobacco. Beer. Talk.'

'I love beer. I adore tobacco. Talking is my life. I will come.'

'Here is my card. Eight o'clock tomorrow. Good-night.' And so I left him.

He came, and it turned out that he worked in a bank from ten to four every day, and played the wild bohemian every night. His beard was a disguise. He spent his evenings seeking for adventure, he said, and apologized to me for earning an honest living. He was really delightful. So are our friendships made; there is no difficulty about them; no diffidence; you try a man as you would a brand of tobacco; if you agree, then you are friends; if not, why then you are but two blind cockchafers who have collided with each other in a summer night, and boom away again each in his own direction.

Over the road there is the Café de l'Europe where, also downstairs, there is an even larger drinking-hall. Huge bizarre pillars support a decorated ceiling, and beneath them there are a hundred tables, with variegated maroon-coloured cloths, stained with the drippings of tankards and wine-glasses. There is a band here, too, in a balcony halfway up the stairs. This place, like all the other cafés, is not exclusively bohemian; we are only there on sufferance, in isolated parties, and it is a curious contrast to look away to the clerks, demimondaines, and men-about-town, sitting at the other tables; faces that have left their illusions with their youth, faces with protruding lips and receding chins, weak, foolish faces with watery eyes, office boys trying to be men, and worn-out men trying to be boys, and women ridiculously dressed and painted. We used to go there most when we were new to journalism, and we found it a great place for planning new periodicals. Eight or nine of us used to meet there, and map out a paper that was to startle the town, and incidentally give us all the opportunities that the present race of misguided editors denied. We would select our politics, choose our leader-writers, and decide to save quarrels by sharing the dramatic criticism between us all. We would fight lustily over the title, and have a wrangle over the form. Some would wish to ape the *Saturday Review*, some would desire a smaller, more convenient shape for putting in the pocket, and others, commercially minded, would suggest a gigantic size that might make a good show on the bookstalls. We would stand lagers again and again, proud in the knowledge of our new appointments, leader-writers, editors, dramatic critics every one of us. And then, at last, after a whole evening of beer and extravagance, and happy pencilled calculations of our immediate incomes, based on a supposed sale of 100,000 copies weekly (we were sure of that at least), we would come suddenly to fact. The Scotch poet, whom we usually elected business manager on these occasions, would smile grimly, and say, 'Now, gentlemen, the matter of finance. There will be printers and papermakers to pay. Personally, and speaking for myself alone, I will give all that I possess.'

'And how much is that?' we would cry, although we guessed.

'Well' – and he would make great show of rummaging his pockets – 'it seems that I was cleaned right out of bullion by that last lot of beer. O'Rourke, it's your turn to stand. Waiter – waiter, this gentleman wants another round of lagers.'

This was the invariable end, and at closing time, having swung from the glory of newspaper proprietorship to the sordid penury of sharing our coppers in order to pay all 'bus fares home, we would walk along Cranbourn Street to Piccadilly Circus, and separate for the night.

Such was Soho as Arthur Ransome knew it as a young journalist and writer, starting out on his career. Throughout the following decades its varied, colourful history continued and it remained raffish and louche by repute. During the Second World War, while the blackout was in force, gangsters moved in to control the vice trade and sometimes, it was rumoured, the local police, who were not averse to accepting back-handers. The 'ladies of the night' were still a visible Soho feature, prominent in doorways and on corners as they touted for custom, till the Street Offences Act of 1959 finally drove them indoors and undercover.

Drinking clubs were also long an aspect of Soho life, most famously represented by Muriel Belcher's Colony Room Club in Dean Street, which attracted generations of artists, from Francis Bacon to Damien Hurst, and various prodigious drinkers; it was a den where alcohol could be obtained by members at the dead times of day when the licensing laws meant the pubs were closed. The Coach and Horses pub in Romilly Street overlapped with the Colony Room in its clientele, which included poets and actors, writers and journalists. Its bar area was reproduced as a stage set for the theatrical presentation of Keith Waterhouse's immensely entertaining play *Jeffrey Bernard is Unwell* (1989), which chronicled the ever-present role played by booze in the life of the eponymous columnist.

As a clearing house for rumour and gossip, the Coach and Horses held a natural attraction for the editorial team of *Private Eye*, being within easy reach of their offices in Greek Street. To this day, after many shifts of personnel through the years, the pub continues to host *Private Eye's* twice-monthly lunches.

In the early 1950s, the revival of traditional New Orleans jazz ('trad') was gaining ground and jazz clubs were springing up as part of the scene all over Soho. Naim Attallah, in his memoir *The Boy in England* (2005), records his own early experiences of the time, when, having come from Palestine, he was willing to have a go at any work he could find. To fill a gap he took on a temporary job as a bouncer in a nightclub off Charing Cross Road. The job involved acting as personal bodyguard to the proprietor, an Oxford graduate who had done a stretch in prison for possession of cannabis. Naim's duties did not begin till 2 a.m. as the venue functioned as a jazz club during the earlier part of the evening.

The club's patrons were mostly committed jazz enthusiasts who appreciated and revelled in its intensely charged atmosphere, and although its success was short-lived, it became known for the quality and brilliance of its musicians, some of whom were later famous. They were keen to use the club as a testing ground to improve their skills and try out their music on a live audience. At 2 a.m. each night, however, the drinkers took over from the jazz lovers, and as chucker-out Naim knew he was likely to sustain a few knocks. One night a hefty Scot, who had been drinking excessively, threatened to set off an uproar and needed to be ejected. Naim moved in to deal with him, noting his inebriated stumblings, but found himself instead on the receiving end of an expert blow, delivered with all the precision of a practised street fighter, that sent him backwards down two flights of stairs. He had to be taken to casualty at the Charing Cross Hospital suffering from an injured back and bruises to both legs. It was a lesson in never underrating an adversary, however the worse for drink they might seem to be.

Among the most positive aspects of Soho was the infinite variety of its gastronomic delights. Where else could one find a deli serving rye-bread sandwiches of warm salt beef with lashings of mustard and large pickled cucumbers, a culinary treat? There were also the continental food shops, some of which had been run by the same families for several generations. They gave an un-English frisson to a Britain not yet used to eating garlic, and imported exotic vegetables like aubergines from the Continent. Life was never dull. Naim's boss at the nightclub was in the habit of getting wind of some bizarre party in progress, and would round off the night by setting out in search of it in the Soho jungle, taking Naim with him. Soho at that time had a particular sort of lurid sleaziness that has completely gone from it today. It formed the underbelly of a sin-conscious Britain, where all that was forbidden could be obtained at a price.

Yet eras in Soho are always destined to come to an end. The Colony Room was a classic example. After Muriel Belcher died in 1979, her successors managed to keep it going for almost another thirty years, but then its door closed for ever. The novelist Will Self wrote its obituary in a piece in the *Evening Standard* (9 September 2008): 'While some may say the Colony represents the old Soho that is being killed off by smoking bans and other sanitizing measures, the truth is that there was another criterion for membership: the hard-core members were first and foremost raging alcoholics' – and perforce were dropping off their bar stools with ever greater frequency. It was the liberalization of the licensing laws that had really done for it, with round-the-clock availability of drink taking away the naughtiness of afternoon boozing.

The problem for Soho today is how any of the essence of it can be preserved as gentrification advances apace, and close on its heels comes the corporation ethos, which, with old leaseholds running out, means the potential escalation of real-estate values, the glossy modernization of pubs and coffee bars, shops and offices. Tradition and character, sadly, are unlikely to stand a chance.

Chapman & Hall were one of the leading and most venerable publishers of Victorian Britain. In the first half of the twentieth century they were based not in Soho but just to the south in the neighbouring district of Covent Garden, in Henrietta Street. Arthur Waugh, Auberon Waugh's grandfather, became managing director in 1902, after establishing a niche for himself as a literary journalist and reviewer and as an author, having written *Alfred Lord Tennyson: A Study of His Life and Work*, the first full-length biography of the poet. The fortunes of Chapman & Hall were founded on the fact that among the authors they had published were William Makepeace Thackeray and Anthony Trollope, Robert Browning and Elizabeth Barrett Browning, Thomas Carlyle and, most crucially, Charles Dickens. They retained the valuable Dickens copyrights through to the fiftieth anniversary of Dickens's death in 1920, when inevitably their cessation created anxieties for Arthur Waugh over how long Chapman & Hall could hope to carry on as a fiction publisher.

As it happened the family connection with the firm was to continue because help was on the way in the person of Arthur's second son, Evelyn. Despite Arthur's misgivings and sensitivities over its sharp and sometimes personal satire, its eye for scandalous comedy, Chapman & Hall published *Decline and Fall* in its first bowdlerized edition in 1928. Arthur was aware of having missed out with a previous best-selling novel, his elder son Alec's controversial *The Loom of Youth*, having drawn back in alarm from the social complications it was likely to set off, with its descriptions of boys' public-school passions and sexuality. The timing in the new jazz age of the 1920s was right for *Decline and Fall*. It was an instant success, though the original text would not be issued till there was a standard Evelyn Waugh edition after Arthur's death. All of Evelyn's subsequent fiction was first published by Chapman & Hall; sometimes he went to other publishers with his non-fiction books.

For Auberon Waugh ('Bron'), Evelyn's eldest son, it was natural to look towards the family firm when, in the early stages of his career, he tested himself out as a novelist. 'Perhaps it would have been more seemly,' he admitted in his autobiography, *Will This Do?* (1991), 'if I had sent it to some other publisher under an assumed name, but I was very short of money...' *The Foxglove Saga*, the first and most successful of his novels in terms of sales, was a project he embarked on when he was in a long convalescence after managing to shoot himself in chest, arm and hand with a Browning machine gun as a National Service officer on active service in Cyprus. The weapon had jammed and Bron gave it a good shake by the barrel, whereupon the gun's mechanism started to fire. He was lucky to survive. *The Foxglove Saga*, published in 1960, while he was still an undergraduate, sold an impressive 14,000 copies in hardback. It was praised by many, including several of his father's influential friends, who tried to emphasize that here was a new distinctive voice; but inevitably his fiction would always be compared with that of his father, whose books had achieved the status of modern classics. Bron wrote four more novels, the last having been published in 1971, and they made their mark in their day, before he decided to give up fiction. In *Will This Do?* he said that, when he came to look the books over again later, he wished he had spent more time and care in working on the writing of them, and, 'It was not so much that I objected to cashing in on the name [Waugh] as that I was not going to be allowed to get away with it.' They are none of them currently in print. With *The Foxglove Saga*'s initial success his father had warned him: 'Regard it as a lucky win at gambling, not likely to be repeated.'

The fifth novel, *Bed of Flowers*, was published just a year after he had joined *Private Eye*, and he suggested in his autobiography that it was his 'last novel to date'. It would in fact be his last. He had ceased to be enamoured with the literary process.

> Novel-writing is a tedious, self-absorbed business, and the main hope which keeps writers going – that somebody will read their work – is in short supply. When the pot of gold at the end of the rainbow – fame, wealth and the affectionate gratitude of an adoring readership – had been reduced to the faint hope of a literary prize, I decided it was time to seek other opportunities. On top of that I now had a huge house to

keep up and four children were approaching the age when I would have
to start worrying about school fees…

Back at the start, *The Foxglove Saga* had the unforeseen effect of blocking
off another early career move when Bron applied to the Foreign Office
and came to be considered for MI6. Though he was turned down, he
made further efforts to join the intelligence services between 1960 and
1963, but was rejected every time. Only later did he learn that a former
army acquaintance, whom he had mercilessly pilloried as a heartless prig
in the *Saga*, had written a reference stating that, to his certain knowledge,
Bron was unfit for the service. The letter had come up on the file without
fail each time he applied. Nevertheless, according to his son, Alexander
Waugh, in his 'autobiography of a family', *Fathers and Sons* (2004), Bron
continued to help MI6 out 'on an ad hoc basis'. What this consisted of
we shall never know. 'The Waughs have, for three generations,' writes
Alexander, 'maintained cordial links with the Secret Services, though
we're not supposed to talk about it.'

As for Chapman & Hall, in the second half of the twentieth century,
when the landscape of publishing altered profoundly with international-
ization and the ascendant rule of accountants and business plans, it went
through an experience shared by many other familiar and established
household names. It was traded and sold, swallowed into the *mêlée* of
a conglomerate, dismantled, reassigned and given a new character. It
still exists as an imprint within a group, where it specializes in books on
statistics and data analysis – exactly the sort of publishing that Bron's
grandfather, Arthur Waugh, loathed the most.

Bron in fact failed to graduate from Oxford, and despite the success
of *The Foxglove Saga* it was evident that writing fiction was not going to
produce a satisfactory income; and especially not when he married young
in 1961. The door that opened naturally for him was the one that led to
the literary journalism that defined his future. His first main chance came
when he joined the team of junior contributors to the Peterborough
'London Day by Day' diary column in the *Daily Telegraph*. To his father's

special pride, he also had a spell contributing political comment to a column in the *Catholic Herald*, managing to be instantly controversial and attracting bundles of correspondence from readers who acclaimed him as a bright new voice as well as from others who thought he should be sacked on the spot. In fact after two years he was fired after Bertrand Russell demanded a retraction and threatened damages over something Bron had written about his deserving to have 'his cup of hemlock'.

An extraordinarily prolific journalistic output characterized these ten years; his work appeared both in daily tabloids and august journals ranging from the *Daily Mirror* to the *New Statesman* and the *Spectator*. He honed his themes, defined his targets, decided on his enemies, expanded his hatreds and sharpened his focus on everything and everybody he found ridiculous and pretentious. It seemed a natural progression when he arrived at *Private Eye*'s offices in Greek Street in 1970 and was invited, according to Bron, by its then editor Richard Ingrams, an old friend from university, to be its first political correspondent. Ingrams isn't sure this was entirely the case (see page 43) but no longer remembers the exact circumstances. He certainly does not consider the magazine ever had a 'political correspondent'. But whatever Bron was, there began to evolve the *Private Eye* diaries, which many think marked the peak of Bron's achievement, and he certainly thought so himself. *Private Eye* had already been going seven years by the time he joined the publication, which was not to be defined by the established politics of right or left, but expressed its ethos as having to do with 'Tory anarchism', where nothing was sacred or beyond ridicule or safe from the weapon of laughter. This was related to 'fogeyism', but it had a cutting edge. Besides Ingrams, its associates included Peter Cook (then proprietor), Barry Fantoni, John Wells, Willie Rushton and Paul Foot, the latter standing out as a consistent man of the left, though in due course he became one of Bron's life-long friends; something that some of Bron's antagonists on the left have found paradoxical.

In this company Bron was at his most free to exercise his gift for scathing invective and bitter vituperation, enhanced by surrealist and absurdist flights of fancy. Those he saw as his enemies were likely to find themselves pilloried as comic turns and grotesque running gags. Welfare politics, career politicians of both left and right, modernism in the arts in all its forms, the working class and old-age pensioners were all grist to his mill; the sight of the aged queuing for their weekly handouts in his local post office in Somerset could inspire an ire in him that was virtually Swiftian in its disgust. If items he wrote in the diary remain relevant today, it's partly because they were also wildly funny.

In his introduction to *Closing the Circle: The Best of 'Way of the World'* (2001), a final collection of Bron's *Daily Telegraph* pieces, Craig Brown agreed with Alan Watkins that 'one of Waugh's great strengths as a satirist was complete absence of restraint and good taste':

> He was a caricaturist, pointing his distorting mirror at a drabber reality, converting self-righteousness into comedy and bossiness into buffoonery. He also had the prose equivalent of perfect pitch. The most surreal and absurd ideas could be carried on the majestic wave of his prose, propelled from beneath by an undertow of fearless vulgarity.

Craig Brown did not seem an admirer of Naim Attallah. He never missed the chance to lambast any of Naim's activities. His review, on publication of Naim's book, *Women*, in the autumn of 1987, was the most scathing of all the many reviews. He told his readers of the *Mail on Sunday* that:

> At 1,150 pages the book called *Women* is much, much longer than any of the classic works of literature on women. It is three times as long as *Madame Bovary*, ten times as long as *Hedda Gabler*, and about as long as all Jane Austen's novels put together. Which publisher has so much confidence that this man who has never written a book before has so much more to say on the subject than the great artists of the past. The answer is, of course, Naim Attallah himself. As the owner of Quartet

Books he was in the perfect position to have his book accepted for publication by them.

Subsequently Brown and Bron had lunch with Naim. It was meant to be a kind of rapprochement, though that was not quite how it worked out. Craig was in the same mould as Bron. Both of them felt passionately about things, and particularly about people. Once they had taken against someone, it would be extremely hard to divert them from their target.

Bron's avowed enemy at that time was Lord Gowrie, and he never missed an opportunity to attack him. The reason (see page 49–50) began for Bron when they were both at Oxford. Bron had lashed out at Gowrie ever since with vitriolic spleen. It took Naim months to persuade Bron to let bygones be bygones and allow him to bring the two of them together.

Though Bron's seemingly never-ending feud with Grey Gowrie was mostly stoked up by Bron himself whenever he saw an opportunity (with Grey remaining largely unphased by the whole charade), it became an irksome problem for Naim, who was a professional and social friend to them both. It faced him with problems over party invitations or other occasions where he needed to make sure they wouldn't cross paths. One day he broached the matter with Bron, who replied, 'Well, he stole my girl at Oxford,' as if no reason could be simpler or more justified. Naim, astonished, proposed that he set up a lunch just for the two of them and Bron agreed. In no time, according to Naim, Bron and Grey were laughing and gossiping together and the malign spell had, after all those years, been broken at last. Lord Gowrie cannot now recall the lunch, though a friendship revived and Bron became very supportive of Grey and would not tolerate a word of criticism against him.

Craig Brown's coolness towards Attallah was something Naim found strange in so far as he could not decipher it. Naim was a supporter of literature and the arts, spending most of his money bolstering endeavours closely related to them, so even if Craig did feel some kind of antipathy towards him, he could not see why that should stop him being more appreciative. So it did not surprise him to see himself featured in Brown's *Evening Standard* column of 28 June 1993, written with his usual blend of satire.

Every now and then a conspiracy book is published which reveals a bizarre new secret dynasty, stretching from either Christ or Napoleon or Hereward the Wake. The authors invariably claim that each member of these secret dynasties is particularly gifted in business, or in fortune-telling, or in the arts. Shock! Horror! I think I have just spotted another such dynasty. Over the past few years, three men and one woman have come under the media spotlight for their penchant for the high life, and their inability to say: 'I've had more than enough, thank you.' From France, Jacques Attali. From Palestine, Naim Attallah. From England, Roy Hattersley. And from the world of fiction, Lady Chatterley. Spooky, eh? And where do they all spring from? Many centuries ago, Attila the Hun was also censured for taking rather more than his fair share of the pickings, and for improper personal extravagance. Attila, Attali, Attallah, Hattersley, Chatterley. Are they by any chance related?

'Looking back over my career to date, and at all the people I have insulted,' Bron wrote in *Will This Do?*, 'I am mildly surprised that I am still allowed to exist.' In summing up the *Private Eye* phase, he said, 'During my sixteen years ... I had endless opportunity to be rude about people, even a requirement to set up three or four new Aunt Sallys a fortnight in order to knock them down. The great problem was always to find enough people I wished to be rude about.' A rare hint of remorse came when he looked back on the example of Michael Foot, his friend Paul Foot's uncle, who was much vilified as Labour leader in opposition to Mrs Thatcher, admitting that 'I have never been anything but rude to Michael Foot in print, dubbing him "the posturing ninny" and much else besides, but he has never been anything but kind to me'; and, he observes, Michael Foot would even agree to write for the *Literary Review* for sums even more paltry than he would have been paid by *Tribune*. 'There is surely a sanctity among the Foots,' Bron concluded.

Bron was also fortunate in the two cartoonists who provided images for his *Private Eye* diary entries, both of them in their different ways convivial to the quality of his imagination. The first, for the years 1972–6, was the veteran Nicolas Bentley, whose penetrating and witty character line drawings were familiar to an earlier generation of readers in both magazines and books, including such authors as Damon Runyon, Eric Linklater and T. S. Eliot (the original illustrated edition of *Old Possum's Book of Practical Cats*), to name only a few; and also Bron's great precursor as a satirical columnist, J. B. Morton ('Beachcomber'), whose prose style was based more on whimsical parody. Nicolas Bentley cut an unlikely stalwart of the left figure, invariably going to work dapper and trim in suit and tie. No one would have suspected him of having been at the 'battle of Cable Street', among those who turned out to oppose the attempt by Oswald Mosley's blackshirts to march through the heart of the East End's Jewish quarter in 1936, but he had been. The integrity of his views earned him respect from Bron, who remembered him affectionately as 'the gentle old left-winger' who had illustrated his column. When he died in 1978, Bron wrote of him in *Private Eye*: 'Nick was a gentle, modest, humorous man, with none of the usual characteristics of the highly individual genius which inspired his quiet professionalism and supreme technical ability.'

For the years 1976–85, William ('Willie') Rushton took over the illustrating of the *Eye* diary column, presenting a more rumbustious image than Nick and bringing to the task his own highly individual style, wild and rudely anarchic. Bron asked Willie to start contributing drawings to the *Literary Review* after he had taken over the magazine's editorship with the April 1986 issue. Rushton would create all the cover images for every subsequent issue, as well as the masthead drawing for the 'From the Pulpit' editorials, until his shocking death in January 1997.

Willie had been a contemporary of Richard Ingrams at Shrewsbury School, along with Paul Foot and Christopher Booker, and so became one of the founders of *Private Eye* as well as an indelible influence on the growth of the satire boom in the 1960s. For ten years without fail he also produced the artwork for all the covers of *Private Eye*, besides penning dozens of other cartoons. He was a natural comedian, who made his mark on television, starting with appearances on the BBC's legendary late-night satire show, *That Was the Week That Was*, alongside David Frost. At the age of fifty-nine, in 1996, he had to go into hospital for a heart operation, but it went wrong for him. His sudden death was a terrible shock for his whole circle and all who loved his work. Richard Ingrams described him as 'the most talented of my contemporaries by far', who had had a 'brilliant sparkling wit' – 'a born cartoonist who had no training. It was completely natural to him.' Willie had detested *The Times* and the Establishment, but, said Bron, 'there was no malice in his hatreds, only amazement. His jokes and drawings could appear merciless', but only if you studied them at length could you realize that 'the driving force behind his work is simple enjoyment'. David Frost said he had been someone who 'just went on getting wittier and funnier with every passing year'. His was a light that went out all too soon.

The *Literary Review* became Bron's major focus when his years with *Private Eye* came to an end, as it gave him a platform, with his editorial 'From the Pulpit' page, from which to express his most cherished opinions and wage war against smug certainties. For Bron, editing the *Literary Review* was a labour of love in the heart of Soho, and he cemented its status as the prestigious and highly readable literary magazine it has continued to be. He worked on it tirelessly till his health failed shortly before his death on 16 January 2001. He was only sixty-one. Since his death no contrarian spirit has arisen to match or replace him on the British literary scene.

ACT ONE

&

The *Private Eye* Years

I

FIRST CULTIVATE YOUR ENEMIES

A UBERON WAUGH AND RICHARD INGRAMS FIRST CROSSED PATHS
in 1959 when they were both at Oxford. Richard Ingrams, a year
ahead of Waugh in his degree course, had taken over the editorship, along
with his friend Paul Foot, of a small magazine owned by the Berry family
(who also owned the *Daily Telegraph*). It was called *Parson's Pleasure* and
was a rival to the more 'official' Oxford undergraduate organs, *Isis* and
Cherwell, its satirical slant being mostly reserved for those left-wing radicals
who, according to Ingrams, 'cannot disagree without condemning. They
rarely laugh. The proverbial fire in their bellies eats away any latent sense
of humour...' But the paper did have a secondary target at which to take
swipes: the rich, privileged miscreant rowdies with whom Waugh, still
possessing a certain callowness, was at that stage associating.

Waugh's recollected view of the Oxford of the time was as he described
it in an interview he gave to Edward Whitley for his book of interviews,
The Graduates (1987):

The Oxford myth I knew was very much my father's ideal – one sees
it in a rather coarse, crude form nowadays – that myth of lotus-eating
and champagne-drinking ... The Oxford Union was going through its
Dimbleby days. [David] Dimbleby was 'General King' and [Peter] Jay was
'Intellectual King'. As a kind of anti-Dimbleby movement, I founded a
ghastly club of Christ Church hoorays ... I remember a party in a room
in Canterbury Quad, where the ceiling was almost as high as this one
[the interview took place at Waugh's Somerset home, in Combe Florey].
One of my friends was sick, but didn't vomit downwards, he stood up

and leaned back and vomited upwards. He produced this remarkable column of vomit which hit the ceiling and left a deep stain, before, of course, coming down.

Bron made an attempt to buy *Parson's Pleasure* from the Berry family, wanting to bring it round to reflecting more the Oxford he wished for. As he describes his intentions in his autobiography, *Will This Do?* (1991): 'I was appalled by how few public schoolboys there were, appalled by the number of earnest, working-class youths whose humourless faces betokened young men on the make; they would never have time to frolic, take risks or make fools of themselves.'

His effort to buy the journal did not succeed, and he penned his revenge in *Isis*, ridiculing Paul Foot and his ilk as 'scruffy men in roll-neck sweaters who lay about on the floor of their lodgings late at night talking left-wing politics, drinking cocoa and trying to seduce girls who were also wearing roll-neck sweaters'. Paul Foot in fact became in future years one of Bron's staunchest friends, 'witty, wise and possibly the only true romantic of my acquaintance'; the integrity of his consistent left-wing stance aroused Bron's respect, even if he found the reasoning behind it preposterous.

Bron then failed his finals and chose to depart from Oxford rather than retake them and suffer another ignominious defeat. He realized he had opted to study for the wrong degree, as he neither liked nor understood philosophy and economics. His economics tutor, Sir Roy Harrod, maintained that his student had been reluctant to believe anything he was taught. Other reversals included a fraught infatuation with a female undergraduate 'with lustrous brown eyes', which ended in despair and her loss to a rival. This left an emotional bruise that was slow to fade. He was careful to guard against revealing her identity and long afterwards called down 'an orphan's curse' on the head of anyone who might attempt to do so. Meanwhile he had completed his first novel, *The Foxglove Saga*, and it was accepted for publication. This convinced him not to retake his humiliatingly failed finals but to leave instead and set off for London to take his chances. In the event his journalistic and literary career got going almost at once, and he would not encounter Richard Ingrams again for several years.

In *Will This Do?* Bron describes what he saw as having been the reasons for his inability to get to grips with his ill-chosen degree course in politics, philosophy and economics (having gone for PPE 'on the grounds that it sounded vaguely clever and modern'), while making the proviso that readers could 'easily skip the next few paragraphs'. The advice still stands, but any reader who does skip will be missing a treat:

> Lesson one in formal logic, which seeks to reduce logical argument to algebraic symbols as a means of testing its validity, concerns a symbol called the hook, thus ⊃. The practical function of the hook might best be translated by the English word 'therefore': A, therefore B, or if A, then B. A ⊃ B. However, neither the consequent nor the conditional role was considered sufficiently formal, so the function of the hook was reduced still further to give A ⊃ B the precise meaning as follows: 'It is not the case that A is true and B is false.' So long as A is true and B is true, the hook is true. If A is true and B is false, the hook is false. So far, so good. Now we come to the *pons asinorum*. If A is untrue, then the hook is true whatever the truth of B. The reason for this is that the hook guarantees only that A cannot be true and B false. However, this restriction removes the hook from all application to truth or reason, and reduces it to a mathematical symbol. There are no circumstances in which 'A therefore B' or 'If A then B' automatically become true statements when A is shown to be false. If the hook does not cover either the consequent or the conditional relationship, but one of its own invention, then its only applied function must be either as a parlour game or as a liar's charter. Formal logic, like so many other things studied in the universities, must surely be a colossal waste of time. Far better play with

Rubik's cube, which might impart a measure of digital dexterity which could be useful in a world threatened by a plague of RSI.

My objection to neo-classical economics was even more elementary. I stumbled and fell at the simple equation that savings equal investment. This cannot be gainsaid, since it is built into the definition of the two words as used by the disciples of Marshall, whereby they seek to create a tautology out of what is plainly an untruth. There are plenty of things to be done with savings which do not involve investment or consumption, the most obvious of which is to put them under your mattress. Although this objection is not central to the whole study of economics, as my objection to the hook was central to the current practice of formal logic, nevertheless it occurred to me that any scientific discipline which worded one of its main propositions so sloppily must be a waste of time.

The success of *The Foxglove Saga* (1960), employment for £9 a week at *Queen* magazine and a successful application for a junior post on the diary column of the *Daily Telegraph* marked the start of his professional writing life. Launching himself into the graft of Grub Street to earn his living and make a name turned out to be not such a rash move after all. In July 1961, still only at the age of twenty-one, he became a married man. His bride was Teresa, the daughter of Lord and Lady Onslow, and there was a reception on the terrace of the House of Lords. His bread-and-butter commissions, however, continued for a few years to be somewhat more dependent on writing for the tabloids than he might have wished. Then, in 1967, Nigel Lawson offered him a leg up into 'higher journalism' by signing him on for a regular political column in the *Spectator*.

Bron joined the *Spectator* that September as its political correspondent, knowing, he confessed, almost nothing about politics. 'My only qualification for the job was a certain scepticism about anything I was told and an unbudgeable suspicion of political motives.' In this he was consistent and Nigel Lawson took him under his wing to guide him through the political thickets of the time; and so, under his tutelage, Bron began to learn about politics. He came to the conclusion that most politicians were 'social and emotional misfits, handicapped folk, those with a grudge'. In a later *Spectator* piece on his reaction in 1984 to a performance of 'Peter Hall's magnificent *Coriolanus* at the Olivier theatre', he commented:

> I never understood the play until seeing Ian McKellen's memorable performance. The play's message is very simple, and even more relevant to modern democratic society than it was in Tudor England, that politics is not a suitable occupation for a gentleman… Politics, as I never tire of saying, is for social and emotional misfits, handicapped folk, those with a grudge. The purpose of politics is to help them overcome these feelings of inferiority and compensate for their personal inadequacies in the pursuit of power. Power, I imagine, is all that democratic politicians have ever been interested in. Those who do not suffer from this urge may have difficulty in understanding it: they may even be reluctant to believe in its existence. Among the lower classes it is generally supposed that politicians are in it for the money, but I believe that they are wrong, and we should all study this phenomenon of the power urge. It seems to cause far more unhappiness than happiness.
>
> The yells and animal noises which the nation listens to on the radio programme *Today in Parliament* have nothing to do with disagreements about the way the country should be run, or how much fuel should be given to old-age pensioners at Christmas time. They are cries of pain and anger, mingled with hatred and envy, at the spectacle of another group exercising the 'power' which the first group covets; alternatively, they are cries of alarm as the group in 'power' sees its territory threatened. Old-age pensioners are mad if they think anyone cares about their wretched coal. Until one understands this one will never understand the confrontational nature of democratic politics. The only thing that any of them is really interested in is the chance to make decisions and see them put into effect – to press a button and watch us all jump.

His attitude to political journalism was likewise rigorous in its contempt. Also from the *Spectator* is this general comment made in 1971:

> The role of journalists is to ridicule, humiliate and generally torment politicians, pour scorn on everything they propose to do and laugh at them when they do it. We should never, never, never suggest new ways for them to spend money, or taxes they could increase, or new laws they could pass. There is nothing so ridiculous as the posture of journalists who see themselves as part of the sane and pragmatic decision-making process.

And in yet another observation from the *Spectator*:

> In several years' sitting through every important debate in the House of Commons, I never consciously heard anyone tell it a word of truth. I never once checked on an answer to a Parliamentary Question without finding it either gravely misleading or a straight lie.

By the later 1960s Bron and Richard Ingrams had been remaking one another's acquaintance. In 1968 Bron nominated Richard for the *Spectator's* Honours List, and Richard realized there was a warmth coming towards him from Bron, and even a regard, that he had never detected in any of the dealings they had with each other at Oxford. It also so happened that they were living near to each other in the country, and since Mary (Richard's wife) and Teresa Waugh took to each other, their acquaintanceship began to ripen into a friendship.

Bron was fired from the staff of the *Spectator* by Nigel Lawson in 1970 for having meddled, in a fit of mischief, with the contents page while he was subbing it at the printers. It was 'a mild prank', said Bron, aimed at his fellow journalist George Gale, whose byline he had altered to read 'Lunchtime O'Gale', the joke being that this was a variant on *Private Eye's*

generic term, 'Lunchtime O'Booze', for a drunken hack with a drink problem. Lawson did not think this at all funny and sacked Bron 'on the spot'.
'It was a sad end to a happy relationship,' wrote Bron in his introduction
to *Another Voice* (1986), his anthology of his *Spectator* pieces, but it would
have various rewarding consequences. He sued Lawson for breach of
contract and ultimately won handsome damages, but before the case had
even come to court, Lawson 'had himself been dismissed as Editor', and

> Mr George Gale had been appointed in his place, and I had been reap-
> pointed to write a weekly column on books – by Mr Gale. When the
> case was eventually heard at St Marylebone Crown Court, Lawson, as
> a sacked editor, had to defend himself for sacking me, who had since
> been re-employed, for insulting the man who had since re-employed me.

In due course the weekly column on books was succeeded in the *Spectator*
by the 'Another Voice' column, which continued for several years and
became home to many of Bron's weightier and more considered pieces
that needed some room for expansion. But also on the day of his sacking,
Friday, 13 February 1970, Bron had taken a walk from the offices of the
Spectator in Gower Street to the offices of *Private Eye* in Greek Street, and
there

> Richard Ingrams hired me as the first political correspondent of *Private
> Eye*. The pay was not particularly generous – £50 a fortnight. 'But I
> imagine that our circulation will increase so enormously now you
> have joined us that we will be able to increase your fees accordingly,'
> said Ingrams.
>
> By odd coincidence, the circulation of *Private Eye* did indeed increase
> enormously at about that time, although obviously not as a result of my
> having joined the team – very few of its readers had the slightest interest
> in politics, except possibly of the infantile left. Although I remained
> at the *Eye* for sixteen years, and wages just about crept up in line with
> inflation, I cannot say that they ever increased much in real terms. But

at least the arrangement gave me an office, a telephone and a home-from-home in London, without which I felt certain I would have gone mad. Living in the country has that effect on people.

Waugh states in his autobiography that he was taken on as the magazine's political correspondent, but Richard Ingrams has queried from his own perspective whether this was the actual intention. He did not necessarily trust Bron on politics. Back in their Oxford days, he had felt that in fact Waugh didn't like him much, and neither could he say he was all that impressed with Waugh. He had the impression Bron was still trying to be too much like his father, Evelyn, and liked 'sucking up to toffs'. Ingrams, on the other hand, was already certain and focused in his views on who were 'the right people' to know; with which Bron's attitudes were often at variance. There is a sentence in *Will This Do?* that might explain Bron's point of view best: 'My father brought me up to believe that if one had to be bored, it was better to be bored by a rich bore than by a poor bore. My children's generation … seems to take the opposite view.'

Where Richard Ingrams and Bron were concerned, Grey Gowrie had a fascinating insight into their relationship as he had perceived it during their days at Oxford. He thought the one character at the university, the one person whose approval Bron sought most, had been Richard Ingrams. Bron had missed out on the first eventful seven years of *Private Eye*, so in 1970 he was joining a settled team in which he had to establish his own space. On whatever terms his and Ingrams's paths began to intertwine at that stage, what can be said for certain is that for his first year or so of working at Greek Street, Bron's initial commission was to write the *Eye*'s political-satire column, 'HP Sauce', this supposedly being the favourite condiment of the then Labour prime minister, Harold Wilson, a preference thought to be shared with the working class in general. Bron did not, as it happened, retain any particularly fond memories of working on the column.

[It] took a certain amount of time to find its feet and was only a moderate success at the end of the day. It was all very well insulting politicians and making up funny nicknames for them, but very few people were interested in politicians, and if ever I got a fact wrong, there was the danger of a writ. More litigious even than the politicians were the other political journalists, with whom I had a running battle …

Although only one libel case ever came to court against 'HP Sauce', there were a number of irritating complaints, two of which had to be settled out of court. Libel actions, generally speaking, are no joke. They are boring, worrying and take up an enormous amount of time.

In saying this Bron is not perhaps being entirely transparent. As will become clear, libel cases always held a fascination for him. Richard Ingrams has recalled that Bron and Peter Cook equally took delight in attending the various libel cases the *Eye* was involved in, both of them sitting in court, making notes and avidly following proceedings. Where 'HP Sauce' was concerned, however, Bron began to find it increasingly irritating, combined with 'an awareness that the column was no longer much good'. He himself suggested to Richard Ingrams that it was time for it to be discontinued. As an alternative suggestion Richard then came up with the idea for 'Auberon Waugh's Diary', which 'ran for the next fourteen years'.

Bron recalled in his autobiography that 'of all the hundreds and thousands of words I have written in a life's scribbling', 'Auberon Waugh's Diary', later collected as *The Diaries of Auberon Waugh*, in two volumes, *Four Crowded Years, 1972–1976* and *A Turbulent Decade, 1976–1986*, 'is the series of which I am the most proud'. Initially created to be a parody of 'Alan Brien's Diary', published every week on the back page of the *Sunday Times*, Bron developed a unique voice of outrageous, suggestive abuse, ostensibly coming from a man about town who, though just up from the country, where he lorded it over the locals, attended every important social function in the metropolis. He described its conceit in his autobiography:

The essence of the Diary, as it emerged, was that it was a work of pure fantasy, except that the characters in it were real. If ever some president or head of state paid an official visit, I was there to greet him. If ever the

45

Queen gave a ball or luncheon party, I was there to dance with her or help her survive the terrible bores who had in fact been invited – their names were often available in the court circular or gossip columns … It worked very well indeed, and I began to think I might have created a new art form. However, its success was [also] partly because there was the slight suspicion in the back of people's minds that I might indeed be very rich and grand, and they could never be absolutely sure when I was pulling their legs.

Alan Brien, as the model that set the series going, became a target for Bron's ire and irritation by 'the simple expedient' of saying Bron's writing in 'HP Sauce' was not funny. Brien, while conceding that 'the political column in the *Spectator* had been funny … could not detect a glimmer of wit in my *Eye* stuff'. 'My revenge,' wrote Bron, 'took two years to get off the ground, but [then] it ran, as I say, for fourteen years.' 'Alan Brien's Diary', by contrast, promptly disappeared from the pages of the *Sunday Times* within a few months. Brien was an unrepentant socialist whose journalistic success could be almost a mirror image of Waugh's, and towards the end of his life, despite the earlier frisson, he was contributing to the *Literary Review* under Bron's editorship. A circle of sorts was thus completed.

Bron shared a cubby hole of an office at the *Eye* with Paul Foot, which he had decorated with William Morris wallpaper. He only ever wrote copy by hand and dictated it to the typesetter – the only contributor that ever did so. The office was next to the ground-floor entrance. A group of angry cult members from Emin (an esoteric movement, formed in the 1970s in the wake of the 'New Age') called in, after an exposé in the *Eye*, written by Halloran (an *Eye* regular), to demand an apology. Bron told them it had been written by Wilfred De'Ath and sent them off to the *Daily Express* to protest their outrage there. He also absent-mindedly threw a lit cigarette from the first-floor window to fall on the hat of a lady who also entered the building to demand satisfaction.

Richard Ingrams thought Bron liked attending the lunches at the Coach and Horses, though he didn't like the pub or the atmosphere very much.

Bron preferred the Beefsteak where he was a member. Ingrams remembered an unusual luncheon which a friend of his father's – an Austrian banker, Gustav Glück – asked if he could attend. Ingrams introduced him to Richard Crossman who, recognizing Glück's face, realized that this was the man who had married his first wife after their divorce in 1934. A strange coincidence, as it was also at that lunch that Tina Brown heard Crossman reveal that he, Aneurin Bevan and Morgan Phillips had perjured themselves in a famous libel action against the *Spectator* (see page 96).

In 1990, Bron agreed to give an interview with Naim Attallah for *Singular Encounters*, a collection of interviews with men to follow up the success of Attallah's first book, *Women*. Talking about his *Private Eye* years Bron reflected:

> When you work for sixteen years on *Private Eye* you really do need enemies. I don't have many, but on the whole I cherish those I've got and go on building them up. My attacks on Lord Gowrie certainly have their origins at Oxford and my being unhappy in love there, but my feelings towards him today are more tied up with my hatred of modern art. If I keep the attack going it is partly out of force of habit, because once you savage the enemy you might as well carry on. I don't really bear grudges. It is only copy, and these things are more like public feuds. I used to have a nightmare, particularly when I worked for *Private Eye*, of entering a room and finding all those I'd insulted there, mostly politicians I've been rude about, such as Wedgie Benn, or that disgusting man Eldon Griffiths, or of course Lord Hailsham, whom I've always mistrusted. That had its origins when I was about fourteen and Hailsham came to [my school] Downside to give a lecture. I thought then what an appalling, affected man he was. Much later I learned about his behaviour to P. G. Wodehouse and decided to go for him, and I've been doing it ever since.

Harry Thompson, in his biography of Richard Ingrams, *Richard Ingrams: Lord of the Gnomes* (1994), reveals Ingrams as sounding a somewhat different note in his feelings about Bron:

I did feel uneasy about one or two of his personal campaigns against individuals, and I think probably I should have been stricter with my blue pencil, looking back on it. Because I think he does pursue personal vendettas against people out of malice, and that is regrettable.

An instance where he consistently used his blue pencil to shield an individual from Bron's mode of attack occurred in the case of Barry Fantoni, the only member of the *Eye* inner circle then who was not a product of the British-public-school tradition. A writer and satirist, cartoonist and jazz musician, Fantoni contributed many of the *Eye*'s best visual and verbal jokes over almost fifty years, including the 'E. J. Thribb' rhyming obituaries, which always began 'So. Farewell now ...' Bron claimed he had no animus against Fantoni, but that he seemed to present as good a target as anyone else, and naturally Bron was constantly in need of targets. Yet whenever he launched an insult in Fantoni's direction, Ingrams cut it out. This simply made Bron itch more to land a shot, and he bided his time till Ingrams was away on holiday; but when the time came he found that Ingrams had anticipated him and posted a sentry to wield the blue pencil in his stead. Bron hinted that this frustration was the final straw that made him feel, after fourteen years, that the time had come to move on from the *Eye*; but then, as we shall see, Bron at different points came up with a multitude of reasons to explain why this critical point had been reached.

So far as his basic relationship with Ingrams was concerned, Bron asserted in his autobiography:

My affection and admiration for Richard will always carry ... a heavy burden of gratitude. Nobody else would have published 'Auberon Waugh's Dairy', let alone kept it going for fourteen years. However ephemeral it is bound to prove, I suspect it will remain my proudest achievement.

And it can certainly be argued that Ingrams has been more influential in the development of an independent press in Britain than any other journalist of his time. *Private Eye* could, it is true, sometimes seem childish, petty, bloody-minded or malicious, but its insistence on exposing hypocrisy and deceit by satire, even creating its own special vocabulary of coded euphemisms – who can forget the phrase 'Ugandan discussions', meaning the temporary absence of someone for opportunistic sex – resulted in a magazine that brought about a fundamental change in public discourse.

That Bron himself was a romantic at heart was shown by the way he could go on sustaining for years animosity towards any other male who had crossed him in a matter of affection. It began back at Oxford with the young woman student – she of the 'lustrous brown eyes' – whose attention had been drawn away from Bron by Grey Gowrie. Bron's at times rabid abuse of Gowrie through the phases of their subsequent careers seemed obsessive and relentless, though Gowrie was actually never troubled too much by it, even when appearing as a black-face grotesque in Willie Rushton's illustrations for Bron's *Private Eye* diary. Should they ever meet (which was not that often), relations were cordial. The one thing with which Lord Gowrie never felt comfortable, however, was the way Bron made continual attacks on the writings of Anthony Powell, Gowrie being President of the Anthony Powell Society [see pages 297–299].

Alan Watkins, writing about Bron in his *Brief Lives* (revised edition, Elliott & Thompson, 2004), made the suggestion that 'there was something a little eerie about the way he pursued his father's dislikes and vendettas, even when their subjects were safely in their graves'. These included:

> Churchill and Duff Cooper (though largely on account of their treatment of P. G. Wodehouse) and Cyril Connolly and, among the living, Stephen Spender, Lord Lovat and Peter Quennell. As a corollary, he treated his father's old friends well on the whole. He was extravagantly admiring of Graham Greene, and was always indulgent to his godfather Lord Longford. There was at least one exception in Anthony Powell, who maintained that Waugh formed dislikes of his father's friends because he had been frightened by his father. But the truth seemed to be simpler, which was that Auberon Waugh considered Powell's [novel sequence

A Dance to the] Music of Time tedious and overpraised – particularly by
literary hangers-on.

Watkins also made the point that sexual jealousy was one of the strands
that provided the driving force for some of Bron's most scurrilous attacks,
often going back, of course, to student days in Oxford. In fact Watkins
was the first to blow the cover on the real reason for Bron's treatment
of Gowrie. Bron' s 'Beatrice' figure, whose name he gallantly sought to
conceal and who was, as he saw it, stolen away from him by Gowrie,
had been Grizelda Grimond, only daughter of Jo Grimond, leader of the
Liberal Party at a critical post-war period, and through her mother's line a
great-granddaughter of Herbert Asquith. For the alert there had actually
always been a clue to her identity in plain sight, since not only did Bron
gift her a necklace of onyx beads to match her eyes, he also included her
in the dedication of his first novel, *The Foxglove Saga*. At Oxford she had
never lacked for suitors, as is clear from the story told in her *Times* obituary notice (29 July 2017):

> She returned to her college one day to find a note on the door that read,
> 'Will you marry me?' To this was added not just the signature of the
> author but the names of several other callers beneath the words, 'And
> me', 'And me', 'And me'.

Grizelda Grimond never did marry, but she fell in love with the film director Tony Richardson, and had a daughter by him. Her name is commem-
orated in a garden area at the National Gallery, created at her suggestion
when she worked there as an assistant to the director.

Whatever the differences in the personalities of Bron and Ingrams, Alan
Watkins considered one point of similarity to be that both 'persisted in
believing something even when contrary evidence was produced': in

Watkins's view, this conviction could be seen as 'at once a strength and a weakness'. Right or wrong, certainty for some can energize all sorts of activity and produce remarkable results. It was Ingrams who made the suggestion that Bron should stand against Jeremy Thorpe in the General Election of May 1979 in the former Liberal leader's constituency of North Devon, for which he was the standing MP. What followed turned out to be one of the funniest pokes in the eye for the English establishment anyone could have wished for.

Thorpe, though somewhat louche, was a wily politician, but he was having to fight the election under the shadow of a trial for conspiracy with others to murder Norman Scott, with whom he was alleged to have had an affair and who had become a persistent thorn in his side and threat to his reputation. It was a story that had been in and out of the press since 1975, attracting much attention in *Private Eye*. In the course of the alleged murder attempt, a hit-man had managed to shoot dead, instead of Scott, his dog Rinka. The *Eye* had played a prominent part in the case which was eventually being brought to court and Bron had been giving regular exposure to the unfolding story in his 'Diary' column. In retrospect the whole extraordinary business has come to be seen as a serious matter into which the spirit of comedy relentlessly intruded, as brilliantly reflected in a recent BBC TV mini-series directed by Stephen Frears.

The Jeremy Thorpe End-of-the-Pier Show

Despite the best attempts of Thorpe's solicitors to get an injunction to suppress it and have Waugh jailed for contempt of court, Bron's campaign address was published in both the *Spectator* and the *Guardian*. It read as follows:

VOTE WAUGH

A BETTER DEAL FOR YOUR DOG

Unaccustomed as I am to public speaking I offer myself as your Member of Parliament in the General Election on behalf of the nation's dog lovers to protest about the behaviour of the Liberal Party generally and the North Devon Constituency Liberal Association in particular. Their candidate is a man about whose attitude to dogs – not to mention his fellow human beings – little can be said with any certainty at the present time. But while it is one thing to observe the polite convention that a man is innocent until proven guilty, it is quite another thing to take a man who has been publicly accused of crimes which would bring him to the cordial dislike of all right-minded citizens and dog lovers, and treat him as a hero. Before Mr Thorpe has had time to establish his innocence of these extremely serious charges, he has been greeted with claps, cheers and yells of acclamation by his admirers in the Liberal Party, both at the National Conference in Southport and here in the constituency. I am sorry but I find this disgusting. I invite all the electors of North Devon, but especially the more thoughtful Liberals and dog lovers, to register their disquiet by voting for me on

3 May and I sincerely hope that at least fifty voters in this city will take the opportunity to do so.

Genesis XVIII 26: And the LORD said 'If I find in Sodom fifty right-eous within the city, then I will spare all the place for their sakes.'

1 Samuel XXIV 14: After whom dost thou pursue? After a dead dog, after a flea.

Rinka is NOT forgotten. Rinka lives. Woof, woof.

Vote Waugh to give all dogs the right to life,
liberty and the pursuit of happiness.

A photograph of the Dog Lovers' Party of Great Britain's candidate had been snapped under a tree in Soho Square.

In an article he wrote for the *Independent* in December 2014 recollecting a period of dalliances with British Liberal politicians, D. J. Taylor remembered the impact made on his adolescent provincial upbringing in Norfolk by:

Auberon Waugh's election address to the electors of North Devon, issued shortly after Thorpe's acquittal on a charge of conspiracy to murder his putative former boyfriend Norman Scott and shortly before Waugh stood against Thorpe on behalf of a single-candidate pressure group called the Dog Lovers' Party. An injunction having been granted, this document, printed in the *Spectator* in lieu of Waugh's weekly column, was instantly recalled, but not before a few copies had made it to the Norwich branch of W. H. Smith.

In *Will This Do?* Bron chronicled his own narrative of the case:

It was two years before the allegations against Thorpe came to a head with his arrest in August 1978 on charges of having attempted and conspired to murder a male model, Norman Scott, with whom he was acquainted, four years earlier. My own first mention of the matter came on 15 December 1975, when I describe how west Somerset was buzzing with rumours after Scott, 'who claims to have been a great friend of Jeremy Thorpe, the Liberal statesman, was found by an AA patrolman weeping beside the body of Rinka, his Great Dane bitch, which had been shot in the head'. I ended my piece on a friendly, encouraging note:

> My only hope is that sorrow over his friend's dog will not cause Mr Thorpe's premature retirement from public life. Jeremy is not only a very wonderful person in his own right, he is also a gifted impersonator of London celebrities like Lady Dartmouth [a footnote added: Later Countess of Spencer *(sic)*] and Mr Heath. Indeed in the whole of fashionable London, I can think only of John Wells as possibly being his equal in this field and Wells, of course, has other disadvantages.

The 'other disadvantages' in John Wells included a tendency to sniff, which I had spotted at an early stage in our acquaintance. But this friendly, encouraging attitude towards Thorpe did not represent my true feelings at that time. Other journalists, like the Cambridge-educated Christopher Booker and the previously mentioned John Pilger [another regular target for Bron's scorn], seem to live in a perpetual state of indignation, but practically nothing made me genuinely indignant, at any rate since the Biafran war five years earlier. Rather to my surprise, I found myself genuinely indignant at the suggestion that murder was to be reintroduced as a means of political advancement for the first time since the Tudors, and even more indignant that the legal and political establishments in all their forms – which included, at that stage, the police – were going to cover up the whole episode. In the event, it turned out that my anxieties were unfounded, as Thorpe was totally innocent of all charges brought against him. But it was this anxiety that sustained me through four years of what may have seemed to be no more than another routine persecution of a politician. It led me to accept Ingrams's satirical suggestion that I should stand against Thorpe in the General

Election of 1979 on behalf of the Dog Lovers' Party of Great Britain, and even after Mr Justice Cantley's extraordinary summing up at the Old Bailey trial and Thorpe's subsequent acquittal on all charges, it led me to write a book about the trial, making whatever points remained to be made. The book, called *The Last Word: An Eyewitness Account of the Thorpe Trial* (London, Michael Joseph, 1980) still strikes me as quite good ... [and he urges anyone who might still own a copy to have another go at reading it].

Meanwhile, my pursuit or hounding of Thorpe followed its usual oblique, crablike course. On the day before the trial of the dog shooter, Andrew Gino Newton, in Exeter, the *Sunday Times* allowed Thorpe to print a violent attack on the defendant including the information that he (Thorpe) was not and never had been a homosexual. On the day the trial opened, [Harold] Wilson announced his resignation [as prime minister] and the Snowdons announced their impending divorce, so the event was rather eclipsed, but the fact that nobody ever mentioned the laws of contempt in relation to the *Sunday Times* article and the trial of Newton made me wonder what was happening.

In November 1977, when Newton was released from prison and was offering his story round the newspapers, Thorpe called a press conference in New Scotland Yard, of all places, to announce his innocence in the face of persistent rumours. I wrote in my 'Diary':

1 November 1977

To New Scotland Yard where Jeremy Thorpe has called a press conference to discuss various allegations that have been made about his sex life. I have many interesting new allegations to make, but they threw me out at the door.

When all the weeping toadies are assembled, only one of them dares to ask him whether he has ever done it. Mr Keith Graves, of BBC TV, who is hereby given the Gnome Award for News Reporter of the Year, has been vilified by every prig and Pharisee in Fleet Street for asking the only worthwhile question.

Poor Jeremy. He is his own worst enemy, but with friends like these he really has no need of himself. The only remaining mystery is why the Liberal Party policy committee decided to murder Scott rather than Jeremy.

In an affectionate moment, Thorpe had written to Scott that 'bunnies can and will go to France'. When the glorious moment of Thorpe's arrest came in August 1978, I was in France, staying at La Pesegado, with Ferdinand and Julia Mount and their children as guests. By sheer good luck a previous tenant had left a television set behind, and as Ferdie was interested in politics we watched the French news [events that were transmogrified into this in the 'Diary']:

5 August 1978

News of Jeremy Thorpe's arrest breaks like a thunderclap over the Languedoc countryside. There is dancing in the streets, ceremonial rabbits are cooked and groups of peasants with lanterns are to be found wandering the lanes far into the night, singing at the tops of their voices and beating the hedges with staves.

… Over here, where people were understandably alarmed by Thorpe's assertion that 'bunnies can and will go to France', a collection is being made to provide some token of their gratitude and relief over the new development.

I suggest that this take the form of a monument to Rinka, the unfortunate [Great Dane]. Contrary to general belief, the French are even more obsessed by dogs than the English are, and a monument subscribed by the Languedoc farmers to stand at the lonely, windswept spot on Porlock Hill, Exmoor, where Rinka was so foully done to death would be poignant testimony to the neighbourly way in which Europeans share each other's sufferings and joys.

A picture of the monument was supplied by William Rushton for my 'Diary' of 30 October 1978, when I describe myself as leading a deputation to the lay-by on Porlock Hill – just fifteen miles from Combe Florey – which 'stands in silence for a while in memory of the dead Great Dane, Rinka, who gave her life to create a better world'.

> All those present pledge themselves anew to the struggle. Rinka's sacrifice will not be forgotten. She will be avenged, and a cleaner, healthier society will arise. Rinka lives on in our hearts.

I sat throughout the week of magistrates' court hearings in Minehead, taking notes. The atmosphere was less formal than at the Old Bailey. Thorpe wandered up to me one morning and said: 'Scribble, scribble, scribble, Mr Waugh', with a sickly grin. It was the last exchange I ever had with him. I did not go down to North Devon to canvass support as Dog Lovers' Party candidate in the General Election, as I had been banned by the courts from publishing my election manifesto or giving any account of why I was standing. Mr Carman, Thorpe's barrister, applied to the Divisional Court to have me committed to prison and my manifesto banned, but the Lord Chief Justice threw [the application] out. On appeal, Lord Denning reinstated the ban, saying he had been reading *Private Eye* and was in no doubt of my intention to pervert the course of justice.

Even so, seventy-nine people voted for me. Thorpe lost his seat, but the most interesting feature of the result was how few Liberals switched their votes. Despite Thorpe's name being dragged through the press every day for a week, with lurid accounts of buggery, financial crookery and attempted murder, fewer than 5,000 voters out of an electorate of 77,000 actually switched their votes away from him at an election which produced a higher Conservative swing elsewhere. He still received 23,338 votes, having received 28,209 in October 1974. One wondered how much harm was really done to anybody by the written word, and how our savage laws of libel can really be justified except as a convenience for the rich and powerful to save themselves from criticism.

3

EXTRACTS FROM THE
DIARIES OF AUBERON WAUGH, 1972–1985

11 November 1972

WHEN I WAS AT SCHOOL A FAVOURITE LARK OF THE ENGLISH sixth form was to send off a letter every month to poor Ezra Pound in his Washington mad house, asking him some earnest question about his ridiculous *Cantos*. Sometimes he would answer with a brief obscenity – always typed, unsigned and undated – sometimes with a long, passionate screed of gibberish. These were read aloud in various satirical voices to great laughter and applause. We always threw them away afterwards ... Perhaps Pound could have written decent poetry if he had tried, and if he had not been surrounded by half-witted sycophants encouraging him to turn out this solemn drivel. There may not be any particular reason to suppose he had a talent for poetry, but we have no means of being sure. Pound was indeed one of the luminaries of what is laughingly called the Modern Movement which has encouraged poets, writers and artists to get away with preposterous rubbish for the last fifty years. Thank heaven that at last we have got the great and good Sir John Betjeman for our Laureate. Soon there will be nobody left in the Modern Movement but a handful of ageing critics...

6 December 1972

We shall probably never know exactly how many contestants for the Miss World title in any given year are actually female impersonators. Unlike the organizers of Olympic and other sporting events which involve women, nobody in the Albert Hall demands on-the-spot inspections or sex tests. Yet it is a curious and undeniable fact that wherever women compete publicly together, a few men are tempted to join in the fray. This may explain the outcry from contestants whenever anybody suggests they should parade in the nude. Certainly it is much more fun trying to spot the female impersonators.

26 January 1973

When I called at her cottage in St Ives, Cornwall, to wish her many happy returns on her seventieth birthday, Dame Barbara Hepworth, who is the world's greatest sculptor since Donatello, reminded me irresistibly of one of her own statues. She stood in the garden on this cold January morning quite still and so far as I could see, completely unclothed. Her stomach, far from showing the expected middle-aged spread, was, in fact, a highly polished cavity, spatially related to the idea of a stomach contained within its void. Her breasts, which grew from her shoulder blades at the back, were surprisingly firm and quintessentially feminine. She answered none of my questions except for one slight moan. I thought I recognized it as middle D in the Vox Humana range with diapason backing. On the other hand, it might have been caused by the wind blowing through her stomach cavity. In either case, it was a most moving and memorable experience.

20 February 1973

I hope someone in authority will look into the current unscrupulous campaign to raise £2,500,000 for LSE's Library of Political and Economic Science. The existing library contains more rubbish than any other single building on earth, and not a word which any sane person would wish to believe. The library's only serious function is to provide a little extra income for LSE students who steal books from it and sell them second hand.

21 March 1973

The first [and evidently the only] time I was taken to tea with Ivy Compton Burnett must have been in 1945 or 1946 when I was about six. She had expressed a desire to meet me, but at that age I had a particular taste for jam tarts, and Miss Burnett neglected to serve them – whether from incompetence or deliberate malice I was never able to discover. To make matters worse she placed me on a high chair like a two-year-old and proceeded to feed me with scones dipped in milk, much to the amusement of Sir Max Beerbohm and Bernard Shaw. Understandably annoyed by this, I bit her finger and proceeded to be violently sick all over the tablecloth and into the lap of H. G. Wells, to whom I had also taken a dislike. Wells died soon after, and Miss Burnett never asked me to tea again, which I can't help feeling a pity, as I am sure we could have got along quite well and had some good fun together once she learned the simple rules of hospitality.

21 April 1973

Sometimes I worry about our children. They sit watching odious, patronizing rubbish like *Blue Peter* week after week, and when a chance comes to get their own back they do nothing about it. The *Blue Peter* Old Folks Appeal for treasures from the attic was a golden opportunity for the nation's kiddies to show their satirical metal. My own attics are a treasury of rotting mattresses, fossilized dog shit, old sets of false teeth, dead bats, broken bulbs and old plastic potties. If only I had heard of the appeal in time, it would have been the work of a moment to send the entire contents round to *Blue Peter*. If enough people had done the same we might have put a stop to this sentimental filth which is perverting the moral awareness of an entire generation.

11 July 1973

Sometimes I curse my strict Christian upbringing which prevents me from suing fellow hacks for libel. In this month's *Harpers and Queen* there is a revolting article ... about literary parties [that] claims that Auberon Waugh, a 'failed novelist', is frequently to be seen at these gatherings which are 'not fit for decent people', being noted for lechery and drunkenness. 'An owlish figure', this Waugh is easily recognizable by having 'straw and animal substances adhering to his tweeds'. In fact, I have only been to one literary party in the last six years – in a dark suit, without straw or animal substances. No impropriety occurred. [In the right hands] this vicious libel would certainly be worth a couple of thousand pounds.

12 July 1973

The great Anthony Burgess, who really is one of the better novelists in the world, has come in for heavy criticism in court where a sixteen-year-old pipe-lagger is accused of murder under the influence of Burgess's delightful and instructive novel, *A Clockwork Orange*. The press has joined in gleefully, and one wonders how many other foolish young men will be tempted to their own do-it-yourself clockwork oranges after reading about it in the newspapers. The long-term answer is surely not to ban intelligent novels, or even cretinous newspapers from reporting these unsavoury things. It is to stop teaching these impressionable people how to read, since they're obviously not equipped to cope with so much emotional and intellectual stimulation.

13 July 1973

Considerable alarm has been caused in government circles by a report of an Ancient Egyptian princess whose mummy when X-rayed now turns out to be that of a baboon. Sir Peter Rawlinson, the Attorney-General, is considering legislation to make it a serious offence to X-ray members of the Royal Family.

22 July 1973

'I am an old-age pensioner aged 84 and live in a bed-sitter. I find my N.H. Pension ample for lunch out every day, postages, newspapers, occasional bus fares and 50 pence for the Offertory on Sunday,' writes a correspondent in the *Sunday Telegraph*. With more careful stewardship, he could probably run a string of race horses, too. Congratulations to the *Sunday Telegraph* for finding this courageous man. So many old-age pensioners are in fear of their lives if they mention how happy they are, or how embarrassed by the enormous sums of money the government pours into their pockets. Stupefied by food and drink, they can just stagger from their restaurants to church where they hope to secure forgiveness for their indolent, luxurious lives on earth by extravagant bribes to the clergy.

30 July 1973

It is a pity the *Sunday Times* poll on which professions are considered most trustworthy, and which least trustworthy, did not include a placing on Roman Catholic priests. Probably they would have come out highest of all... On the other hand, if the findings rated RC priests lower than might be hoped, the *Sunday Times* was quite right to suppress them. Needless to say, journalists were thought least trustworthy by the greatest number, although to read the *Sunday Times* headlines and report one might not have gathered as much. What is really alarming in these figures is that four per cent of the people still think Members of Parliament trustworthy. Have all my efforts in this field been fruitless, or are these four per cent simply the insanely obstinate, the deaf and dumb, whom one can only hope to reach through prayer?

15 March 1974

News of the Archbishop of Canterbury's retirement will come as a sad shock to all satirists.

24 March 1974

The present [Labour] government has already added a footnote to the English language by its use of the expression 'national unity' to mean taking away more of my hard-earned cash and giving it to the lower classes. The louder Mr Wilson talks of his unity, the faster we should count our spoons... So far as any of us have any interest in politics, we should surely direct it towards seeing that the lower classes do not get any richer than they already are and make the country more hideous than it already is with their transistor radios and plastic accessories. I see it may be my patriotic duty to do no work at all next year.

10 April 1974

The new law introduced by Michael Foot that anyone meeting a strike picket has got to stop and talk to it may seem progressive but could easily become another instrument for oppressing the masses. The great problem for the ordinary, law-abiding citizen is going to be what he can talk about to these people. The weather always seems a trifle lame but they seldom have much interest in art, religion, philosophy or literature. Perhaps the government will produce a green paper suggesting likely subjects and providing useful information about football matches, recent television programmes, etc. The crunch is going to come when a minority of wreckers decides to engage them in conversation about Kierkegaard or the novels of Alain Robbe-Grillet. An uncle of mine who is a philosopher suggests that what really enrages the masses is not so much any suggestion that other people may be richer than they are, but that other people may be superior to them. So this policy of enforced conversation may be a double-edged weapon so far as making any of them happier is concerned. I am not at all sure about this, but it may be worth trying.

23 April 1974

It is the kindest thing one can possibly say of a politician that he changed nothing.

28 April 1974

I wonder how much the *Sunday Times* has paid Jan Morris for the very wonderful, searing story of how she changed sex? It is little known that I am the only human being in the world who has changed sex and then changed back again. My reason for changing sex in the first place was a general feeling that at thirty-four it was time for a change. My reason for changing back was the ghastly boredom of women's conversation after dinner.

12 June 1974

Poor Spike Milligan is up before the beaks for shooting a marauder at his home with an air rifle. His mistake was to let the brute get away. Every house of any size in Somerset has its graveyard of would-be burglars. Usually their graves are unmarked, but some landowners with a sense of humour put up rather touching little headstones: FIDO, a faithful friend; DAFFODIL, not forgotten; PUSSIKINS, the best mouser ever.

30 June 1974

As the storm clouds gather and the threat of proletarian dictatorship looms ever nearer, many of my neighbours in Somerset have been building machine-gun emplacements and investing in anti-personnel landmines for their parks and parterres. This puts me in something of a dilemma, as I do not want a bloodbath, but obviously can't leave my dear wife and children completely unprotected against the day the working class marches up my drive to take possession of my marble halls. Probably the best thing would be to invite them in and poison them with paraquat, but this involves always being present to receive them. After much thought, I issue each of my dependants with a World War II gas mask and a supply of Milk of Magnesia tablets against the disgusting food they will have to eat in the new era of social progress. Ear plugs would probably be useful too, against the noises these people make and the terribly boring things they say. But not even the wives and children of the rich can expect everything. What did the good Lord give them fingers for?

13 July 1974

The Finer Report on single-parent families, which I've now read from cover to cover, recommends vastly increased assistance for unmarried mothers, as one would only expect. But it ignores the most crucial issue: have the children of unmarried mothers the right to describe themselves as 'Honourable' if their mother is subsequently given a life peerage? King Charles II's bastards certainly used courtesy titles as well as inheriting their mother's honours. But perhaps this is not an exact parallel. Until Mr Wilson sets up another Royal Commission to investigate the matter, the nation will remain in doubt.

The death at ninety of Dame Sybil Hathaway, the Dame of Sark, removes the only person in the British Isles whom I still wanted to meet. Unfortunately, she rejected all my advances. She was a model ruler for our times, forbidding not only cars and aircraft on her island, but also trade unions, taxation, female dogs, divorce, and most of the troublesome manifestations of our age. I had always hoped to persuade this admirable lady to take England under her rule when our parliamentary system finally disintegrates. Now she is dead I think I shall leave the country for a time – probably for a very long time. I can see no hope.

23 August 1974

Today [Sunday] being the Feast of St Lawrence, the whole neighbourhood is given over to dancing, drink and fornication. The priest who declared the orgy open in church this morning proposed that Wednesday should be observed as a day of fasting and penance in expiation for the excesses of the next forty-eight hours. After Mass I went round to shake the priest's hand and give him some money. This is always a painful experience. Nobody has ever explained satisfactorily to me why the hands of Catholic priests are so horribly soft. Some say it is a product of their sacramental powers, others that they use cold cream. My own theory is that they are made to sleep in boxing gloves, although I have never been able to think of a reason why this should be so. If any reader has an opinion on this curious phenomenon, I should be delighted to hear it.

2 October 1974

Whenever the subject of football hooliganism comes up, I rack my brains trying to think of a punishment which is bad enough for these dreadful people … until suddenly, today, I see the light. When Fritz Stangl, commandant of Treblinka and supervisor of some million murders, was arrested in Brazil in 1967, no one could think of a bad enough punishment for him, so they just put him in prison. Four years later he was visited by Miss Gitta Sereny, described as 'a slight woman in her fifties with an abrupt jarring way of laughing'. Miss Sereny was researching a treatise on the extermination camps which has now appeared – *Into That Darkness*. In it she reveals how the man who had personally supervised these atrocities without turning a hair was reduced to a shadow of himself by seventy hours of conversation with Miss Sereny. Nineteen hours after she had left him, he was dead. 'He had finally faced himself and told the truth,' she said. Obviously the way to end football hooliganism is to let it be known that Miss Sereny is researching a book into its social and emotional background. Anybody convicted of these offences will be required to spend up to five, or even ten, hours with her alone. Every football ground will carry posters showing her face and, as a special refinement, police riot squads will be equipped with loudspeakers and recordings of her high, jarring voice.

16 October 1974

What a miserable election it has been. [The General Election of October 1974 was narrowly won by Labour, giving Prime Minister Harold Wilson a majority of just three seats.] In the new spirit of austerity I take an Underground train from Islington to Tottenham Court Road. One would have thought that at least the lower classes would look happy to have won again, but they look absolutely wretched. Perhaps they always do, but in that case the whole thing seems a waste of time.

18 October 1974

Today I drive up to Bewdley, in Worcestershire, a delightful small town with a three star barmaid in the George Inn. I have come to interview Mrs Mary Whitehouse [the moral crusader] on behalf of the *New York Times* – an intelligent, articulate and charming woman, not at all the monster we are given to believe. In fact I watch television very seldom and cannot know what she is talking about much of the time, but when she mentions a programme on Florence Nightingale which I happen to have seen I have to agree with her wholeheartedly. I turned it on – no doubt like many others – because I have an interest in the period, but all we saw was some fatuous rubbish about two moronic twentieth-century students rubbing up against each other in bed. If Mrs Whitehouse can do anything to keep these conceited boring young men of the BBC and ITV in their place she should have the support of us all.

16 November 1974

I see the Novosti News Agency in Moscow has expressed admiration for Thames Television's series *The World at War*, which I mentioned at the time in connection with a long paean of praise to the Red Army's 'liberation' of Eastern Europe. Thames Television must be proud that their finished work comes up to the very exacting standard required by the Russian propaganda services. It would be a terrible shame, while so many pro-grammes are having to cut down on their budgets, if British know-how lost the opportunity of leading the world in Russian propaganda films.

16 January 1975

A visit from Miss Angela Levin, of the *Observer* colour section, who is interviewing the nation's top workers to discover the source of their exceptional energy. My secret is very simple. For breakfast, I touch nothing except a couple of young partridges (in season) or a fat capon, washed down with a quart of barley wine. I never eat aubergines, scotch broth or shellfish at breakfast. For lunch, I prefer to sit in a convenient church (or in the churchyard, if the weather is fine) to eat my cheese sandwiches with a bottle or so of whisky to help them down, while I ponder the eternal verities – life and death, beauty and pain, yin and yang, etc. After April, I will probably have to make do with a bottle of methylated spirits. In the afternoon, if my work involves heavy intellectual strain (VAT accounts, for instance, or an important game of bridge), I may drink a bottle of crème de menthe frappé on crushed ice. Tea is not taken seriously in any of my houses (thin cucumber sandwiches, followed by a hot meal or eel pie – even sausage and mash at a pinch – and ice cream). Dinner is the most important meal for the intake of energy by essential food supply. Here one tries to be as varied as possible, but a typical meal might start with pigs' blood pudding followed by demoiselles of goose, cold lobster or stuffed carp, roast suckling pig in honey, redcurrant-leaf sorbet, roast beef or venison, artichoke soufflé, orange or raspberry tart, snipe's entrails on toast, fruit jelly with cream and nuts. I think my agreeable complexion comes from the fruit jellies, while nuts are well known to be good for sexual performance.

25 January 1975

Prince Philip has asked me if anybody I know would like the job of being his personal valet. His present man, George Tribe – formerly of the Welsh Guards – is retiring and all applicants for the job so far have turned out to be pooves. Being a simple naval fellow, Prince Philip finds this worrying. If only he knew what the rest of us have to put up with in the way of domestic servants: drunken Irish cooks who have chased our dear wives round the kitchen table with a carving knife; Italian butlers who have gone mad and tried to murder the daily women; nannies who have grown horns and lost all their hair. I know nobody who is at the same time neat, deferential and sexually normal, but anyone interested should write to the Comptroller at Buckingham Palace, SW1, for further details.

12 February 1975

So [the new leader of the Conservative party] is to be Mrs Thatcher. As the only one of the five candidates in the final round who has ever dared to attend luncheons at *Private Eye*, she was undoubtedly the one who deserved best... Obviously Mrs Thatcher owes her election to the chivalrous instincts of the backbenchers... But I can't help feeling that chivalrous instincts are misplaced in politics and these new developments may mark the death of chivalry. If it is unbecoming in a man to wish to be Prime Minister and boss the rest of us around, it is doubly unbecoming in a woman. I blame Dennis Thatcher, whoever he may be, for not keeping his wife under control. Anybody else whose wife showed these distressing symptoms would shut her in her bedroom on bread and milk for a few days, sending her to a nursing home if she persisted. It is the wretched husband who should be blamed for all the troubles ahead.

5 April 1975

A new W. H. Auden Memorial industry seems set fair to rival the Churchill Centenary racket [with *W. H. Auden: A Tribute*, edited by Stephen Spender]. I hear Weidenfeld & Nicolson are seriously thinking of giving away little plastic busts of this wrinkled old bachelor, each one personally signed by Stephen Spender, to anyone who will buy his extraordinarily expensive volume of tributes. Auden certainly deserves a memorial or two, but I wonder who will be left to pretend that Stephen Spender was a great poet. Yet it really is quite a distinguished thing to have lived for sixty-six years as a poet without producing a single line which anybody could possibly wish to remember. You would have thought, by the law of averages, he would have written one such line, if only by accident.

19 April 1975

This evening, to my dismay, I find I have agreed to give a talk [in West Somerset] to the combined meeting of the Lydeard St Lawrence and Stogumber Young Wives. I suppose it was the idea of young wives that attracted me, but on my arrival in the village hall I find there is nobody who answers this description. My talk is on the theme, 'It is high time we had a Civil War in this country.' I point out the threat that exists to that most sacred of British Institutions, the Strike, arguing that when our industrial 'workers' find that there is no more work for them to refuse to do, they will suffer a severe identity crisis, after which anything might happen. I warn them that it doesn't matter which side they're on, but unless they are prepared to fight they will find their homes occupied by ferocious dwarves from the Midlands who will insist on keeping coal in their baths.

21 April 1975

In these unhappy times when all forms of dope are so ruinously expensive, I sometimes draw comfort from eating daffodil bulbs. After a few one has the agreeable sensation of floating on air; and after a great many one can sometimes imagine that one has been turned into a giraffe with a beautiful long, furry neck.

14 *December 1975*

'Vulgar, crude and dirty', are the words used by Marge Proops, the *Daily Mirror's* magnificent old Duchess of Holborn Circus, to describe a new pamphlet issued by the Family Planning Association, called *Getting It On*. This purports to teach less gifted members of the under-privileged social groupings how to put on a male contraceptive. 'The pamphlet is written in a style they will understand,' says a spokesman for the Family Planning Association. I very much doubt it. In my experience it is almost impossible to communicate anything to these people by means of the written word. But if by any chance the pamphlet succeeds, a much more horrible situation may arise. When I telephone the Family Planning Association headquarters in a state of some agitation, a cool young lady in the Press Office agrees there are no instructions given for taking it off again. She does not seem to think it part of her job as Press Officer to make any suggestions either. This failure on the part of the FPA to provide clear instructions strikes me as a grave abdication of responsibility. One dreads to think what the consequences will be for all the bemused young men who have followed their instructions so far. I am happy to report that Gnome House is rushing out a second pamphlet, *Taking It Off Again*.

21 *December 1975*

To Skinners' Hall where I have been invited with other Companions of Literature to celebrate the 150th anniversary of our Royal Society. We are a funny collection, when all is said and done, but everyone is very friendly. I am in the middle of talking to a deaf old woman about ladybirds when somebody comes up behind me, covers my eyes and asks in a pretty, refined voice: 'Guess who?' You could knock me down with a feather. Among all my acquaintances, the one I least expect to meet at a Lit. Soc. 'do' is the Queen of England. When I ask her if she has read any good books lately she puts on her haughty look and says yes, she is quite enjoying Mr Heath's book about sailing. The deaf old lady I was talking to thinks she said 'Gide', and launches into a long harangue about the morals of the French avant-garde between the wars, a subject on which she holds vehement opinions. The Queen mentions that she read Georges Duhamel's *Le Notaire du Havre* in the schoolroom, but is too diplomatic to say whether she enjoyed it or not. I still don't know why she bothered to come.

25 December 1975

For dinner, we have a goose which has ingeniously had a pheasant put inside it. Inside the pheasant is a duck, inside the duck a woodcock, and inside the woodcock no doubt a grasshopper, although I do not care to enquire too closely.

26 December 1975

Still no newspapers. But I find I can understand practically nothing which is said on television nowadays. Today it is full of comedians with incomprehensible accents imitating other comedians I have never heard of. In desperation we turn to *The Magic Flute* sung in Swedish – a very good joke to play on the lower classes on Boxing Day. At least I can recognize a few of the tunes.

11 February 1976

It is quite untrue, as widely reported in the gutter press, that my visit to Cambridge last week had anything to do with the University's difficulties in finding a new Chancellor. In fact, as I revealed at the time, I was engaged in a survey of sexual behaviour at King's College. Unfortunately, the results were too nasty to publish.

25 August 1976

Sir John Betjeman's seventieth birthday is a glorious moment, to be compared with the Diamond Jubilee of Queen Victoria's reign in 1897. No wonder the whole country seems intoxicated with joy. The only poet writing in the English language who has a genuine passion in his soul, a true anger and a true charity, he is also one of the very few who has stayed aloof from the drivelling, doomed experiments of the Modern Movement... Betjeman's success reveals that there are still 100,000-odd intelligent, educated and civilized people left in this country. He also reveals that it is still (just) possible for a poet of genuine passion and sensibility to break through the elaborate minefield of pseuds, charlatans, left-wing fanatics and assorted creeps who monopolize the serious newspapers and have virtually destroyed poetry in this country as a result.

17 November 1976

Philistines in Leeds have beaten up two artists who were planning to shoot at budgerigars with an air pistol in an attempt to extend the frontiers of art. This is the sort of thing that makes my blood boil. Of course it is a delusion that the public can ever be educated in an appreciation of the arts. But what on earth is the Arts Council's purpose if not to protect artists from the need to ingratiate themselves with the vulgar throng? In Somerset we have no such difficulties. With the help of generous grants from the Somerset County Council, the Ewart-Biggs Memorial Fund, etc., our budgerigar shoots are strictly private affairs. Luckily, as chief landowner in the village, I do not only have *droit de seigneur* or *jus primae noctis* over the village maidens (a right seldom exercised now that their average age is ninety-three) but have also retained full shooting rights. This means I can order any old-age pensioner I choose to bring out her budgerigars for me and my friends to shoot at. If the old dears are upset by this, I comfort them by saying: 'Ars longa, vita brevis.' If they go on complaining, I point out how lucky they are it is only their budgerigars I have chosen to shoot.

25 December 1976

A wonderful surprise at Christmas luncheon [in times of the privations of a Labour government]. My dear, clever little wife serves roast meat, having procured it at an amazingly low price from a man she met in the bus queue. He said the beagle had fallen off the back of a lorry, poor creature. Our four tins of Kit-e-Kat are simmered in Madeira and then flared in brandy to make a very passable crayfish sauce. The animal itself has an agreeable tangy flavour. Beagle should be marinated for twenty-four hours in old Burgundy with rosemary, thyme and bay-leaves, then roasted in a slow oven and served with dumplings.

13 January 1977

There is a photograph in today's *Daily Express* of a plump, homely middle-aged woman in slacks and bedroom slippers sitting on a sofa. She is not topless or anything like that, but I find myself eyeing her appreciatively and wondering if we have not perhaps met somewhere before. Then I look at the caption and find myself reeling back in amazement: 'A relaxed Mr Heath at his home.' It says much for Jean Rook's tact – or perhaps for her short-sightedness – that she conducted the interview without apparently noticing anything different. I suggest it is time the *Daily Express* bought Miss Rook a new pair of spectacles.

14 January 1977

Only twenty days after Christmas and our guests are beginning to leave for their various employments. It has been an expensive and debilitating business keeping them drunk enough to lose when I play them at ping-pong. The season has been marred by ugly squabbles over the Stilton cheese – between those who prefer to scoop it out and those who say that the only sane or civilized approach is to slice it like Cheddar. I have no strong feelings on the matter, but this year I've noticed a sinister dogmatism and aggressiveness on the part of the slicers. Next year we had better order two Stiltons if we are to avoid bloodshed. Or perhaps we shall have none. God knows what the future holds at a time when the overweening truculence of the workers is met by a middle class so hideously divided.

12 February 1977

It is a little known fact that the Queen has a marvellous sense of humour, especially if one tickles the soles of her feet with an ostrich feather.

6 May 1977

for the religious revival. The clotted blood of St Januarius, the
[ma]ry martyr and patron saint of Naples, has liquefied again. Even
more remarkable is a discovery by doctors at King's College, Denmark
Hill, London. In a project financed by the World Health Organization,
they found that an extract from the urine of Italian nuns, called Pergonal,
allows infertile women to have babies without risk of a multiple birth.
For my own part, I never doubted the miraculous properties of nuns'
urine. Where the nun is Portuguese, her urine may be used in place of
anti-freeze in motor cars. Make friends with a German nun, and she will
show you unusual ways of polishing silver.

10 May 1977

I do wish the Queen would learn how to pronounce the word 'Jubilee'.
Until this shameful year, nobody put the stress on the last syllable. We
expect the politicians to get it wrong, and media men, and ice-cream
saleswomen in Blackpool, but we expect the Queen to do her homework.

22 July 1977

I have an open mind about queer-bashing. From one point of view it
seems rather cruel, although from another I can see it might be necessary
on occasions. I simply don't know. But if it has to be done, it should be
done properly on Wimbledon Common and not in an underhand way
at the Old Bailey.

20 August 1977

Last night, I spent from midnight to dawn lying on my back in the
Languedoc countryside staring at the sky. This was because the *Daily
Telegraph* had promised a 'spectacular fireworks display' caused by mete-
orites streaming from a comet named Temple-Swift which has just passed
near the earth. According to a Harvard scientist quoted in the newspaper, 'A person not expecting it may find it frightening.' I am determined
not to be frightened and have invited a large party of local landowners,

government officials and fun-loving young persons to watch the phenomenon. We watch for hours, seeing innumerable bats and a *chouette*
or screech owl which frightens two young Ugandans by the side of the
swimming pool. But no sign of a meteorite. Probably it was a practical
joke by the *Daily Telegraph*'s science correspondent... If so, I take my hat
off to him. But if we can't believe the *Daily Telegraph* one might as well
become an Existentialist.

4 September 1977

Tomorrow I must be in London for the Open Day at the Lambeth
Crematorium – a once in a lifetime opportunity.

6 October 1977

The culture shock of finding oneself once again among hungry, dirty,
dishonest Englishmen is immense. Many of the beggars in the streets have
open, gangrenous wounds from the recent fighting; hospitals have been
closed by their 'ancillary workers'; many newspapers are failing to appear
or appear in garbled, incomprehensible form with the new pupil-oriented
spelling. In Blackpool the Trade Union Congress deliberates its next programme of theft, chaos and destruction in the name of Workers' Power.
But the Tooting grounds of Lambeth Borough Crematorium prove an
island of tranquillity. Here, for the very reasonable fee of £13.50, dead or
allegedly dead workers are taken, injected with formalin in case a spark
of life survives, and then burnt in a gas oven. Then their bones, teeth,
etc., are put into a 'cremulator', or bone-crushing machine, the residue is
scattered tastefully over municipal lawns and their names are recorded by
hand in a 'Book of Remembrance'. When everything in Britain is breaking
down, and nobody does anything properly, the operation is marked by
the efficiency and quiet enthusiasm of its staff. I think I will give up everything and come to work at Lambeth Crematorium. If they have no other
job available for me, I will set myself the task of learning all the names
in the 'Book of Remembrance' by heart. In that way, at least, someone
will remember them.

4 October 1977

The Labour Party Conference has decided by six million votes to abolish the House of Lords… If they really intend to abolish the Lords, many of us will have nothing left to live for. What is the point of making pots of money, robbing widows and orphans, grinding the faces of the poor and making children cry on their way home from school if there is to be no peerage at the end of the struggle?

13 February 1978

An unpleasant postcard has arrived from a Cornish 'artist' called Patrick Hughes. 'I have cancelled my subscription because I can't stand that humourless prick Auberon Waugh. I just had to tell you …' I know nothing about Patrick Hughes and have never heard of him before, but somebody has a theory he may be married to Molly Parkin. If so, it serves him bloody well right.

7 April 1978

To the Savoy for my annual Press Award [commended as Critic of the Year]. Once again I am chagrined to hear no mention of my campaign against the ordination of women in the Church of England – one of the longest campaigns ever to have been waged in the British press and, so far at least, the most successful… Many women are beautiful, kind, affectionate, soft, loyal and generous. Only a tiny unrepresentative minority wants to make an exhibition of itself in church pulpits. A good counter-measure, I understand, is to release a few mice at the beginning of every sermon.

22 August 1978

Now there has been an epidemic of botulism among old-age pensioners in Birmingham, all struck down by eating American tinned salmon. A few years ago they had the same trouble with Russian tinned crab. Surely it is time the National Health Council stepped in to discourage these gastronomic experiments among the old. They should stick to their traditional diet. In Somerset, I always feed my OAPs on Kit-e-Kat. It keeps them sleek and frisky. Eight out of ten OAP owners say their OAP prefers it. For my own part, if I didn't give my OAPs regular helpings of Kit-e-Kat they would leave home, I know they would.

17 September 1978

Exciting news that Mr John Sparrow is to stand for the Professorship of Poetry. Since he was appointed Warden of All Souls in 1952, this blameless and beautiful man has been a model to us all for his benign inactivity... After Mr Sparrow has been elected perhaps the Arts Council will take the hint and in future pay people *not* to try and write poetry.

12 April 1979

[In Rome, at the Vatican] A simple enough meal: borscht, green sausages, sauerkraut, cold beer and bitter black bread which tastes of conkers. The Pope says that as it is Maundy Thursday he must go to St John Lateran and wash the feet of twelve poor men. When I ask why they can't wash their own feet, he replies that the act is a symbolic one, going back to the Last Supper. If the poor are genuinely unable to wash their own feet, then of course the Pope is doing something useful and kind. But if it is merely symbolical, I urge him to think again. There was a time when it was considered a beautiful and unusual thing for the Pope to wash the feet of the poor. Nowadays the poor expect it as a right, and many not only refuse to wash their own feet but refuse to have them washed by anyone under the rank of air vice-marshal or suffragen bishop.

29 July 1979

Snowbum [as Bron referred to Lord Snowdon, then married to Princess Margaret], it always seems to me, is the last of the great Welsh heroes. Born to be small and without any obvious advantages, he now enters placid middle age with an earldom – probably the last of those agreeable things to be created – and a pleasant, pretty wife to go with it... Now he can amuse himself for the rest of his days designing [motorized] invalid chairs [as he did] which will overturn on corners, thus adding enormously to the gaiety of the nation. Other jokes one might try in his position are crutches and wooden legs made of India rubber, wigs which stand on end, false teeth which glow beside you in the tumbler at night and sing the *Marseillaise* to call you in the morning. Disabled persons' lavatories should be left well alone, on the other hand. The country is not yet ready for jokes in this field.

27 August 1979

A long heart-to-heart conversation with Prince Charles [then still a bachelor] on the subject of marriage. His problem, he says, is that his bride must at any rate appear to be a virgin. It would never do, as he puts it, if Martin Amis or Jonathan Aitken, or some enterprising merchant banker in the City, were able to go around boasting that he had screwed the Queen of England. The trouble, he claims, is that the only virgins left are Roman Catholics, and he is prevented from marrying a Roman Catholic by the Royal Marriages Act. Must he remain celibate all his life, amusing himself with divorcées and suchlike rough trade? I put it to him that if he advertises his problem there are many sporting girls who will play for high stakes and keep themselves *virgines intactae* on the off chance.

22 December 1979

Shooting at Orchardleigh with my old friend Alexander Chancellor, the immensely distinguished Old Etonian editor of the *Spectator*. All the birds seem to be flying backwards, which is strange. An old boy called Major Chamberlayne makes a gallant attempt to engage Chancellor in conversation over lunch: 'Have you left school yet?'

14 April 1980

I seem to be the only person of any distinction in Britain who is not mentioned in Cecil Beaton's will. Where can I have gone wrong? One would have thought that he might have left me a little lace handkerchief to clutch. Greta Garbo once said of Beaton: 'He was the only man I ever

78

allowed to touch my vertebrae.' I once touched them without her consent when I was posing as vascular dermatologist in New York City. Her secret is that she was really a female iguana. Although I never revealed this she has never forgiven me for discovering it. I feel like a murderer.

21 June 1981

There are some bad pitfalls in Debrett's new book on *Etiquette and Modern Manners*. Practically none of the really important changes in polite behaviour have been noticed. For instance, it used to be normal when arriving at a country house for the weekend to bring a little gift for the hostess. Nowadays guests are expected to bring a present for the host – usually a case or two of sound Burgundy or claret. More than five cases is sometimes thought ostentatious, but the more modern-minded host will overlook such transgressions.

22 November 1981

After a three-week fact-finding tour of the Far East, I find myself in Manila with time on my hands to buy a few servants for my dear wife and eat a dog or two. They do not taste at all bad – the Filipinos are brilliant cooks. I think I will propose it for the menu of the next annual dinner of the Dog Lovers' Party of Great Britain. We meet at the Imperial Hotel, Barnstaple, on 4 August every year – the anniversary of Jeremy Thorpe's arrest [see pages 53–57] – to drink long and solemn toasts to the memory of Rinka.

28 February 1982

Jeremy, Jeremy, bang, bang, woof, woof. How nice it was to have Mr Thorpe back in public life. I had been missing this blameless and distinguished man more than I can say. People who complained that he was not the best person to head the British section of Amnesty International are missing the point. Amnesty's purpose is to rescue people from prison, and nobody in the country has better experience of staying out of gaol than our Jeremy.

9 March 1984

Dr Germaine Greer has a beautiful face, a pretty wit and a warm heart, but she will always remain a mystery to me. I doubt if I will ever get underneath the dough to the jam at the centre. When in *Sex and Destiny* (Secker & Warburg) she describes the male attitude to sex as 'squirting jam into a doughnut', she is in fact quoting some foreigner who made the observation first. What neither of them seems to realize is that the jam is not put into doughnuts this way. You lay your dough flat, put a teaspoon of jam into the middle then wrap it round the jam before deep frying. Germaine may be the greatest expert in the world on the politics of human fertility, but she knows nothing about making doughnuts. I wonder if this explains why she is still unmarried – and whether, in fact, she really understands how babies are made.

15 May 1984

The moment John Betjeman died the sun went in and the heavens opened. Like so many other Englishmen at this time of desolation, nursing their private grief, I wander around my rain-soaked acres killing adders. When a great nobleman dies we are all diminished. But with the death of Betjeman even the fields and churches of Somerset seem to have shrunk.

6 July 1984

To Westminster Abbey for John Betjeman's memorial. It is conducted with as much decorum as the age can muster. None of the priests is obviously suffering from AIDS, and none dies in the course of the service. A minor diversion is caused by the entry of Lord Gowrie, Mrs Thatcher's swarthy, panther-like Minister for the 'Arts'. Goodness knows what he is doing here. A curious buzzing comes out of his wild bush of tightly curled hair. Perhaps a swarm of bees has made its home there. It is most distracting. But when I scowl at him he gives me the most piteous look and I relent. No doubt he is just thinking. He has had this unpleasant idea of charging people a sum of money – to be called Gowrie's Groat – whenever they visit a museum, and obviously he finds it very exciting.

8 September 1984

The Queen's hatred of Margaret Thatcher is becoming so obsessive that I look forward to the times when the Royal Family is at Balmoral. She keeps urging me to attack Mrs Thatcher mercilessly in *Private Eye*, but I have to tell her the *Eye* is not that sort of magazine. Mrs Thatcher may be bossy and irritating, as well as profoundly ignorant on most of the subjects that matter, but one can scarcely expect anything very different in her job... In any case, we on the *Eye* are not interested in politics. If Ma'am has any good stories to tell us about bishops and actresses or homosexual clergymen, she will be paid the usual rates.

25 December 1984

With all the dreadful things happening around us, it is no wonder that so many families have decided to stay home this Christmas and sniff glue.

1 May 1985

[The last piece Bron wrote for the *Private Eye* 'Diary' concerned the finally married Prince of Wales and his bride.]

The best magazine in Italy – its equivalent of *Private Eye* for fearless observations, etc. – is called *2000*. It has discovered that the Prince of Wales has arranged for his bedrooms to be sound-proofed during his stay in Italy: 'Lady Di has decided – I want from Charles a baby made in Italy,' it announces, revealing that the princess has taken some black shortie nighties with her. It hazards that the prince will not make much use of the two pairs of silk pyjamas he has packed. 'Charles loves to sleep naked,' the princess is alleged to have remarked. Sound-proofing has been ordered, it says, 'To avoid even the most delicate whimper being heard by indiscreet ears.' The truth, I'm afraid, is somewhat different. The Prince of Wales's new passion is for singing. He has to practise every night and is understandably embarrassed that anyone may overhear his terrible warblings. What the Princess of Wales thinks about all this is not known. I am not in her confidence.

4

See You in Court

The Colonel Brooks Let-Down

'IN THE HIGH COURT OF JUSTICE ALL DAY,' WROTE BRON IN HIS 'Diary' entry dated 24 November 1974. 'The bottom-slapping libel action brought by Colonel Brooks against the *Sunday People* has been advertised as a show that is going to run and run – two weeks is the lowest estimate, at a minimum cost, I should imagine, of £18,000. I will be here throughout to ensure that the money is well spent.'

John Elliott Brooks was a former mayor of the Royal Borough of Kensington and Chelsea, of which he had been an alderman for twenty-three years, and was himself a lawyer. He had, it was said, paid a young woman, Miss Susan Carr, a nineteen-year-old student he had met through placing an advertisement for 'good-natured young ladies' in *Private Eye*, for taking off her knickers and submitting to being spanked on his private yacht on the Thames. Having spanked her, Colonel Brooks afterwards rubbed whisky on to her bottom to numb the sting and drove her back to town in his Rolls-Royce. Miss Carr then sold her story to the *Sunday People*, which in its write-up declared Colonel Brooks to be 'a menace to young girls'. The colonel hoped to net substantial damages for this slur on his reputation and Bron was particularly pleased to see the *Sunday People* having to defend itself in court, *Private Eye* having suffered a libel claim from the paper in the past. Now, he hoped, it would be deemed to have committed 'the filthy and revolting offence of libel' and was going to be 'taught a very sharp lesson'.

In fact this so promising case turned out to become one that presented Bron with peculiar difficulties, the main problem being that the reality of whatever then went on in court from the outset constantly upstaged whatever absurdist spin a satirist might try and put on it. It was hard to know which side to take, said Bron. 'Generally speaking, one hopes that the plaintiff in a libel case will lose, since there is nothing so funny as a person demanding money to which he is not entitled in recompense for an injury to his reputation which he has not sustained.' In this instance, the fact of the plaintiff being a lawyer made it even better – or it should have done.

Colonel Brooks's advocate, Roger Gray, QC, set the tone on day one by arguing that 'every healthy, normal, vigorous male is a bottom-slapper in mind if not in deed'. Bron commented that he had never been so tempted himself. He conceded that pouring whisky on a girl's behind might be quite jolly in the right circumstances, but in fact he wondered whether what Mr Gray really meant was that 'every healthy, normal, vigorous male *lawyer* is a bottom-slapper at heart'. Meanwhile, in court, Mr Gray's client was robustly asserting that he did like to spank young women, but only with their consent. In fact he had over the years, he thought, spanked at least fourteen young women, and in his opinion he was and always had been 'perfectly normal'. 'As long as it is absolutely with the girl's consent,' he declared, 'it is nothing more notorious than the Italian habit of bottom pinching.'

The national press descended on the proceedings as a gift to headline writers and cartoonists that swiftly emptied the news-stands. 'The Case of the Slap and Tickle Squire' blazoned the *Daily Mail*. Bron, however, prepared himself to bow out on day two, having become curiously dispirited. 'I don't think I can stay here much longer,' he wrote. 'Already I find myself eyeing the pigeons in Trafalgar Square rather oddly during the lunch break.' He was not therefore in court to hear the judge, at the end of five days, commence his summing up to the jury by saying, 'Members of the jury, your minds may have boggled once or twice during this case'; or musing, when it came to handing down his judgment on the sixth day, the following Monday, 'Such is the colonel's ego and character that I doubt very much that the publicity has adversely affected his reputation in any significant degree.' The verdict of the jury went against the *Sunday People*, which meant the paper had to pay all costs. Colonel Brooks was awarded damages of the absolute minimum: one penny. 'We have had some fun in this case,' Mr Gray had said himself, but Bron had not been a part of it.

Bron and the Shrimsley Brothers

The knockabout farce of the Colonel Brooks hearing perhaps bored Bron, or it failed to produce the kind of grist that worked his mill. Richard Ingrams, however, was not the only journalist who suspected that Bron in general enjoyed attending libel actions. In the midst of an acrimonious letter to the *Spectator* of January 1981, attempting to join battle with Bron, the former *News of the World* editor Bernard Shrimsley hinted at something of the kind. Under the heading 'The Futility of Waugh', he wrote a response to a Bron *Spectator* column, in which Bron had commented on an out-of-court settlement of a libel action Shrimsley had brought against Waugh and the *Eye*:

> 'Come, Sir!' a judge once said to counsel whose histrionics were less likely to sway the Appeal Court than the Royal Court, 'if you look at the jury box you will see there isn't anybody there.' I suppose counsel's chagrin must have been much the same as that of Mr Auberon Waugh upon discovering last summer that the ego trip of his dreams had been torpedoed. There was to be no headline trial of Shrimsley v. Waugh and Others. No chance for Auberon Mitty, conducting his own defence, to show that here was the greatest amateur advocate since Portia. And, alas, no best-seller. For a judge in chambers had given my counsel leave to settle a statement in open court to end the matter: a right the

law may allow libel victims whose motive is vindication rather than compensation. Denied the Queen's Bench Division, Mr Waugh was fortunate (was he not?) to have available the *Spectator*'s jury of 36,000 good men and women and true. I don't know if his solo ('Shrimsley's End', 13 December) [Bron's column heading to the article Shrimsley is countering] had 'em yelling for more. But it ought to have done, since this jury had not the usual advantage of hearing the plaintiff (leaving aside objections that Mr Waugh's preposterous version admitted no judge, no rules of evidence, no cross-examination – and even contrived to omit the words that were the essence of the libel).

It was a somewhat strabismic [a word more commonly used by oculists, describing cross-eyes or squints] account: false suggestion vying with suppressed truth. Mine will be more illuminating than his, though it will have a job to be more illuminating about his nature. It begins on Boxing Day 1979. I was having a festive drink at my brother's [Anthony Shrimsley, a political editor] when he came back from the telephone looking anything but festive. During the previous days, he had been visiting [a journalist colleague] Patrick Hutber, who was in a coma after a crash. Patrick's wife was calling from hospital. She felt sure he had squeezed her hand. But though she was desperate for hope, we knew there really was none; and from that moment the party was no party any longer. Then came the *Private Eye* piece Mr Waugh categorizes as [having been] 'mildly tasteless'. [Patrick Hutber had joined *NOW!*, the short-lived attempt to create a news magazine by Sir James Goldsmith, long an enemy of the *Eye*, of which Anthony Shrimsley was editor]. It was the day Patrick died. I felt rage at Mr Waugh's gloating cruelty, so I wrote the following item in the *News of the World* [Shrimsley was then still editor. Of the item he chooses to recall only the first two sentences]: 'If there is a 1980 Rat of the Year contest, it has surely been won in the first week, by *Private Eye* magazine columnist Auberon Waugh. While Patrick Hutber, that much admired financial writer, lay at death's door after a car crash, Waugh chose the moment to make fun of him in his poisonous little piece.' Waugh knew perfectly well the truth about poor

Hutber's condition. 'It seems touch and go whether he will live or die,' he wrote in the course of putting the boot in. Hutber, in fact, did not live to read the sneers. He died in a coma on the day Waugh's column was published. He leaves a widow and four children.

Mr Waugh's response was to wipe the toe of his boot and aim it at me. 'Inquiries reveal,' he lied in the next *Private Eye*, 'that Bernard Shrimsley is too idle or illiterate to write his own column and has hired a hack to write it for him.' I took counsel's opinion and issued a writ. The defendants made no attempt to justify. Instead, there followed for the whole of 1980 a vile campaign against me in *Private Eye*, even spilling into Mr Waugh's column in the *Spectator*.

Truth is the first casualty of Waugh, who declares that I was 'dismissed [as *News of the World* editor] a few days after' his April article in the *Spectator*. Well, it is also legend that Mr Waugh fell off a camel a few days after my January article; but that wasn't cause and effect either, and anyway I was not 'dismissed', with all that is meant to imply. Had this really been so, and as the result of Mr Waugh's campaign, my damages could have made the *Guinness Book of Records*. He also insists that my brother and I are 'sometimes distinguished by the unkind and apparently pointless nicknames of Toady and Slimy'. It is modest of him to hint that the credit for this myth might be anyone's but his. He goes on to smirk that the statement of settlement was made 'in an almost empty court'. Of course it was, since there was to be no contest and no speech from the scaffold by Mr Waugh. The point is that newspapers throughout the land (presumably even in Combe Florey) published the statement and thus nailed the lie.

Mr Waugh's wanton disregard for facts and the delight it gives him to fabricate them; his appetite for the vocabulary of the lavatory wall and the images of the sewer – all these make me uneasy about finding myself in any agreement with him. But he is right that the libel laws no longer work; although my view is that this is because they provide action for damages as the only civil remedy. One cannot simply seek an order for a published correction of lies in terms approved by a judge – which is all one ought to want in the average (I said the average) libel case. For my part, this was the third such action I have had to bring to protect the reputation upon which my living depends. In each case I settled for a statement in open court. In no case did I take damages. The *Spectator* well knows this, since (under an earlier regime) it was one of the defendants. If you sue, your jaws are dripping at the thought of a tax-free jackpot. If you don't sue, you are a flabby-faced coward. If you settle, giving to charity the cheque Waugh & Co. paid into court, you 'took the money and ran'. If you don't settle, you are gambling for high stakes. Let us, by all means, pray for reform of the libel law. But, first, let us pray for reform of Mr Waugh.

Bron did admit in his memoirs, *Will This Do?*, that the Shrimsley libel action had started 'with the nasty spectacle of the diarist being caught with his trousers down' in an article that was itself ill-considered.

A journalist Patrick Hutber, whom I knew slightly and who had been to at least one *Private Eye* luncheon, joined Goldsmith's ill-fated news-magazine *NOW!* (usually called *TALBOT!* in *Private Eye* for some long-lost reason [actually, *TALBOT!* was chosen as it was also an ancient car manufacturing marque used to relaunch a disastrous range of motor cars which was spectacularly unsuccessful], but always *TOADY!* in the 'Diary', after its ill-fated editor [he died in 1984], Tony 'Toady' Shrimsley, who used to say that he was 'enthused' by the thoughts of its proprietor, Sir James Goldsmith). The *Eye*, which was conducting a campaign against *NOW!* saw this as something of a betrayal, although I'm not sure why. Returning from a Christmas party at the *Sunday Telegraph*, where he had been city editor, Hutber was involved in a car crash. My information was that he was only slightly injured, but I decided to ham it up and announce that he was hovering between life and death. In my 'Dairy' entry, I put the blame for this sorry turn of events on his quest for grocerish gold (Goldsmith, in those days, was best known as a grocer) and ended my piece with a few verses from Chesterton's 'Song against Grocers'. In fact Hutber had been grievously injured and died a few days after [that issue of] *Private Eye* appeared, leaving a widow and a young family.

Such catastrophes are an occupational hazard for the vituperative artist... In response to my ill-considered piece, Anthony Shrimsley devoted a whole page of *NOW!* to denouncing me... as being worse than vermin... not fit to be received in the company of decent people. He challenged me to sue if any of these statements were untrue. In fact, as he must have known perfectly well, there was nothing remotely libellous in them. They were statements of honest opinion. Next his brother, Bernard (nicknamed 'Slimy' for reasons which I have now forgotten) Shrimsley, who was Editor of the *News of the World*, printed an attack in his New Year leader page in the John Field column, denouncing me to the seven million-odd masturbating readers of his disgusting newspaper as 'Rat of the Year'.

During my days on the *News of the World* this column had always been written by the Editor, Mr Stafford Somerfield, a fine upstanding west country Liberal. Enquiries suggested that nowadays it was normally written by a hack whose name I have forgotten but whose various sackings and other misadventures had been chronicled in the *Eye*. In the course of denouncing the hack, I presumed that the [then] present Editor (Bernard 'Slimy' Shrimsley) was too idle or illiterate to write it himself.

It was this presumption that led to Bernard Shrimsley's writ because, in fact, he had written this particular item himself. Even so, his case was a weak one. He had denounced me as 'Rat of the Year', and he did not normally write the John Field column. His motive in bringing the action was presumably to throw as much dirt as possible over the Hutber episode as a simple act of revenge. But a certain amount of dirt inevitably accumulates around the ears of any editor of the *News of the World*, and I set myself the task of digging it up in the months while we awaited trial, and printing it in my *Spectator* column.

Eventually Bernard Shrimsley grabbed the £250 we had paid into court and ran with it. Once again I seem to have been stricken with remorse. On 1 October 1980, while judging the great *Private Eye* Newsagent of the Year competition (for the newsagent who had most reduced his order for *NOW!*), I wrote in my 'Diary':

> Poor Toady. I feel I may have been beastly to him in the past, and to his dear brother Bernard ('Slimy'), the former editor of the *News of the World* whose pathetic climb down over his libel action should be seen as a cause for commiseration rather than glee.
>
> Alas, I fear there is no truth in the rumour that the two brothers are thinking of joining the Roman Catholic Church. At any rate it seems unlikely that there is any truth in the rumour as I have just this minute invented it. But history is often moulded by poetic visions of this sort, and I think I will send Lord Longford round to see them. For myself, I propose to make a pilgrimage along the paths of the old crusades, lighting candles in all the churches on the way to advance this pleasant idea.

Evelyn Waugh v. Nancy Spain

Bron's feelings over libel actions might well have been influenced by his father's experiences. According to a report in the *Daily Telegraph* for 20 February 1957, '... one of [Evelyn] Waugh's less serious ventures for raising tax-free money was to scan the papers for possible libel and vigorously to pursue any likely quarry in the courts'. His most successful action was perhaps the one he took against the *Daily Express* journalist and book critic, Nancy Spain, who one day in June 1955 arrived uninvited at Piers Court. It's a story worth re-telling. Nancy Spain was, as one of Evelyn's more recent biographers, Philip Eade, describes her (*Evelyn Waugh: A Life Revisited*, 2016), an 'exuberant early television "personality" known for her mannish clothes and proudly lesbian love life – numbering Marlene Dietrich among her various girlfriends'; and also 'a lively, if not very literary, book critic', to quote an obituary after her death in a plane crash some years later.

Waugh had in earlier days been supremely happy at Piers Court, the house he bought in Gloucestershire in 1937 with money given as a wedding present by his bride's grandmother; his departure from it came about almost twenty years later, triggered directly as a consequence of Spain's unexpected visit, though in fact it was more like the last straw in a growing disillusionment as the neighbourhood came under the threat of plans for road-widenings and urban development. When Miss Spain arrived at Piers Court with a companion, Lord Rufus Noel-Buxton, in tow, Waugh showed them the door. Nancy Spain then published a description of her visit in the *Daily Express* and within weeks Waugh had put Piers Court on the market. 'I felt it was polluted,' he told Nancy Mitford. Late in 1956, the family moved to the manor house in the Somerset village of Combe Florey and made it their home thereafter.

Spain's newspaper account could not in fact be said to have been all that discourteous:

... So up we went to Piers Court.

A genteel residence indeed. The gravel sweep was dainty as anything. The lawns were trim. Beyond a battlement of urns the dim blue Severn could be faintly seen. And by a neat flower bed was a notice board: 'NO ADMITTANCE ON BUSINESS'.

I rang the bell. Mrs Waugh, a beautiful woman in a twinset and slacks answered immediately, sighed deeply and leaned against the door jamb.

I said who we were. She said she was afraid we couldn't stay, when I heard a voice calling: 'Who is it? What is it?'

Mrs Waugh replied: 'Lord Noel-Buxton and Miss Nancy Spain.'

'Tell them to go away! You read the notice, didn't you? No admittance on business?'

Rufus is rather a tall man (in fact he was six feet, three inches tall). He stood his ground, blinking, looking down at Mr Waugh, who is rather a short man.

'I'm not on business,' said Lord Noel-Buxton. 'I'm a member of the House of Lords.'

'Go away,' repeated Mr Waugh, who once held a commission in the Royal Marines, generally showing that we were not wanted.

So we went back to the car and climbed in and started to run away.

'Oh, Nancy,' said Rufus. 'Do stop. He's coming to apologize.'

So I stopped. But not on your life. He had come out of the house merely to shut two wrought-iron gates and bolt them too.

'So much for our literary pilgrimage,' said Rufus.

And so ended our attempt to gate-crash my favourite idol.

When Nancy Spain's article appeared it put Evelyn in a state of considerable rage. He at once wrote a piece with the intention originally of placing it in *Punch*, a plan thwarted when its editor, Malcolm Muggeridge, became worried about libel. After some judicious changes the piece duly appeared in the *Spectator* and Evelyn gave it the heading: 'Awake my soul! It is a Lord.' It began:

'I'm not on business. I'm a member of the House of Lords.'

These moving and rather mysterious words were uttered on my doorstep the other evening and recorded by the leading literary critic of the Beaverbrook press. They have haunted me, waking and sleeping, ever since.

Waugh then took a swipe at the newspaper, suggesting that the fifty or sixty thousand people in Britain who alone support the arts would not be going to Lord Beaverbrook's critics for guidance, but the centre of his wrath was reserved for the recalcitrant Lord. He has discovered, he tells his readers, that Lord Noel-Buxton was not on the pay-roll of the *Daily Express* and was the second generation of one of Ramsay MacDonald's peerages. The peer was not strong, 'poor fellow', he suggests, in that he'd been invalided out of the Territorial Army at the beginning of the war, and since then had spent much time paddling in rivers. (In fact he occasionally got himself a mention in the press for testing out a theory he had about historical river crossings, most famously in 1952 when he attempted to prove that the Thames was 'fordable' beside the Houses of Parliament by wading across on a submerged gravel bank at low water. Unfortunately the river current took him off his feet and he had to swim part of the way.)

Evelyn's penultimate paragraph ridiculed Noel-Buxton's suggestion that to be a member of the House of Lords meant that one has no interest in business. There are 'many types of lord in this country, lords haughty, affable, lavish and leisurely, dead-broke, and hard-working,' the article ends. 'In Lord Noel-Buxton we see the lord predatory. He appears to think that his barony gives him the right to a seat at the dinner table in any private house in the kingdom.'

His lordship himself duly came up with a reply:

Sir, I have met Nancy Spain several times. I am a long-standing friend of Mr John Masefield, the Poet Laureate. One of Miss Spain's ambitions had always been to meet Mr Masefield and I duly arranged this. We had tea with Mr Masefield and then went on west because I gathered that Miss Spain had some business with Mr Evelyn Waugh. At Mr Waugh's front door we had a brief conversation with Mrs Waugh, who told us that we could not come in. During the quiet conversation there came from the room immediately on the right of the hall a cry: 'Tell them to get out.' So we turned away. As we did so, Mr Waugh roared out and shut the door in our faces. He then came out of the house and barred the gates.

This incident was, a day or two later, inflated by Miss Spain into an article in the *Daily Express*, which would certainly have angered me if I had been Mr Waugh. It angered me in my own character because Miss Spain put into my mouth words which I certainly did not utter; namely: 'I am not here on business. I am a member of the House of Lords.' I should like here to point out categorically that there was no exchange of any kind between Mr Waugh and myself. Mr Waugh is entitled to be angry with Miss Spain; whether he is entitled to accept her version of my own part in the affair and to compose in consequence such an ill-mannered diatribe as you published in last week's issue is quite another matter. I admit that I am partly responsible for any misunderstanding that may have occurred in that I did not trouble to correct Miss Spain's falsifying of the incident – largely because it seemed to me that her piece, however irritating, was of no consequence what-ever. As to Mr Waugh's observations on my family, your readers will already, no doubt, have formed their own opinion. – Yours faithfully,

NOEL-BUXTON

In Waugh's diary entry for Saturday, 16 July, he writes that at dinner with friends, including Anthony Powell, they talked of Lord Noel-Buxton, who, in his letter to the *Spectator*, had rounded on the lady he escorted to Piers Court and had publicly called her a liar. 'Has she no brother with a horsewhip?' In Waugh's letter sent in response, printed in the following week's *Spectator*, he ends his opening salvo by turning this single question into two. 'Has Miss Spain no brother? Has the editor of the *Daily Express* no horsewhip?'

Waugh had also been discussing the incident via letter with 'the other Nancy', as Nancy 'the literary critic' rather presumptuously referred to Nancy Mitford, who was amused enough to put in her own contribution:

Sir, Mr Carlisle says that 'Mr Evelyn Waugh's article is the worst example of bad manners to be granted space in your columns since the Sitwell correspondence.' I do not recollect the subject of the Sitwell corre-spondence, but I would like to say here and now that it is no wonder if elderly writers become bad-tempered. Dogs which are constantly baited turn savage and writers are supposed to be more highly strung than dogs.

Alongside these letters from Waugh and Mitford was one from the first Nancy:

Sir, I have read in your magazine Mr Evelyn Waugh's account of my visit to his house and now I have read Lord Noel-Buxton's account of the same thing. I would like to point out for what it is worth that the day after our visit Lord Noel-Buxton rang me up. I read out to him and actually explained the relevant passage in my piece. Not only did he raise no objection. He actually applauded me.

NANCY SPAIN, *DAILY EXPRESS*,
FLEET STREET, LONDON

In January 1957, Waugh had his revenge on the Spain–Noel-Buxton intrusion by winning libel damages of £2,000 from the *Daily Express* and Nancy Spain. The offending libel occurred in a quite different article by Spain which suggested that sales of Waugh's books were much less than they actually were and his worth, as a journalist, was low. His brother Alec Waugh had recently hit the best-seller jackpot with *Island in the Sun*, sales of which had been boosted as a result of a puff Miss Spain had given it, she rather misleadingly claimed, so that it 'dwarfed' all of Evelyn's first-edition sales put together and left him an embittered, unsuccessful writer. The judge perceived that she was 'rather overstating the case' when it came to assessing her own influence and concluded that certain other of her assertions were 'hopelessly inaccurate'. The money from the damages was a welcome addition to Evelyn's finances to help with work that needed to be carried out on Combe Florey.

A curious coda to this whole saga came when Bron requested Richard Ingrams invite the adopted son of Nancy Spain and her lover, Joan Werner Laurie, along to a *Private Eye* lunch so conclusions could be drawn about boys brought up by lesbians, by spending some time with one who had been.

MPs as 'Pissed as Newts'

In a quite different context, there was another *Eye* lunch that Bron mentions in *Will This Do?* which also had libel connotations, in this case quite unexpected:

> It was to the sixtieth birthday party of the *New Statesman* that I happened to take Tina Brown as a nineteen-year-old undergraduate from St Anne's College, Oxford. I had met Tina a few weeks before when she came to Combe Florey to interview me for *Isis*, bringing a young man in tow – Stephen Glover – who later became editor of the *Independent on Sunday*. She expressed a desire to attend a *Private Eye* lunch, and I naturally complied. It was plain that this extremely attractive young woman was going to go a long way. Tina was later to say that these two events – the *Private Eye* lunch and the *New Statesman* party – altered the whole course of her life. She happened upon the famous *Private Eye* lunch at which Richard Crossman announced that he, Aneurin Bevan and Morgan Phillips, General Secretary of the Labour Party, had all perjured themselves in their famous libel action against the *Spectator* which had jocularly suggested that they had been drunk at a socialist conference in Venice: Phillips at least had been as drunk as a skunk throughout it. This point had not particularly impressed itself on Tina, but she wrote an extremely witty account of the lunch party in *Isis* which so pleased all the journalists mentioned in it that in no time at all she was the toast of London.

This epic lunch, with its startling disposure, was to generate continuing interest. Bron had cause to mention the incident in one of his *Spectator* columns, which prompted Lord Goodman, the solicitor whom Bron had retained when he sought compensation for his dismissal from the *Spectator* and who was used by many Labour politicians when personal problems needed legal advice, to suggest that Bron was not being entirely accurate in his account of what was said at the lunch.

Patrick Marnham, long a friend of Bron's and, according to *Will This Do?*, convinced of Bron's 'partly Jewish ancestry' (as a result of which he 'always makes secret Jewish signs to me when we meet'), wrote a letter to the *Spectator* dated 29 April 1978:

> Sir, Lord Goodman suggests that Auberon Waugh's 'recollections of a conversation five or six years old describing an incident fifteen years before that' may be unreliable: on the contrary. The conversation took place over lunch in Soho on 3 May 1972. Apart from Mr Waugh, at least three other people present at that lunch remember Richard Crossman's remarks quite clearly. When Crossman was invited to agree that – despite having won handsome libel damages from the *Spectator* for the allegation that he, Aneurin Bevan and Morgan Phillips were drunk at a conference in Venice – he, Crossman, had indeed been drunk, Crossman replied: 'Yes. But they said we were drinking whisky. You don't drink whisky in Venice.' The conversation then moved on to embrace Lord Goodman's role in the case and his great skill in general.
>
> So fifteen years after the famous victory in *Bevan and Others v. The Spectator* (1957), Crossman was indeed happy to boast that the libel action had been founded on a complete lie. Lord Goodman, in support of his contrary view, makes three points.
>
> 1. That none of the plaintiffs ever admitted to him that they had been drunk.
> 2. That all three of them gave evidence on oath asserting their sobriety, and therefore ran the risk of a criminal conviction for perjury if their evidence was refuted.
> 3. That the *Spectator* never pleaded justification (or truth), which suggests that it lacked the evidence to do so.
>
> On the first point, Lord Goodman's credit is not so low that he has to mention this.

There are many people in the world who would take it for granted that Arnold Goodman would never have prosecuted a cause in libel knowing it to be based on a lie. His second point is incorrect. Risk of prosecution for perjury merely because a jury does not believe one's evidence in a libel action is nil.

His third point is also incorrect. Any supporting evidence the *Spectator* might have produced would have been weighed against the contradictory assertions of three public figures on oath. The chances of an English jury disbelieving such a trio would not have been so great as to justify the risk of incurring aggravated damages which is run by libel defendants who unsuccessfully advance the defence of truth. The dice, as usual in libel, were heavily loaded against the defendants.

Any action before a jury involves a degree of bluff. Lord Goodman is too experienced a solicitor to suggest that libel actions are an exception. Bluff evidently saw Bevan, Crossman and Phillips through against the *Spectator*. Perhaps it is merely bluff when Lord Goodman mentions the possibility of extending our over-restrictive libel laws to include dead plaintiffs?

In any case, to return to Auberon Waugh's simile, Lord Goodman cannot after his stated enthusiasm for the present libel laws be the example (in an age of air crashes) of the good Jumbo which has landed safely. I fear that another of our Jumbos is missing.

PATRICK MARNHAM
34 GREEK STREET, LONDON W1

But the last word went to an eminent witness who had been proprietor of the *Spectator* at the time of the libel case.

29 APRIL 1978

THE BEVAN LIBEL ACTION

Sir: I have never before written about the Bevan libel action against the *Spectator* in 1957. It is a distasteful subject in that all of the following came out of it badly: the *Spectator* and myself, the three plaintiffs, Messrs Bevan, Crossman and Morgan Phillips, and the judge, Lord Goddard.

Another reason for silence has been that many of the people involved died fairly soon after the case, and not even Mr Auberon Waugh's fascinating revelation tempted me to break it. But, since Lord Goodman's letter would, if unchallenged, tend, in his words, 'to allow a mischievous legend to gain further ground', it requires an answer.

Lord Goodman tries to refute Mr Waugh's recollection of hearing the late Dick Crossman admit that 'he and Bevan had been pissed as newts', by saying that, had the *Spectator* possessed any evidence to back up the libel, 'they would certainly have adduced such evidence'. Yet, as one of the best libel lawyers of the day, Lord Goodman must know perfectly well that to plead justification in a libel action is highly dangerous (since it is liable to multiply the damages), and therefore that a defendant's failure to plead justification does not necessarily mean either that what was written was untrue or that there was no evidence for it. In fact the *Spectator* could have presented quite a lot of evidence. But, as our leading counsel, Mr Fearnley Whittingstall, told us: 'We cannot expect an English jury to prefer the evidence of Italian journalists and Italian waiters to that of a British Privy Councillor and two other leading British Politicians.'

The other reason why we did not plead justification was that, although the reference to the three politicians' drinking habits à la Venice was fairly light-hearted, we thought we should not have published it. Finally, there was also some doubt as to whether the article had been wholly fair in bracketing Crossman with the other two.

The *Spectator* did in fact apologize, but our apology was not accepted. In retrospect, I think we should probably have grovelled and given the sort of unblushingly untruthful apology that newspaper defendants are often compelled to offer. We did not grovel because we thought that would be unfair to the late Jenny Nicholson, the highly reputable writer of the article. Besides, to do so would have meant libelling her. Above all, it never occurred to us that, when it came to the point, any of the Plaintiffs would want to commit perjury for money. That was naïve. As a result, the *Spectator* defended the action without pleading justification. And that was stupid.

Nevertheless, it nearly worked. Crossman told me afterwards that he and the others had very nearly accepted the £500 which the *Spectator* had paid into court for each of the defendants, but that they had been dissuaded by the promise from a Socialist millionaire to compensate them for any possible losses.

When I saw Crossman at a party after the case, he clearly felt guilty about the part he had played. That may have been because he had revealed in court private 'without prejudice' conversations. More probably, however, in view of Mr Waugh's article, his guilt had a more fundamental reason.

To complete this unedifying story, Mr Fearnley Whittingstall wrote to me: 'Goddard was quite shocking and, having ranged himself on Beyfus's side, the latter needed no courage to be as offensive as he was irrelevant.' (Mr Beyfus was counsel for the plaintiffs.)

But of course the original fault lay with me and the *Spectator* for publishing the two offending sentences.

IAN GILMOUR, HOUSE OF COMMONS, LONDON SW1

Ballsoff and Other Pranks

Two more scrapes with libel were to engage Bron at the *Eye*. The first concerned Nora Beloff, who was one of *Private Eye*'s habitual targets; while the second was Claire Tomalin, who was never a target, but who came within range through no fault of her own when a practical joke worked only too well. Miss Beloff, a long-standing *Observer* political correspondent who specialized in Eastern Bloc matters, was represented by Mr Carter-Ruck when she sued for libel after Waugh jested in his column that she was frequently found in bed with Harold Wilson and other members of the cabinet, but 'it was thought that nothing improper occurred'. Beloff won damages of £3,000, though she lost a separate case against *Private Eye* over the magazine's publication of a memorandum she had circulated within the *Observer* about the former Tory Home Secretary, Reginald Maudling. The costs, estimated at £10,000, were awarded against her.

As Bron recollected of this case in *Will This Do?* '…it was the only writ the *Eye* ever had to defend in court on my behalf …'

Our lawyers thought it too preposterous to stand a chance in court, but they reckoned once again without the extraordinary workings of the British legal system. I think the judge, Mr Justice (later Lord Justice) O'Connor, may have had a son at Downside with me, which would not have helped.

The background to the Ballsoff affair, as it was known from *Private Eye*'s unfortunate nickname for Beloff, was a curious one. Paul Foot had been investigating the Poulson case, involving a northern architect and developer who had been paying out large sums of money to politicians on both sides of the House, and in local government, in exchange for services which were not always entirely clear. One of Poulson's beneficiaries was Reginald Maudling, an intelligent and able man who had occupied most of the main offices of State in various Conservative administrations and was currently Home Secretary and deputy Prime Minister. He had been paid quite a large salary by Poulson as some sort of consultant.

Suddenly, out of the blue, Beloff printed a violent attack on *Private Eye* for questioning the honour and integrity of Maudling. She described the magazine as a political comic and promoted Maudling as the next Prime Minister who would definitely succeed if Heath fell under a bus.

It looked, to the sceptical observer, as if she had fallen head-over-heels in love with him. Foot secured possession of an internal *Observer* memo which she had sent to the editor, who was then David Astor, describing a meeting with Maudling. Foot printed it, and she sued for breach of copyright. The *Observer*, to its eternal shame, backed her in the action, which was thrown out by Mr Justice Ungoed-Thomas, of holy memory, on the technical point that she did not own copyright.

Unfortunately, I, too, had put my little oar in with a whimsical piece introducing Beloff as 'delicious 78-year-old Nora Ballsoff who sometimes wrote under the nom-de-plume Nora Bailiff ... Miss Bailiff, a sister of the late Sir Alec Douglas-Home, was frequently to be seen in bed with Mr Harold Wilson and senior members of the previous administration, although it is thought that nothing improper occurred.' This was obviously intended to be humorous because Douglas-Home (always called Baillie Vass by *Private Eye*, for reasons lost in the mists of antiquity) was not, at this stage, officially thought to be dead. Nor was Beloff yet seventy-eight.

One did not need to know, or even to have seen Beloff, to understand that this suggestion was obviously made in jest. The essence of a libel is that it must lower its victim in the estimation of right-minded or sensible people. No ordinary person, reading the piece, could possibly believe that it accused Beloff of being found in bed with Harold Wilson and other senior members of the previous administration. This did not stop her counsel, Tom Bingham, QC (now Lord Justice Bingham), expressing the utmost indignation at this foul aspersion. One QC, Anthony (now Mr Justice) Lincoln, had turned the brief down because he happened to come to dinner in my house the day before it was offered him. Bingham was not put off by being a friend of my sister, Margaret, and her husband Giles Fitzherbert. He seemed genuinely appalled that such a wicked assertion could be made against a maiden lady of spotless character. Bernard Levin, writing about the case afterwards, said he was amazed Bingham could keep a straight face throughout, as he quoted an Irish ruling of the 1830s to the effect that those who commit libel in jest, jest at their peril. The judge, who was, of course, Irish, was profoundly impressed. Beloff was awarded £3,000.

The second libel furore that engaged Bron's total involvement, and gave him yet another of his reasons for deciding to leave the *Eye*, was best described by him in his *Spectator* column, 'Another Voice' (12 October 1985), at a point when the case was still unresolved. He begins as a preamble to his theme:

> All Fleet Street has been laughing for a fortnight over the excellently successful practical joke played by journalists from the *Mail on Sunday* on that bastion of NewBrit pomposity, the *Sunday Times*. Its butt was in fact the one section in that general encyclopaedia of ignorance, boredom and conceit which is quite readable, the 'People' page written by my friend Henry Porter, himself a bit of a wag.
>
> Porter was summoned to the Ritz to interview a woman posing as Meryl Streep, the actress, and duly published an interview in the course of which he accused Streep of lying to the press in order to promote a false image of herself to the public. It would be hard to imagine a more damaging libel on an actress of Miss Streep's reputation. Had Mr Porter a tit, jottle or scintilla of evidence for this disgraceful allegation?
>
> No, Porter had been the victim of a practical joke. As soon as he discovered his mistake, he apologized prettily: 'I did not, I am ashamed to admit, carry out an instant fingerprint test nor even ask for her dental records, as is customary on these occasions.' I have not heard that Miss Streep proposes to pursue the matter in the High Court, which may indicate that she has a sense of humour.

Then he continues:

> I wish I could say the same about the equally successful and amazingly similar practical joke played by an employee of the *Sunday Times* on me. In October 1983, as regular readers may remember, I received a letter on *Sunday Times* paper which purported to come from Mrs Claire Tomalin, the newspaper's literary editor. It enclosed a disgusting paperback of 'Lesbian and Gay fiction' edited by Mr Adam Mars-Jones,

a homosexualist and friend of Mrs Tomalin. The letter asked for a 600-word review, ending with the sentences: 'Before starting please phone me to let me know what sort of review you are going to write. I understand you are sympathetic to the gay movement and I would expect a generous piece.'

It was a curious letter, and I decided that the most likely explanation for it was that Mrs Tomalin, in uncharacteristically skittish mood, was trying to make a joke. I did not, I must admit, carry out an instant handwriting test, as may be customary on these occasions. Instead I wrote a humorous entry in my *Private Eye* 'Diary' rebuking her for trying to influence a reviewer's judgement and ending with the waggish sentence: 'It makes me wonder about all those crazy Somerset majors who say there is a left-wing homosexual conspiracy in the media.'

No sooner had the *Eye* appeared than all hell broke loose. Mrs Tomalin, who knew nothing of the forged letter, might reasonably have been puzzled by this rebuke from out of the blue. She went and put her affairs in the hands of the *Sunday Times*'s legal department, whose manager is called Antony Whitaker.

Whitaker may be familiar to *Spectator* readers from a lively correspondence between him and the *Spectator*'s charming, witty and bold former editor, Mr A. S. Chancellor, when Whitaker was trying to extract money 'to reflect the seriousness and gravity of this totally outrageous suggestion' – on behalf of another *Sunday Times* employee, called Simon Freeman, whom he claimed I had libelled. On that occasion, after a fairly robust letter from Chancellor telling the Legal Manager of the *Sunday Times* what he could do with Mr Freeman's complaint, the correspondence ended on a distressingly acrimonious note:

Dear Mr Chancellor, I have your letter of yesterday. Your patronizing off-hand and sneering response to Mr Freeman's complaint is as degrading as it is disillusioning. Do you wish to nominate solicitors, or should the proceedings [be] served at the *Spectator*'s offices?

However, the *Sunday Times* reporter later assured me verbally that he had only been joking.

On this occasion the *Sunday Times*'s legal department wasted no time writing to the *Eye*'s editor. A writ arrived on the Tuesday after publication with a letter from the *Sunday Times* solicitors, Messrs Theodore Goddard, demanding a retraction, apology and damages for what was 'as gross, baseless and hurtful libel as it is possible to imagine'.

As soon as I realized what had happened I published – in the next issue of *Private Eye* – a total retraction and apology. Oddly enough, although people often suppose that working for the *Eye* involves endless argy-bargy with lawyers, it is the only apology which has ever appeared as a result of my 'Diary'. In nearly fourteen years of its life, the 'Diary' has attracted only three writs – all from journalists staked by their employers, two of them paid for by Rupert Murdoch. Perhaps he enjoys paying for his journalists to sue other journalists in this way. Certainly the legal department of the *Sunday Times* seems to spend a fair amount of its time using his enormous resources to threaten small magazines like the *Literary Review*, the *Spectator* and *Private Eye*. The *Eye*'s file of writs from Messrs Theodore Goddard – mostly on behalf of the sensitive Harold Evans – will make an amusing coffee table book one day.

My own judgement of *Tomalin v. Waugh, Ingrams, Pressdram and Others* was that once again the legal department of the *Sunday Times* was going to fall flat on its face. Having read very carefully through all the papers, I could not believe – and still cannot – that any British court would award Tomalin more than 5p in damages once it had the facts of the case before it.

Most unfortunately Ingrams, having started the case full of robust enthusiasm, charming, witty and bold, had in the meantime taken on an idiotic, doomed case against a Welsh solicitor. Damages of £20,000 were aggravated by costs of £180,000. Ingrams put on a mooncalf face, said he had lost faith in British justice, and announced he was going to try to settle Tomalin, agreeing to pay £2,500 to a charity of Tomalin's choosing and Theodore Goddard's costs of over £8,000. Or so I read in the *Standard*, although the 'charity' aspect is a fairly recent development.

The case is still not settled, twenty-four months after it began. At present the parties are squabbling over the details of a Statement in Court, but for my own part (if I had the resources of Mr Murdoch behind me) I would be happy to let a British jury decide whether my own or the *Sunday Times's* judgement of the case is the sounder. Perhaps I am guilty of libel 'as gross and baseless as it is possible to imagine'. I do not know. It seems to me that if one loses one's faith in the ultimate common-sense of the courts one might as well become a crook or a politician. Poor Ingrams, I feel he may be dying or going mad. I am worried also that Meryl Streep, as an American, is not showing more interest in the opportunities open to her. But others will be delighted to learn they can buy ten years of these miraculous diaries in a book just published: *A Turbulent Decade: The Diaries of Auberon Waugh 1976–1985* (Deutsch, £4.95). It is so cheap, the best thing might be to buy a couple of dozen and give them to all your friends for Christmas.

In his memoirs Bron described the case as having been 'rather a sad one' and confirmed by admission that it 'contributed as much as anything else to my decision to leave *Private Eye*, if only because it showed the way the wind was blowing in matters of libel'. After explaining the hoax – 'its origins were farcical enough' – he continues:

It did not occur to me that the letter was not genuine, although I was puzzled that it started 'Dear Auberon Waugh', rather than 'Dear Bron'. I did not know Claire well, and she belonged to a different literary tradition, but we had always enjoyed cordial relations. I liked and admired her husband, the journalist Nicholas Tomalin, who had been killed on the Golan Heights by a Syrian sniper. There were various tragedies in Claire's life, not least, in my view, an attachment to Michael Frayn, the dreaded Cambridge humourist. But I had nothing against her and rather admired her in several ways.

In the normal course of events I receive quite a number of letters every day, like many other people in my business, and it would surely be a sign of incipient madness to start suspecting that a letter from an acquaintance was, in fact, a forgery. Still, it was an odd letter. Claire had never asked me to review before, which was scarcely strange as I had been holding up the *Sunday Times*'s book pages as a general hate focus for as long as I could remember, and the proposal was not an entirely serious one.

I decided that Claire was making a rare excursion into the fun-and-games department, and instead of answering the letter to say that most unfortunately I was too busy to review her homosexual anthology, I wrote in the 'Dairy' as follows:

Journalists cannot afford to be too choosy about the newspapers they work for. I think I have written for nearly every newspaper in Fleet Street, drawing the line only at the *Sunday Times* and the *Sunday People*. To be fair, I must admit that the *Sunday People* has never asked me.

Today a strange letter arrives from the Literary Editor of the *Sunday Times*, Ms Claire Tomalin, enclosing a smutty paperback with a picture of two Lesbians on the cover. It describes itself as an anthology of recent Lesbian and Gay fiction.

She wonders if I would like to review it for her. I seldom look at the books page of the *Sunday Times*, but I suppose that is the sort of book its ghastly readers enjoy. But the oddest thing about Ms Tomalin's request is contained in her last two sentences: 'Before starting please phone me to let me know what sort of line you are going to take,' she writes. 'I would expect a generous review.'

As I say, I have written for some pretty odd publications in my time, but I do not think I've ever received instructions from a Literary Editor about the sort of review I was to write. It makes one wonder about all those crazy Somerset majors who say there is a left-wing homosexual conspiracy in the media …

As soon as I learned I had been the victim of a practical joke, I printed a craven, although unagreed, apology – the first and only one which ever appeared in the 'Diary'. It is the custom of libel solicitors on these occasions to demand an apology which destroys any possible defence in the subsequent libel action, and then plead aggravation when you refuse to print it. This is the apology I wrote:

Claire Tomalin

> Claire Tomalin, Literary Editor of the *Sunday Times*, wishes me to state that the letter bearing her name from which I quoted in the last issue was a forgery, written without her knowledge or consent. In the circumstances I am happy to withdraw and apologize for everything I said about her.

Technically, an agreed apology is valueless either in satisfaction or in mitigation of damages, but a jury might not accept that. I hoped it might mollify Tomalin, and it seemed to show common sense, not to say common decency, to explain myself. But once lawyers had been brought in (and the *Sunday Times* had agreed to take over the case) nothing is quite so easy as that. My enemies on the *Sunday Times* plainly reckoned they had caught me with my trousers down ... [and] after a first conference in chambers, I decided to present my own case in court ...

This is always a tremendously unpopular thing to do. It brings an element of anarchy into the smooth process of the law, dedicated to fleecing the public according to its own sacrosanct procedures. Ingrams decided (quite rightly) that there was an element of exhibitionism in my decision, which he deplored, but agreed to go along with. The decision had been taken to defend the action. We would probably lose, since defendants always lost, but the *Eye* could not go on paying out money without ever defending a case. The elements of absurdity in the case, and the curious picture which would emerge of the plaintiff, should discourage other plaintiffs, and damages, in the context of a genuine misunderstanding immediately acknowledged, should be small.

As the wheels of justice slowly turned and nothing happened, Bron wrote a letter to the then *Private Eye* solicitors, Messrs Bindman & Partners, dated 3 September 1984:

> It seems to me that the time has long since passed when Tomalin could accept the £250 paid into court … I would like to sketch the Defence which I propose to present on my own behalf so that you can check it against the Defence we have already entered and ensure that everything is included in the dossier available to the Plaintiff.
>
> My Defence is as follows:
>
> 1. I did not say what she claims I said.
> 2. Even had I said it, it would not have been defamatory.
> 3. What I said is not capable of implying any of the consequences she attributes to them; nor, if I had said what she claims I said, would it be so capable.
> 4. Even if the words complained of are held to be capable of a defamatory meaning, the damage to Mrs Tomalin's reputation was initially so small, so briefly current and has been so reduced by a prompt apology and unqualified retraction, the circumstances of the misunderstanding having been explained and a generous payment having been paid into court, that Mrs Tomalin's suit must be seen as a waste of court time and meriting only nominal damages.
>
> In support of paragraphs 1, 2 and 3 I would make the following points:
>
> (a) There is nothing corrupt or dishonest in a literary editor's inquiring in advance about the likely attitudes of a reviewer. This is fairly normal practice. I am never troubled by such inquiries myself because my attitudes are already well known. In support

of this I would attempt to call various literary editors and reviewers as witnesses.

(b) The words complained of do not in their natural or normal meaning or in any other meaning, state or imply that Mrs Tomalin is
a lesbian. What they say is that the evidence of a forged letter
made me wonder about some Somerset majors, admitted to be
crazy, who claim that a left-wing homosexual conspiracy exists
in the media. The reference is plainly jocular, nor is there the
slightest suggestion that Mrs Tomalin, although possibly part
of such a fantastic conspiracy, should herself be a lesbian. [Bron
then mentions the various shenanigans that had to do with
Jeremy Thorpe and the killing of Norman Scott's dog, cf. pages
53–59] ... belonging to that Liberal conspiracy ... inspired to
benefit the Liberal Party and its leader, paid for by Liberal money
and supervised by a deputy treasurer of the Liberal Party, none of
the three people I have named were ever members of the Liberal
Party. To put it less elegantly, Tomalin might perfectly easily have
been a fag hag, or heterosexual patron of homosexuals.

(c) There is nothing disreputable in the desire to further the cause
and interests of homosexuals.

(d) None of these accusations, even if they had been made and were
true, make her unfit to be a literary editor.

5. The apology, explanation and retraction was prompted by an earnest
desire to set the record straight as soon as possible before my going
abroad. It covers not only everything I said, but also everything which
Mrs Tomalin or her lawyers in their wildest flights of fantasy might
claim I said. The original apology suggested by Messrs Theodore
Goddard was obviously, and I suggest deliberately, unacceptable for
three reasons, of which the most important was that it put into my
mouth untruths in the form of the admission that I had accused
Tomalin of homosexuality. Since publication of Theodore Goddard's
apology carried no guarantee that the matter would not be pursued
to court and since the issue of damages was left outstanding, there

could be no possibility of publishing it, as they must have well known. The other objections were that it was too long, taking up considerably greater space than the words complained of, and written, apparently *in propria persona*, in such a constipated style as no self-respecting journalist could have accepted.

By way of documents I would like to produce, if I can contrive one, an affidavit signed by at least four Somerset majors agreeing that they feel the possibility of a left-wing and homosexual conspiracy in the media requires a public inquiry in the matter; an article by Marje Proops in the *Daily Mirror* pointing out that there is nothing disgraceful in lesbianism; two issues of the Greater London Council Women's Committee *Bulletin* Nos. 17 and 18, number 17 describing itself as a special lesbian issue. In this we can see that an entire committee of the democratically elected, and increasingly popular, Greater London Council, spending £7 million a year, is publicly committed to promoting and furthering the cause and interests of homosexuals.

Further witnesses should be able to establish that there is nothing illegal or disreputable in this activity; that homosexuality is not a disqual-ification from literary editorship; that there is nothing disreputable or against journalistic ethics in editors promoting their own causes.

Bron admitted in his autobiography that 'looking at the huge file on this case, which went on for two years, I see the enormous amount of work I put into it, writing the equivalent of a book in letters to solicitors, letters to potential witnesses and articles in the *Spectator* taunting the plaintiff and her backers'. As Waugh became increasingly determined, he noticed (according to *Will This Do?*) that 'both Ingrams and Tomalin began to get cold feet ...'

Tomalin offered to settle for £2,500 plus £5,000 towards costs. It was very tempting to settle an action so cheaply, and Ingrams eventually decided to settle – I am not sure of the final terms – despite his earlier assurances to me that he would not do so. I made several attempts to sabotage the settlement by writing inflammatory articles about the case in the *Spectator*, but Theodore Goddard, Murdoch's solicitors who have acted in numerous cases against me on behalf of Murdoch employees, would not rise to the bait … Claire behaved honourably, giving the money to charity. I behaved rather less so, publishing 'In Tomalinam' (all the speeches I would have made in court had I been called to do so) in the next edition of the *Spectator*.

Claire Tomalin's autobiography, published in September 2017, reports that she earned £30,000 from the case, money which went to various writers' charities, and that she told her daughter that Auberon Waugh might be glad of a handout from one in his old age. She bore no grudges and suggests, in the manner adopted by many feminist writers when describing similar male behaviour, that it had all been some silly little schoolboy prank, not worth the time of day. One could be listening to the opening bars of *Cosi fan Tutte*.

Henry Porter, the true originator, remembering Bron after reading and hearing comments made after his death, recollected the consequences of his prank in a *Guardian* article dated 18 January 2001.

… the case dragged on and became more and more bitter. Meanwhile nobody at *Private Eye* or the *Sunday Times* had the slightest idea who had written the letter. I kept my head down for two years while Bron fought it out with the paper's lawyers. Huge bundles of letters accumulated as he argued that he had not accused Tomalin of being a left-winger or a lesbian, but that even if he had, it would have been insulting rather than damaging. At length Bron guessed I was the author and confronted me in the mildest possible terms at another *Private Eye* lunch. When I confessed he just laughed, a reaction that contrasted to the eruption that took place at the *Sunday Times*, where I was required to make a shaming public apology to Tomalin, the other victim of my idiotic hoax.

When the case was over and the settlement agreed upon, I took

Bron out to lunch by way of an apology. The whole affair had left him rather weary and cross about the libel laws, but he didn't take it out on me. Instead, he gave me a long lecture about effective lying. 'The thing is,' he said, 'you should tell the truth as often as you can, but in such a way as people don't believe you or think that you're being funny.'

What is often forgotten when Bron's journalism is remembered is that alongside the grim satire and patrician scorn there lay a genuine, radical fury at a world often run by dishonest fools. The irony was fetchingly remembered by a much younger journalist writing in the *New Statesman* in 2001. In an article headed 'Auberon Waugh, Hero of the Left', Neil Clark recalled a Balkans event of a few years before:

Spring 1999. A group of very left-wing, very disillusioned ex-pats sit in a dingy bar in Budapest as above them fly B52s on their way for another night's bombing of neighbouring Yugoslavia. Who will be the target of the 'smart' bombs tonight, we all wonder. Another passenger train? Another embassy, or even some civilians on a bridge? The shame felt as our own country takes the lead in a brutal, illegal attack on a sovereign state that threatened no other is too strong to bear. To make matters worse, all the papers from home seem full of support for this shameful war, with the *Guardian* the most hawkish of all.

But wait, what's this? A piece in the *Daily Telegraph*, of all papers, calling the continued bombing by Nato an 'atrocity', denouncing the 'lying propaganda' and calling for the arrest of Tony Blair and Robin Cook for war crimes.

All of a sudden, our mood changes. Who was the writer of such a stirring, heroic piece? A veteran hack from the anti-Vietnam movement? Some crypto-Marxist columnist who had somehow been smuggled past the *Telegraph*'s ideological sentinels? No, it was none other than Auberon Waugh, commonly considered the most reactionary journalist of his generation. It was his writing that had so cheered up our little band of erstwhile revolutionaries.

An 'Unofficial Auberon Waugh Appreciation Society' was formed there and then. A letter was sent to him, care of the *Daily Telegraph*, pledging our wholehearted support. We received a reply from Combe Florey. 'Thank you for your letter. Would it give you comfort if I suggest you call yourself the Official Auberon Waugh Appreciation Society? I know of no rivals.'

So that is how, to a group of thirtysomething leftist romantics in eastern Europe, Waugh became a hero, his popularity outstripping even our previous idols – George Lansbury, General Nasser and Fidel Castro.

But (*pace* Polly Toynbee) how can anyone on the left hold in esteem a man who hated socialism in all its manifestations, who was proud to call himself a class warrior and who, in 1984, suggested the police offer a £50 bounty for every miner's scalp, thus saving redundancy payments and 'giving the unemployed of Liverpool a chance to earn a little more beer money'?

The first answer is that, by lampooning the left's most ludicrous and humourless excesses, he provided an invaluable service to the longer-term interests of the movement. In the *Guardian* in 1993, Philip Norman, a long-term Waugh adversary, wrote that, 'far from being a bulwark against political correctness, Waugh's writings give it precisely the ammunition it needs to justify itself'. Wrong way round, Norman. Those on the left who couldn't see the joke and laugh along with the funniest satirist in the English language since Swift demonstrated the very boorishness Waugh set out to ridicule.

G. B. Shaw once remarked: 'We should have had socialism already, but for the socialists.' Douglas Jay was a case in point. In 1939, Jay wrote: 'In the case of nutrition and health, just as in the case of education, the gentleman in Whitehall really does know better what is good for people than people know themselves.'

Waugh saw it as his life's work to lampoon such outrageous pomposity. At first, he thought politicians to be merely self-important and silly, but it was his experience of the machinations of the Labour government during the Nigerian civil war in the late 1960s that convinced him of their innate wickedness, too. 'In their quest for power and self-importance,' he wrote, 'to compensate for whatever feelings of social inadequacy or sexual insecurity, they are prepared to perpetrate something which is hard to distinguish from mass murder, if they think they can get away with it.'

As a result, countless 'power-mad' politicians suffered from Waugh's poison pen, starting with the 'bully' Richard Crossman and finishing, thirty years later, with the 'twerpish' Tony Blair. Yet those politicians who Waugh felt were genuinely activated by nobler motives than the desire to boss the rest of us around – such seemingly disparate figures as Eric Heffer, James Callaghan, Sir Geoffrey Howe, the 'fragrant' Lady Olga Maitland and, in later days, the 'saintly' Michael Foot – received different treatment.

Waugh opposed socialism because socialists always seemed to want to ban things or to discourage people from activities they enjoyed, such as hunting, boxing, drinking or smoking. He was first and foremost a libertarian, who felt as out of place with the hang 'em and flog 'em brigade at the Tory Party Conference as he would have done at a strike committee of the National Union of Mineworkers.

Coloured by his experience of the Fleet Street print unions, he was sceptical of the idea that unions were the blueprints for building the caring, sharing socialist utopia. Similarly, he doubted that the welfare state and transfer payments would in themselves produce kinder, nicer people. While Ferdinand Mount may have gone too far in describing Waugh as a 'prophet of a generation', it is surely true that Waugh helped to provoke a critical and much-needed self-analysis on the left; at the very least, he guaranteed that there were no taboo topics.

The other major reason why I believe Waugh can be held up as a hero of the left was his consistent opposition to the US / British 'world policeman' foreign policy role that developed after the end of the cold war. Nato may once have been necessary but, in Waugh's eyes, after the Berlin Wall came down it served no useful purpose, and its metamorphosis into a crusading 'human rights' war machine left him mortified. Being sceptical of all politicians, Waugh was not fooled by the war-mongering hysteria of the Gulf War. He wrote: 'I have stuck resolutely to my thesis that there is no Gulf crisis, it has all been cooked up by self-important politicians.'

Over the following decade, he was equally unimpressed by British and American justifications for sanctions against Iraq. In 1998, he wrote: 'How can any intelligent person be expected to believe that a country of 15 million people, mostly impoverished desert dwellers, poses a threat to world peace?' In 1999, the 'moral imperialism', as Waugh saw it, went into overdrive with the bombing of Yugoslavia.

It took a man regarded as the most conservative columnist of his generation to see through the 'lying propaganda' that preceded the campaign to bomb a developed European country back to the Stone Age. In April 1999, very few people were brave enough to state openly that Serb 'atrocities' had been 'deliberately exaggerated'. Waugh said it. And we are still waiting to see the evidence that a quarter of a million Albanians were indeed killed by Yugoslav forces, as British and American officials claimed.

For all his *Private Eye* diary entries, rants about miners and affected snobbery, Waugh did not see humanity divided along class lines. 'My grand philosophical conclusion at the end of the day,' he wrote, 'is that humanity does not divide into the rich and poor, the privileged and the unprivileged, the clever and the stupid, the lucky and the unlucky, or even the happy and the unhappy. It divides into the nasty and the nice. Nasty people are humourless, bitter, self-pitying, resentful and mean ... saints may worry about them and even try to turn their sour natures, but those who do not aspire to saintliness are best advised to avoid them whenever possible, and give their aggression a good run for its money whenever it becomes unavoidable.' Waugh took the latter course, making it his life-work to give aggression a good run for its money, whether it came from politicians, union leaders or military alliances. Hero of the left or not, may he rest in peace.

This makes a fitting conclusion perhaps to Bron's *Private Eye* years, but before we start on our second act – his *Literary Review* years – an account of his last great battle with the libel laws, which greeted him within weeks of his assuming the magazine's editorship, belongs here rather than as part of the next act. It concerned a libel complaint against the *Literary Review* brought by the Countess of Dudley that had its origins from before there was any involvement in the journal by Bron, but it possessed aspects that once again raised fundamental points of controversy over the way the libel laws of the country operated.

The Route to the Literary Review

There are those who see being on the receiving end of slings and jibes in *Private Eye* as recognition of the mark they are making on the general scene. Naim Attallah had certainly come in for his share of gratuitous insults. Sometime during the summer of 1982, however, he received a letter from Auberon Waugh: an invitation to a lunch he was hosting at the Gay Hussar restaurant in Soho. The objective of this gathering was to bring together the leading publishers in England to ask them to debate the merits of their respective imprints and provide fodder for a lengthy article Bron was writing for the *Sunday Telegraph* magazine. Naim declined the invitation, but not because of any past animosities. His feeling about Quartet's position in the publishing hierarchy was that there was not so much an outright rejection as a tacit non-acceptance of its status as an integral part of their world. Quartet was perhaps seen as being on the fringes of the industry, and he did not want to stir the pot by attending, convinced as he was that he would only be plunged into a situation not of his choosing. As it turned out, he could have been right.

Details of the lunch were given in the 'Bent's Notes' column in the *Bookseller* of 7 August, which listed the publishers who were there: Tom

Maschler of Jonathan Cape, Lord Weidenfeld of Weidenfeld & Nicolson, Christopher Maclehose of Collins, Alan Brooke of Michael Joseph, Matthew Evans of Faber & Faber, André Deutsch of André Deutsch, Christopher Sinclair-Stevenson of Hamish Hamilton and John Murray of John Murray. Among those invited but who failed to turn up, the report concluded, was Naim Attallah of Quartet, who declined to join 'a bunch of Zionists and left-wingers'. When Naim read this unwarranted distortion of the truth he was furious and demanded that the *Bookseller* retract the statement. 'Bent's Notes' of 21 August duly made a gentlemanly response:

> I apologize. I referred to Naim Attallah of Quartet declining an invitation from Auberon Waugh to lunch with Tom Maschler, Lord Weidenfeld, Christopher Maclehose, Alan Brooke, Matthew Evans, André Deutsch, Christopher Sinclair-Stevenson and John Murray. He had not, as I wrote in my column of 7 August, declined to join 'a bunch of Zionists and left-wingers' – that was the paraphrase put on it at the lunch but not what Naim Attallah had said. He had, in fact, replied in these courteous terms: 'My own view concerning publishing is alas not one that other publishers would share and I therefore feel inadequately placed to cope with established figures whose motivations rarely coincide with mine. Their world is one which I feel neither comfort in nor draw any comfort from.' I apologize for any distress or embarrassment I may have caused him.

In the finished article for the *Sunday Telegraph*, which appeared later that year, Bron, whom Attallah had personally never met up to this point, was very complimentary about the literary quality of Quartet's output and about him personally:

> When Naim Attallah of Quartet started publishing six years ago, he gave the impression of being concerned by what he saw as the excessive Zionist influence in British publishing. But his list, which includes among its greater successes Nigel Dempster's *HRH Princess Margaret: A*

Life Unfulfilled, does not really support the idea of a holy crusade. There is a surprisingly pleasant and relaxed atmosphere at Quartet under such a dynamic man (Attallah is also the financial director of Asprey's, the jewellers) but the list is unmistakably one of the more interesting around. Currently they are chiefly excited about the recent publication of *Red Square*, a faction novel by Edward Topol and Fridrikh Neznansky, about a supposed plot to topple Brezhnev.

Two years later, in January 1984, Naim received another letter from Bron, whom he had by now met casually on a number of occasions, though without ever really getting to know him. In this letter Bron asked Naim to consider interviewing his elder daughter, Sophia – beautiful and fresh out of university, said her father – for a possible job at Quartet Books, an outfit he always referred to in the press as 'Naim Attallah's seraglio'. Naim duly responded and asked Sophia to come and see him at Namara House, his office in Soho. She arrived simply dressed and seemed totally confident and relaxed. Attallah was won over by the sheer warmth of Sophia's personality and had no hesitation about offering her a job. Her response was spontaneously joyful as she accepted it on the spot and said she was prepared to start as soon as possible. Instead of shaking her hand as she left the office, Naim bent forward and kissed her. Unbeknown to him, she had already attended another job-seeking interview, with Alexander Chancellor, the editor of the *Spectator* and a close friend of her father's. He, too, had offered her a post, and according to his account she had said she would take it. When the news broke that Sophia would be joining Quartet, Alexander complained to her father over his disappointment that she was choosing a book publisher over the *Spectator*. Auberon was forthright in his response: 'You should have kissed her as Naim did.'

Towards the end of September 1985 Naim was planning the launch of an entirely different venture, having created two new perfumes called respectively by the unashamed names, he admitted, of 'Avant l'Amour' and 'Après l'Amour'. He also thought in retrospect that the blurb contrived for their publicity might have been rather over the top in flowery qualities:

Enter my fragrant world and discover the age-old secrets of perfume's seductive spell … For the woman whose nights of passion dissolve into clear mornings of tenderness and tranquillity, I bring Avant and Après l'Amour … They are created out of love, created for women who enjoy love and dare to show it.

Bron, in an account of a press preview of the perfumes, had already described them as 'indescribably delicious', competing 'tantalizingly with each other'. Considerable interest in these new scents was stirred up in the press in general; and for the launch party itself Bron joined the high-powered guest list, accompanied by his daughter Sophia. It was indeed an exotic affair, master-minded by Charlotte Faber, whose creativity knew no bounds when it came to turning publicity events for Namara and Quartet into unforgettable occasions. She had dressed eight of the girls from Namara and Quartet in rubber dresses with laces up the back and velvet at the hem and collar. Four of the dresses were in white rubber, the other four in black. The girls got through a great deal of talcum powder in squeezing themselves into the garments, but with much giggling they struggled and helped each other to success. Once the girls were in, they looked weirdly evocative, 'rather like Sloanes in bondage' as one journalist (not Bron) commented. Then a problem arose that no one had foreseen. If one of them needed to go to the loo, she was going to have to take her dress off first, and there was no way she would be able to cope with this on her own. 'You'll just have to go in twos,' Naim advised.

After the perfume launch, from that point on references in *Private Eye* by 'Grovel' to 'Attullah–Disgusting' had the epithet 'the seedy perfumier' added on. Bron, on the other hand, evidently decided that there was wholesome fun to be had in Naim's vicinity and was consistently loyal and generous in his appreciation of whatever schemes and projects were being attempted that had Naim's name associated with them. An example was provided by an unusual new venture announced in the middle of October 1989, which involved Naim's wife Maria. A shop was to be opened in Shepherd Market, Mayfair, and called 'Aphrodisia'. Maria was to run it and assemble the stock herself. The idea had its roots essentially in the premise that products that are life-enhancing promote a healthy well-being, and that this, in turn, enhances one's love life. Artificial aids and stimulants found no place in this scheme of things. Nature's way was to be the answer.

Aphrodisia's diverse merchandise would all be guaranteed to combat the stress of modern living. Handcrafted gifts and natural products would be evident everywhere. Rare honeys, both bitter and sweet, gathered from a variety of locations from the Mediterranean to the Pacific, would be placed alongside the finest ginseng and pure mineral sea salts. Chocolates to excite the palate, based on an exclusive Aphrodisia recipe, would be available, as would cold-pressed olive oils, full-bodied and rich in aromas, with jars of wild berries to make the mouth water. The shop would be an Aladdin's cave with love as its theme and *raison d'être*. Maria's natural artistic flare was ideally suited to the exercise. She had acted as sole interior decorator for the Namara Group and had won unequivocal praise for her ingenuity and good taste. The new undertaking would give her the opportunity to display her many talents in a field primarily aimed at boosting the romantic side of life.

The London *Evening Standard* was thoroughly taken with the whole idea of Aphrodisia:

> I'm delighted to hear that the publisher Naim Attallah is to set up his wife in an aphrodisiac shop in Shepherd Market, the notorious stretch of Mayfair so enjoyed by businessmen and authors. The excellent Maria Attallah is sometimes forgotten in all the excitement of the publisher's famous gaggle of nymphets at Quartet Books, so it is heartening to find that Naim is redressing the balance. Among the shop's products will be a 24-carat-gold powder to sprinkle on your bread-and-butter pudding.

Three months later the shop opened, and among the first of the illustrious customers to come through its door was Auberon Waugh. After his visit, writing in his column in the *Spectator*, he first bemoaned the loss of innocence, then went on to tell of how he had 'chanced on a shop in Shepherd Market called Aphrodisia'.

It is kept by Maria Attallah, wife of the Palestinian philanthropist, whose purpose, she tells me, is to sell things which make men and women feel natural and good. Some are toilet preparations, but there are books, too: *The New Sensual Massage: Learn to Give Pleasure with Your Hands*; *Love Spells*; *Shakespeare's Sonnets*; *The Japanese Bath*; books on roses; love poems; foods of love; books of pretty Edwardian nudes; beeswax candles; green-apple candles ... 'all my objects point towards sensual passion', says Attallah. Single ostrich feathers; silk damask copes with gold fringes for those with religious fantasies; pretty painted-wood putti; Japanese tea; honey from Hawaii; hearts made of crystal, yellow and rose quartz; amethyst matrices, silver hearts, eggs of agate; little trinkets of affection; gold love chains; ginseng roots pickled in vodka and brandy ...

At 25 Shepherd Market, Maria Attallah has collected everything that is innocent and pure, everything worth saving from the Sixties. There is a philosophy and a truth in sensuality which need to be separated from the destructive guilt which once supported the drug culture. Apart from anything else, I felt that all my Christmas-present problems are solved as long as Aphrodisia lasts.

No one could have described the shop better, or with greater friendliness, which takes us back to the passages in *Will This Do?* where Bron gives a vivid description of Naim Attallah in his account of their first personal encounter:

I first met Naim when he was kind enough to employ my elder daughter, Sophia, in his publishing firm, Quartet Books ... Through Sophia I met

Naim and his delightful seraglio of pretty, cheerful, well-born young women, who use him as their springboard into London life. He is happy to be so used, and the system seems to work, as Quartet, although outside the mainstream of London's dismal, introspective publishing scene, produces some excellent books.

On first impression, Naim appears as a bubbling pixie, full of strange and wild enthusiasms. Articulate and outgoing, he seldom wastes a sentence, although he speaks a lot. His favourite word is 'wonderful'. On the few occasions when things are not wonderful, he scowls and goes into an angry speech until the matter is cleared up, and then he finds something new which is wonderful to laugh about. When he is upset – and although he does not seem to mind being lampooned in *Private Eye*, he is surprisingly sensitive to signs of hostility from any other publication, and particularly upset by any display of ingratitude – he has to be comforted by sympathetic and pretty women. But behind the little-boy façade he has a quick, shrewd mind which is never at rest, whether thinking of how to make someone happy or advance a friend, or of some commercial opportunity for one or another of his myriad enterprises ...

A Christian Palestinian from Haifa, he made his millions, it is thought, by playing the exchange rates, and invested them shrewdly – in, among other things, the bricks and mortar of his Poland Street headquarters, and 51 Beak Street, where the *Literary Review* offices are situated, as well as the group design department, the Academy Club, the group's accountant and various other enterprises. Nobody looking for a smaller literary magazine to edit could have hoped for a pleasanter office.

Naim's offer to Bron, in January 1986, to become editor of the *Literary Review*, certainly arrived at a point where it reinforced his feelings that his time at *Private Eye* was drawing to a close. He had worked there for sixteen years, and as he told Harry Thompson: 'I had rather been looking around for something else.' The libel action brought by Claire Tomalin (as described above) had been settled out of court a few months earlier, frustrating Bron's intense wish to have his say in the dock; a fact which Richard Ingrams felt also played a part in Bron's decision. But according to *Will This Do?* there was an accumulation of unwelcome changes in the air:

> Footie [Paul Foot] had left the *Eye*, and so had Marnham [Patrick Marnham, an old friend of Waugh's – they had shared an office at *Private Eye* in the early days] ... [Nigel] Dempster had quarrelled and left. [Peter] McKay was in a strange limbo, still attending *Eye* functions as a sort of official enemy. The magazine had moved from Greek Street to new offices in Carlisle Street just when the atmosphere was beginning to deteriorate. Ingrams seemed to be taking less interest in the magazine. A new employee, O'Hanrahan, made rude noises and insolent faces every time any of the public school-educated contributors walked in or walked out. It was plainly time to move on.

There was a farewell lunch at L'Escargot given in March 1986 for the entire *Eye* staff and a few others. At the end of an affectionate tribute to Bron's contribution, Richard Ingrams astoundingly announced his own retirement and the appointment of a new editor for the magazine. Bedlam ensued. 'The announcement,' wrote Bron, 'came as a thunderbolt.'

> Emotional scenes broke out ... I pleaded with Ingrams to remain, offering to sack the *Literary Review*; Hislop then walked out in a huff, saying I had insulted the young. Only William Rushton growled: 'High time, too!'

There followed a frenzy of speculation, sniping and old-score settling in the media. For a long time Bron would maintain he could not remember Hislop's name, but he did tell Harry Thompson:

> At the time I thought the change was unnecessary and a great shame, and I thought the magazine would collapse without Ingrams, but in

fact it jolly well hasn't as anybody can see. It's rather good, actually. Young what's-his-name has pulled it together and it's really scarcely distinguishable from what it was.

In March 1987, three years after it was first presented, the Countess of Dudley's libel complaint against the *Literary Review* finally had a hearing. It went back to the time before Auberon Waugh became editor, but now the magazine needed to defend its position in court. The passage causing the commotion occurred in just a few sentences of a 1,700-word review by Alastair Forbes of Anne Somerset's book *Ladies in Waiting* in the July 1984 issue of the magazine. Two years further back still, the countess had acted as an 'unofficial' unpaid lady-in-waiting to Princess Michael of Kent on a 'flag waving' tour of the United States. In the wake of that trip her husband, Lord Dudley, took to reciting a scurrilous poem about the princess, which he called 'Our Val', in the privacy of London clubs and smoking rooms. It was 'biting, bitchy and along the lines of "Eskimo Nell"', as the *Daily Mail* described it without contradiction. The poem then unintentionally took on a life of its own by being retailed on the social circuit, on one occasion, it was said, making Princess Margaret fall off her chair with laughter after she heard it. When word of all this got back to Princess Michael, she naturally became upset. Alastair Forbes referred to the episode in his review, saying how the Earl of Dudley had spent much of 1983 giving 'Tennysonian after-dinner readings of his most un-Tennysonian tirade against poor Princess Michael of Kent'.

> [The princess's] only offence had lain in her proven unwisdom in inviting Dudley's humbly born but avid countess to accompany her to the United States as a lady-in-waiting, who would be expected to pay her own way.
>
> Dudley's scurrilously bad poetasting, coarse and clumsy attempts to clothe criminal libel in Clive Jamesian mode, had the effect in due

course of winning considerable sympathy [for the princess], not least from the Queen.

The unprecedented outcome was that Dudley received a *lettre de cachet* from the palace solicitors that has since effectively zipped his wife's lips.

Dudley had then done the least he could do and written a letter of apology to Princess Michael, which was delivered in person to the royal solicitor by Lord Goodman. Subsequently it came into the public domain when part of its text was printed in the *Mail on Sunday* in 1985:

> I write on behalf of my wife and myself to place on record our most sincere regret for the grave distress and embarrassment which we have caused you, Prince Michael, and your family and we unreservedly express our deep apologies. We acknowledge that the statements are untruthful and should never have been made. We undertake that we will never repeat or publish this offensive material again or anything similar relating to you or your family.

Later Lord Dudley, when questioned by the press, put out a statement that he was confident no copy of the poem had got out at the time. 'All copies of it were destroyed.'

As Lady Dudley's lawyer told the press: 'Our action concerns allegations in the review about the countess's attitude.' The burden of their case was that Alastair Forbes's article, by stating that the countess's lips had needed to be 'zipped' by the Queen's solicitors, implied she had fed libellous stories against Princess Michael to her husband and verbally stabbed the princess in the back, while other parts of the review portrayed her as 'vulgar, greedy, grasping and pushy'. It had, claimed her counsel in court, been 'a scurrilous and damaging attack' on Lady Dudley's character. 'It is quite a serious attack on her loyalty, her integrity, and her character as a whole.'

There were undoubtedly social sensitivities involved in the Dudley family background. Lady Dudley herself was irked by the tendency of the press to refer to her as a former 'Rank starlet'. The publicity arising from the libel hearing compelled her to circulate a CV to the editors of Fleet Street to correct any misapprehensions: '... my claim is that I should be regarded as having been a serious actress and dancer who only appeared in leading roles in films, on the stage and on television'. As Maureen Swanson, a talented twelve-year-old schoolgirl from Glasgow – the daughter of a hairdresser's assistant – she had arrived in London to study with the Sadler's Wells Theatre Company and moved on to graduate as a dancer from the Royal School of Ballet. From there she was talent-spotted for stage and screen, gaining a part in the first London production of *Carousel* at the Theatre Royal, Drury Lane, in 1950. The following year John Huston cast her for a role in his film *Moulin Rouge* and she began to widen her social circle, becoming a friend of Dr Stephen Ward before he was engulfed and destroyed through his links with the Christine Keeler–John Profumo scandal.

Later films in which she had supporting roles included Jack Lee's *A Town Like Alice* in 1956, with Peter Finch and Virginia McKenna, based on Nevil Shute's novel; and in the same year there was a film version of A. J. Cronin's novel *The Spanish Gardener*, with Dirk Bogarde, in which she played a 'sultry peasant girl (strangely endowed with vowels of purist Pinewood)', in the words of the commentator, Hugh Montgomery-Massingberd, in the *Daily Telegraph* on 1 April 1987. In the 1950s film fans were not so troubled by such incongruous inauthenticities as they tended to have become half a century later. Then, in 1957, she had a role in Jack Lee's *Robbery under Arms*, with Peter Finch and Ronald Lewis. The promising acting career ended, however, in 1961, when she married the 4th Earl of Dudley after a six-year courtship and joined the long tradition of show girls to have merged into the aristocracy. There had been a delay to their marriage taking place till the earl's divorce from his first wife became absolute.

The actress had therefore 'metamorphosed into the peeress', but the 'finest performance of her career', in the words of Mr Montgomery-Massingberd, basing his judgement on the way she handled her evidence during the libel hearing before a jury, had now become as the Countess of Dudley.

> The vision of the Countess of Dudley crying in court over Mr Alastair Forbes's uncomfortable revelations, published a mere three years ago in the *Literary Review*, could well provoke polemics on the gross absurdity of the libel laws or the sickening hypocrisy of the upper classes, but it also affords a striking example of the apotheosis of the 'actressocracy'.

Both Bron and Naim Attallah had confidence in the total logic of the magazine's defence, which was that Alastair Forbes's words, as given in the *Literary Review*, were not capable of bearing the meaning complained of. The hearing lasted four and a half hours and the jury, consisting of seven men and five women, retired for a further two hours to consider all they had seen and heard. The next day, on 31 March, the *Daily Mail* printed a headline that told the whole story: 'Earl's wife in tears after she wins "zipped lip" libel case'. The spirit of the 'actressocracy' had won the jury round, and a 'tearful countess was comforted by her husband after the hearing at which she was awarded £5,000 damages and costs estimated at £20,000'. 'I feel absolutely vindicated,' said Lady Dudley. 'It was just the result I wanted.'

> Writer Auberon Waugh, recently appointed editor of the *Literary Review*, said after the case: 'We are very sad indeed because it all depended on whether the jury understood English or not. Obviously it didn't.' Asked if there would be any problems in paying the award and legal costs, he replied: 'I imagine there will be, but I am keeping quiet about that.'

Bron also won himself a place in 'Quote of the Day' in the *London Daily News* the following morning: 'Our defence was that what we said was true, but that we didn't say it.' The result of losing the case initially got him down and 'Londoner's Diary' in the *Evening Standard* drew a depressed response from him, finding him 'trying to talk himself out of a job'.

Though the proprietor, the parfumier and publisher Naim Attallah, sings in his sweet Palestinian voice that he'll find the money somewhere – and he shouldn't find it difficult – Waugh says it might be the time for the mag to go to the great library in the sky.

'It should have gone under years ago,' he sighs. 'I have put the subscription up to £15 but haven't got any in yet. The future is parlous.'

The only thought that cheered Bron up a little was that, if the magazine folded, the countess was going to have to start all over again with a fresh action 'against Attallah or the printers if she wanted her money'. Meanwhile Lady Dudley was complaining that Naim Attallah had not stayed to shake her hand in a sporting way, but had 'slunk' off after the verdict, and fuming against Bron for his 'élitist attitude' in patronizing the jury with his assertion that they did not understand English. It was a theme Bron was not going to let drop in a hurry. He returned to it with fresh vigour in his column in the *Sunday Telegraph* of 5 April, saying how he observed that 'three of the jurors had some difficulty in reading the jury oath and one could not do it at all. It was read to him by the Clerk.'

The case revolved around the meaning to be put upon some words in a fairly abstruse piece of literary criticism. The countess claimed that they suggested she was a 'greedy and vulgar woman' who, despite an undertaking to do so, refused to pay her expenses on a trip with Princess Michael, but instead furnished her husband, the Earl of Dudley, with material for a scurrilous poem which he wrote about the princess and circulated until requested to stop by the palace.

The *Literary Review* ... pointed out that the words meant nothing of the sort. Since that was the point at issue, the judge, Mr Justice Drake, declined to take sides. The jury decided after [two] hours that the words were indeed capable of some such meaning ...

I do not know what governs Parliament in its choice of qualifications for jury service, but even a Labour government should be able to understand that a case involving interpretation of the written word is unlikely to be helped by a juror who cannot actually read. This was undoubtedly the case with one juror, but several others had the utmost difficulty. Perhaps, in the great explosion of illiteracy which has been observed since the education reforms of the last decade, court officials might divide their cases into those which require an ability to read and those which don't.

Mercifully enough, said Bron, the hearing had lasted less than a day.

In summing up, Mr Justice Drake seemed to invite the jury to share his disappointment that the *Literary Review* had not mounted a more comprehensive defence. But he must have been aware that tiny mag-azines like the *Literary Review* cannot begin to afford the cost of such an enterprise. At the time of the alleged libel – long before I became editor – its circulation was apparently only 2,000 copies. The sum at stake in this one-day hearing – about £20,000 as it turned out – may be noth-ing to the Dudleys, who are extremely rich, but to the *Literary Review* it represents the entire annual revenue from 2,000 subscriptions ... There is hope that something good will come out of this sorry little episode. I had supposed that immediately after the result, Lady Dudley would announce she was giving the £5,000 to charity. Unfortunately the announcement seems to have been delayed, but when it comes it will prove even more conclusively than the jury's decision that she is neither 'greedy' nor 'grasping' nor any of the horrid things of which she thought she had been accused.

Lord Dudley mounted a counter-attack in a letter printed on 19 April, summarizing Bron's case and adding that readers of the *Sunday Telegraph* would be surprised to know that Alastair Forbes had 'admitted over two years ago in a letter dated January 24, 1985 to Naim Attallah, owner of the *Literary Review*, of which I have a copy, sent to her by the *Review*'s solicitors, that the passages in his article objectionable to my wife did in fact carry the meaning she attached to them; ... and apologized to my wife …' Auberon Waugh, he accused, had unhesitatingly used his access to the press to portray the defeat in court in a less unfavourable light while hinting at a 'possible mistrial'. His advice to Lady Dudley on how to use her damages had only added insult to injury and his comments had already involved the Dudleys in extra legal expenses. They were therefore instituting a 'fighting fund or Waugh chest, fortified by the jury's award'.

Then, as a challenge to a further account of the hearing Bron had given in the *Spectator*, Lord Dudley wrote a letter to that journal too, quoting at greater length from Alastair Forbes's apology:

> Having too credulously but in perfect good faith accepted as author-itative a circumstantial account of the matter from a cousin of the sovereign whom I mistakingly assumed to be in a position to know, I hinted in my review that the two ladies had subsequently fallen out … over the matter of expenses incurred … I have since been informed that this was not the correct *casus* … I unreservedly accept … that 'filthy lucre' played no part … I apologize to Lady Dudley for my inadvertently inaccurate interpretation.

Bron and Naim must therefore have known, Lord Dudley asserted, that the words complained about did carry the meaning Lady Dudley had imputed to them, which meant we were now paying dearly for an error of judgement. Auberon Waugh had been a 'liar' when he wrote that Lady Dudley 'wept in the dock [*sic*] while describing how she had six children' and that she 'did not give the impression of quick appreciation of the English language'. Bron had made the assertion that an effective defence could have been mounted for costs of a hundred thousand pounds, and Lord Dudley challenged him to substantiate this 'untrue and defamatory innuendo'.

> If he is unable to respond to my challenge, and to justify those passages in his article in which I accuse him of deceit, lies and unfair innuendo, he will condemn himself in the eyes of readers of your periodical,

and the wider readership that has access to it, as a bad loser and a bad sport, all whose past comments on the case are attributable to these defective qualities.

There must be more honest and honourable ways of defending the *Literary Review*'s reputation, thought the earl, than more mud-slinging at Lady Dudley or attempts to 'take the edge off her well-deserved triumph'. 'Auberon Waugh,' added an editor's note, 'when asked to comment, groaned.'

At this point Naim Attallah stepped into the firing line and wrote his own letter from Namara House to the *Spectator* on 25 April:

Sir: I was amazed by Lord Dudley's partial quotation ... from a letter Alastair Forbes wrote to the *Literary Review* on 24 January 1985.

If Lord Dudley wishes people to know why the *Literary Review* never published the letter, then I suggest he quotes it in full; or, better still, he could challenge the *Literary Review* to publish it.

In the *Sunday Telegraph* of 26 April, a letter, also written by Naim, clarified the position over this further:

What [Lord Dudley] does not divulge is that the same letter also contained inflammatory material about the Dudleys which the *Literary Review* quite rightly chose not to publish. The magazine was not prepared to find itself embroiled in a family squabble not of its making.

Much fuss has been made of the original review of which Lady Dudley complains; the reality of the situation is that all could have been settled amicably had the Dudleys, at the outset, chosen diplomacy rather than heavy-handedness.

Simultaneously, Alastair Forbes was joining in the letter-writing fray, denying Lord Dudley's claim that there had ever been an admission from him that the passage complained about did indeed carry the meaning Lady

Dudley saw in it. He had, he said, admitted no such thing. In his view, Lord Dudley was attempting to bamboozle and mislead the *Sunday Telegraph*'s readers by disingenuously quoting out of context. He greatly hoped that Lord Dudley would take up Naim's challenge to print in full the text as he originally wrote it. The part that was true, he told the *Spectator*, was that

> after refusing to provide the grovelling apology and withdrawal demanded by Lady Dudley's solicitors, I sent to the latter a copy of the 'Apology and clarification' I had thought it appropriate to offer to the *Literary Review* ... In this document I corrected and apologized for a minor error, attributing one cause of the admitted 1982 dispute between Princess Michael and Lady Dudley ... to a tiff over tipping in a British Embassy.
>
> My clarification reminded readers of the *Literary Review* that Lady Dudley was only one of 'the sixty or so persons, titled and untitled, to have received appropriate contextual mention' in my notice of *Ladies in Waiting*. 'Likewise her husband,' I went on, 'who, it has nowhere been disputed, was the author and publisher of a scurrilous libel and slander grossly defamatory of HRH Princess Michael of Kent whom Lady Dudley at one time accompanied as companion and unofficial lady-in-waiting on a most successful fund-raising trip to the US undertaken by the princess, both roles being performed to the latter's satisfaction ... I have since been informed that this [i.e. the tiff over tips] was not the correct *casus* of the Dudleys' bitterly belligerent ballad ... I unreservedly accept Lady Dudley's assertion that "filthy lucre" played no part in the genesis of her husband's filthy poem ...'

I went on to suggest that nevertheless the princess had been ill-advised to choose as companion 'anyone capable of suddenly becoming so avid of encouraging the public pillorying and ridicule of a member of the royal family, whose much-loved parents-in-law, I cannot help recalling, began their honeymoon as guests of Lord Dudley's father at Himley Hall.'

It was a pity, he concluded, that the jury had heard nothing of all this background, or of the letter of apology written by Lord Dudley to Princess Michael.

At the end of April there was an 'At Home' party for the *Literary Review* at the Groucho Club, ostensibly to mark a change of staff and to boast about the enrolment of the five-thousandth subscriber, though really as 'a riotous excuse for authors to meet authors and for hacks to play in the conversational surf', as 'Londoner's Diary' in the *Evening Standard* reported it.

> Guests included novelist Piers Paul Read (a bit of gravitas there), for foreign glamour Count Adam Zamoyski, for beauty the bevy of Waugh girls and for respectability Jeffrey Bernard.
>   *Literary Review*'s publisher, Naim Attallah … waved aside suggestions that the costs of the recent Lady Dudley libel case may sink the mag. 'It's an occupational hazard,' he said with painful grandeur.

Lord Dudley returned to the lists with a final letter to the *Spectator* on 2 May, apparently unaware of how it reflected on the way the hubris of his uncouth calumny against Princess Michael must continue to haunt him long after he had lodged his apology.

> Alastair Forbes speculates in his letter, and in his review, about the contents of my poem, of which he knows nothing from me, nor, I suspect, from any other source. Unlike his defamatory article, no jury has been asked to decide if it was libellous. It reflected my anger more than four years ago at what I believed to be unfair treatment of my wife, as explained in the covering letter to Prince Michael accompanying my apology, subject to a legal agreement that the contents should remain confidential to those persons having heard or read the poem.
>   I firmly deny that the poem could justifiably have been compared to 'Eskimo Nell' in style, meter, or content, as anyone with knowledge of

it would confirm. Otherwise I continue, despite the leak of my apology, to honour my side of the agreement.

I can also state as a positive fact for which I have conclusive evidence that there was no 'unprecedented outcome' to the existence of the poem, as stated by Alastair Forbes in his book review ... and that it is untrue that my wife's lips were effectively zipped up by any such letter, or that any letter exists likely to have influenced the jury to reach a different verdict.

Finally, on 16 May, Bron put on a demonstration of how formidable he could be when roused. He gathered up and summarized all the implications in an article for the *Spectator* headed: 'Time for Dudley to act like an earl and belt up'. While away in Spain for a week, he had debated whether maintaining a dignified silence was really appropriate in the face of a letter that accused him of 'deceit, lies and unfair innuendo'.

To say of an established member of the journalistic profession that he is a deliberate deceiver, etc., is a fairly dangerous thing, especially if it is based on a single matter whose truth is easily established. In my experience of the libel law, which may be more extensive than Lord Dudley's, I would put it at £20,000 in out-of-court settlement, and any sum you care to mention after litigation. Perhaps someone told him that respectable journalists do not sue for libel unless they are accused of treason or taking bribes. That has always been my rule...

But dignified silence does not always work, either, as I found to my irritation when returning from abroad, by which time another long, tendentious and, I am sorry to say, rather misleading letter from Lord Dudley had appeared ... My earlier silence was inspired, more than anything else, by an earnest desire not to bore *Spectator* readers with a continuation of other people's troubles. However, they have already been bored to tears, and I now feel I have an obligation to explain to them, in as unboring a way as possible, what it is all about. So here goes.

In October 1982 Lady Dudley ... was asked to accompany Princess Michael of Kent on an American tour. In the course of that tour, they spent a weekend at the Washington Embassy where certain events either occurred or did not occur – I do not know whether they did or not – which caused Lord Dudley to write to Mr John Barratt, Prince Michael's secretary, in August 1983 that criticism of his wife's conduct had been made by Princess Michael as early as the previous November (1982), 'when she told Mrs Jonathan Aitken that the British Ambassador in Washington (Sir Oliver Wright) had told her, Princess Michael personally, that my wife's conduct in Washington had been so odious and outrageous that the Ambassador would never invite her to the Embassy again'.

That is Lord Dudley's account. Mr Barratt gives a slightly different one. Whatever the rights and wrongs of it, Lord Dudley under 'emotions of deep resentment', as he described them in a letter to Prince Michael, and feeling that his wife had been unfairly treated, composed and circulated a poem about Princess Michael, which was variously described as scurrilous and obscene. I have not read it. What is possibly the only surviving copy of the poem is now in the safekeeping of Sir Rex Williams, senior partner of Messrs Clifford Turner, the royal solicitors.

It was Alastair Forbes's reference to this incident in his article in the *Literary Review*, said Bron, which attracted the letter from Lady Dudley's solicitor and led to the libel action.

The second string to Lady Dudley's plaint, and the one on which I judged that a defence of fair comment would have been available to the defendants, if they could have afforded the gamble, was where Forbes claimed that activity by the royal solicitors had 'effectively zipped his [Lord Dudley's] and his wife's lips'. Lord Dudley challenged me to produce the letters which would support this opinion under threat of being thought a deceiver by *Spectator* readers.

'I can also state as a positive fact for which I have conclusive evidence,' he wrote to the *Spectator* on 2 May, '... that it is untrue that my wife's lips were effectively zipped by any such letter, or that any letter exists likely to have influenced the jury to reach a different verdict'. He also states as a 'positive fact' for which he has 'conclusive evidence' that no letter was ever received from 'the "Royal" solicitors or any other solicitors'.

Very well. I suppose I had better produce the letters. On the second point, I have in front of me the photocopy of a letter from Sir Rex Williams, Princess Michael's solicitor, to Lord Goodman, Dudley's representative, dated 20 December 1983. He acknowledges receipt of Lord Dudley's letter to Princess Michael and confirms that his client will not pursue her complaint or seek any further remedy in return for indemnification of her costs and the surrender of copies of the poem by Lord Goodman's client.

On the first point, on whether or not Lady Dudley's lips were effectively zipped, it is true that we have not seen any letter from solicitors making a complaint, but we have seen Lord Dudley's own letter to Princess Michael, delivered to her solicitor and written 'on behalf of my wife and myself', in which he places on record their most sincere regret and unreservedly expresses their deep apologies for the poem. Lord Dudley's letter continues: 'We acknowledge the statements are untruthful and should never have been made. We undertake that we will never repeat or publish this offensive material again or anything similar relating to you or your family.'

I do not think it unreasonable to argue that Lady Dudley's lips were effectively zipped up by this letter, which was plainly written at the royal solicitors' insistence. Perhaps Lord Dudley puts some other interpretation on his own words.

Perhaps he was advised by his lawyers that these letters were somehow 'privileged' and unable to be produced. If so, he was badly advised, but in any case it would have been an act of extreme folly to rely on such advice in denying their existence, of which he was perfectly well aware. Perhaps again he sees himself as some knight in shining armour, vicariously defending his pretty, sensitive, unvulgar, ungreedy wife against the calumnies of Princess Michael, and joining in Lady Dudley's 'well-deserved triumph' against the *Literary Review*. Has he no friends who can tell him he is pushing his luck?

The whole dismal affair had been blown up out of all proportion. The Dudleys were unwise to persist in suing a literary magazine that was struggling to survive, especially since the spat was not of its own making. The dispute could easily have been settled in a civilized fashion without resorting to an acrimonious display in court and in the press verging on the ludicrous. Their insistence, as it appeared, on airing their complaint through the law courts did neither party any credit. On the contrary, washing one's dirty linen in public invariably ends in tears, as was the case with Lady Dudley when she seemingly became overcome with emotion during her cross-examination on the witness stand. Whatever her motives may have been – and one can only speculate about those – they won her no friends. The Goliath-like approach the Dudleys adopted towards a small magazine committed to literary excellence was perceived by many to be excessive and uncalled-for. The magazine lost the case, but nevertheless emerged with much of its sympathy enhanced. In the process, it had thrown into question a form of judicial procedure that was greatly in need of reform.

ACT TWO

❦

The *Literary Review*

I

CAPTAIN OF HIS OWN SHIP

W HEN, TOWARDS THE END OF 1985, NAIM FIRST APPROACHED Sophia Waugh, Bron's daughter, to ask if he should try sounding out her father to see if he would agree to take on editing the *Literary Review*, to his utter delight she replied positively. She knew Bron was thinking about leaving *Private Eye* after many years and was feeling the urge to take a new direction. The *Literary Review*, she thought, could be just the stimulus he was looking for; but then again, she warned, he might say no. She offered to speak to her father, who was already at Combe Florey in Somerset for the Christmas break. In response Bron phoned Naim to say he would give the matter some thought over the festive season, suggesting they meet for lunch in the New Year. Though he was being noncommittal at that stage, Naim began to feel a cautious optimism.

When they did meet early in January, Bron was beaming with excitement and ready to spill the glad tidings: he would be willing to fill the post of editor to the *Literary Review*. This left only the matter of fixing a salary, and apologetically Naim mentioned a figure far too modest for such an appointment by anyone's standards. Brushing the figure aside, Bron said he would not accept it. It was far too high and ought to be reduced by a third. If Naim was agreeable, he would be able to start as soon as he had given the usual terms of notice to *Private Eye*. Once he had taken the editorial chair at the *Literary Review*, he said, he would no longer be able to continue with his contributions to *Private Eye*. In this way the matter of Bron's salary was settled, and it was to remain exactly the same throughout the years of his tenure. Whenever the question arose of a wage increase he always refused it. There were others, he said, who worked for the *Literary*

Review out of devotion and were more deserving by far. The amount of any suggested increase should be distributed among them.

Bron could never have survived financially if editing the *Literary Review* had been his sole source of income. He was only able to do it because he worked prodigiously hard and had other strings to his bow, including regular columns in the *Daily Telegraph* and the *Spectator*. Since he could always be relied on to make provocative comments, he was much in demand to contribute occasional pieces or reviews across an extraordinarily varied range of publications. He was, his son Alexander Waugh wrote in *Fathers and Sons*, 'what would nowadays be termed a workaholic'.

> He was the most prolific journalist in England. At home he slogged at his desk from the crack of dawn until lunchtime, was back in the library after lunch until supper, and often retired there after supper as well. He never took a holiday and wouldn't stop even on Christmas Day … He could not live without his work, and on the rare occasions when he rested, would feel distinctly queer. 'For a week I have done no work at all,' he wrote in his diary, 'and marvel at the stamina of the English, who somehow manage to do none all their lives. After a few days, I found myself in a state of nervous exhaustion and moral collapse.'

It is an indication of how important the *Literary Review* was to him that he could summon up so decisive a portion of his energy to give to it. The difference, of course, was that in writing for other publications he was operating under the management of others, but with the *Review* he had the luxury of being captain of his own ship. Certainly Naim felt that a new epoch began the day Bron came into his life. Securing Bron as editor for the *Literary Review* was a remarkable coup. He honed his wit in the first piece he contributed to the magazine, written in the old year, before he had actually taken over the editorship:

> By the time you read this, you will probably be in the middle of your two-week Christmas 'break'. The Institute of Directors has now urged

factories and firms to stop work for a fortnight after Christmas. It all seems lamentably boring. In the old days, when the majority of Christians believed that God had taken human flesh in Bethlehem, the feasting was all over by Boxing Day. Now, when the majority of bishops and theologians do not believe that Jesus was God, and doubt whether he ever went near Bethlehem, we are all obliged to celebrate for a fortnight. At least the problem of presents was solved for me this year by the proprietor of this paper, Mr Naim Attallah. I have given most of my close friends boxed sets of the stunningly alluring Avant l'Amour scent, with its accompanying Après l'Amour. Clearly, this stuff works! I have had a most suggestive thank-you letter from the ever-lovely Suzanne Lowry [journalist; for a time women's editor at the *Guardian*], suggesting that we spend a two-week break together on a Hebridean island, watching the crones weaving tweed underwear on the looms. I will let you know how we passed this *vacance* in the next issue.

Bron was always supportive of his family and friends, so it was typical of him to have plugged Parfums Namara, Naim's recent venture into the fragrance market.

When the news of the appointment broke, the press was surprised and intrigued. Headlines varied. 'Bron Sacks *Private Eye*' was how the *Sunday Times* expressed it, while Peter Hillmore in *Punch* referred to what was going on as a 'Waugh Game', adding that all sorts of fierce disputes with Richard Ingrams were being cited as the reason for Bron's departure. Bron himself stated that there was no animosity between him and Richard, who apparently told him that 'it is stupid of you to go and work for Naim', who 'is a madman'.

From his side of the story, as recorded in *Will This Do?*, Bron recollected that, 'The Tomalin settlement was in November 1985. In January 1986 I accepted Naim Attallah's offer to take over the editorship of the *Literary Review* from Emma Soames, who was moving to become editor of the *Tatler*.' Actually Bron's memory is slipping up here where Emma Soames's onward movements were concerned. As Kathy O'Shaughnessy's recollections (which follow below) make clear, Emma was actually leaving to be features editor of *Vogue* at Anna Wintour's invitation. He did remember, however, that he had first been told about the *Literary Review* by his sister Margaret ('Meg') FitzHerbert three to four years before when she discovered it herself and enthusiastically pronounced it better than *Books and Bookmen*, for a long time the leading magazine in Britain for those readers wishing to be kept up to date with what was appearing on the literary scene. At that stage Bron was irritated by this claim being made for what looked to him suspiciously like an upstart newcomer. The *Literary Review* had been founded, he said, 'only' in 1979, by Anne Smith, an Edinburgh academic, 'as a counterblast to the academic approach to literary criticism'. But then, he admitted, she had 'made it respectable'.

> The next editor, Gillian Greenwood (from the *Books and Bookmen* stable, as it happened), made it lively. The third, Emma Soames, made it smart. The idea was, I think, that I should make it successful...

This ambition turned out to be not so easily attained, at least in terms of making it profitable. An effort which doubled the print number to 10,500 copies still did not lift it out of making consistent long-term losses; the flow of advertising it attracted remained too sluggish. Five years into the job of editor Bron was clear in his mind that it was only Naim Attallah's enthusiasm (and financial support) that had been keeping the magazine afloat.

He had arrived at his desk to find Kathy O'Shaughnessy there to guide him through the skills and tricks of editing a literary magazine, something in which he had little or no experience. Kathy had been deputy editor to both Gillian Greenwood and Emma Soames, and Bron thought she seemed slightly miffed at being passed over for the editorship herself, which he attributed 'perhaps accurately to the fact that she was not nobly born and did not have grand connections'. In fact, however, she greeted him 'with all the warmth of her generous nature, did not make me feel like an intruder at all as she took me over the most elementary first steps in magazine production'. She had, he observed, 'rather strict views on things like politics and feminism, the greatest contempt for those who relied on parental help or influence ... but was too intelligent and too nice, as well as having too much sense of humour to let any of these interfere with the normal enjoyment of life'. When Kathy left four months later to improve her pay and prospects elsewhere, Bron confessed he was heartbroken. Many of his friends assumed she must have left because she found him intolerable, but Bron thought the real explanation was that her enjoyment in the job had been blighted by her missing promotion and the limits it placed on fresh opportunities. Kathy had her own chance to describe her time at the *Literary Review* when Naim Attallah asked her to contribute her recollections for inclusion in his memoir, *Fulfilment and Betrayal, 1975–1995* (2007).

Life at the Literary Review

KATHY O'SHAUGHNESSY

I hadn't spoken to Naim for years, when out of the blue came a phone call, asking me to write a piece about the *Literary Review*. Within minutes I was experiencing his personality in full, just like in the old days. He was telling me not only I could write anything I liked, but – 'If I was a monster, you can say I was a monster!' (voice rising to an excited, already indignant little scream).

'Only a very benign monster,' I replied, but I was laughing away, as Naim's enthusiasm and unEnglish lack of restraint took me back twenty years. He was far and away the most enthusiastic employer I ever had, with a generosity, theatricality and warmth that was extremely endearing, and a long way from corporate publishing as it is today.

I was twenty-three when I went to work for the *Literary Review*. I had abandoned my post-graduate degree at Oxford on Byron ('See you at the end of the term,' my supervisor had said on day one, somewhat dispiritingly) and begun writing book reviews for *Time Out* and the *Spectator*. Shortly after that I heard about an impossibly perfect vacancy – deputy editor at the *Literary Review*. I applied and was interviewed by Gillian Greenwood, the editor, who seemed at once interesting, funny, lively – the sort of person you'd like as a friend, let alone to work for. Happily she took me on, and the next day I went to meet the already legendary Naim. 'Welcome to the family!' he said, as he vigorously shook my hand. My eyes were wandering, however, to the far end of the office, where a stupendously good-looking blonde had materialized as if out of nowhere; and this was to be a recurring feature of working for Naim: beauties popping up in doorways and offices and desks like hallucinations, each more splendid than the last.

The *Literary Review* offices were above a hairdresser's and a strong-smelling restaurant: you had to climb three flights of rickety stairs to get to the two rooms in question – one for editorial (Gillian and myself), one for business (Bridget Heathcoat-Amory). And that, beguilingly, was it – so small-scale, so DIY, so very hands on! On one trestle table lay the books ready to be reviewed. Gillian sat at the large leather-topped boss's desk; I sat at a suitably smaller desk facing the traffic of Goodge Street, and so began my career in literary journalism. (So, too, my intense career as a passive smoker, as all of the magazine's editors smoked with a will, a few feet away from me; yet I have to admit to a nostalgic fondness for that smoky office of the past, with its piled-up books and tottering, over-spilling ashtrays, redolent of a more relaxed and less health-'n'-self-obsessed era.)

It was a dream of a job for a twenty-three-year-old. Each morning began with a pile of post: cardboard-encased books, which, like a cluster of presents, looked all the more promising for being wrapped; and the copy – typewritten, of course. It was a thrill to open the envelope and discover the copy. The typewritten pages had a presence and shadowy sort of character that today's computer print-out could never aspire to – maybe the n's didn't print properly, the page might be clotted with inky crossing-outs; the very letters bore the imprint of effort expended. Then, if the copy was unexpectedly funny, or clever, or just felicitous, you had the feeling of treasure-in-the-making. If it was flaccid or lack-lustre – well, cutting and editing could accomplish a lot. This was my editing apprenticeship, and I loved it.

Gillian was my first and main boss at the *Literary Review*. Like most fine editors, she was herself a gifted writer, and I learnt all about editing and commissioning and putting a magazine together from her. It was a tiny operation, just the two of us, and it felt lucky to be part of this two-man or rather two-woman team – the job so enjoyable it was like being a child in a sweetshop. I soon began writing for the magazine myself, as well as helping with the commissioning. But then we had to do everything: sometimes even driving round London and dropping off batches of the newly printed issue at the not-so-many booksellers that took it at the time; and always spending one exhausting but satisfying day a month putting the magazine to bed at 'the printers'. The printers were in fact a husband and wife team, Ken and May, operating out of a small house in Chatham, Kent. There we spent many hours in the dank and indeed dark basement correcting the final proofs as the magazine went to film. It was a bonding experience and we became close friends.

Part of the job was of course meeting the writers. Broke! solitary! talented, not so talented – satirical – worthy – brilliant – the whole gamut passed through the doors of the *Literary Review*; and if they didn't pass through our office they very likely appeared at Naim's parties or at his dining table in Poland Street, where you might meet Ryszard Kapuściński on one day, J. P. Donleavy on another, Hilary Mantel on another, and so on. In the early days our contributors included, to take a random sample from the time: Francis Wheen, David Profumo, A. N. Wilson, Colin MacCabe, A. L. Rowse, John Lahr, Carlo Gebler, Max Egremont, Geoff Dyer, Sheila MacLeod, John Orr, Christopher Hawtree, Martin Walker, Antony Beevor, Richard Williams, Christopher Hitchens, Grey Gowrie, Lucretia Stewart, Neil Berry, Kyril Fitzlyon and others. For their pains, they were paid the princely sums of £10 or £20! But the world of books was different then: there was less money around, marketing was less to the forefront, and those mergers between the publishing houses were still an evil mirage on the horizon.

The magazine's offices were in Goodge Street, busy and lively with its sandwich bars, Italian delis, shoe shops, bikers dashing in and out with their important packages and Charlotte Street with its restaurants round the corner (the Spaghetti House being our top budget outing). It was a short walk from there to Naim's office, where we would either have lunch (his cook Charlotte was a maestro of the kitchen as well as a beauty, *ça va sans dire*); or debate the perennial problems of circulation, advertising and distribution; or receive Naim's advice, and above all, almost intravenously it was so intense, his enthusiasm. Clapping his hands, exclaiming, he would tell us his idea for a mischievous article that would stir up controversy, and so help the magazine's ailing circulation; and indeed circulation was part of the aim, but so, it must be said, was Naim's badly concealed and infectious joy in taking on the British establishment.

At a certain point the *Literary Review* moved its offices to 51 Beak Street, future site of the Academy Club. But wherever we were, the spirit of Naim was always hovering around. He would ring up on the telephone, and somehow his voice lingered in the office, with its rolled r's, and his favourite phrases – 'at the end of the day' – or, my particular favourite, the exclamation, 'Bobby's your uncle!' In short, the experience of working on the *Literary Review* could not be disentangled from the experience of working for Naim, because you were always conscious of the increasingly wide-ranging activities of your unpredictable impresario boss, who had this protean fund of energy and will, to the point of metamorphosis. One moment he was publishing books, the next he was launching perfumes with the titles Avant l'Amour and Après l'Amour, unmistakable variations on a certain theme, and doubtless there would be a party held in some splendid arena such as the Reform Club or the Travellers' Club. As Naim held one party after another, London seemed to open its doors to reveal an endless number of potential party venues.

The *Literary Review* filled a niche determined in part by its competitors. The *London Review of Books* clearly occupied the intellectual high ground; *The Times Literary Supplement* had its firm allegiance to matters academic; and so the *Literary Review* was there to be perhaps more comfortably on the ground, not highbrow, but not lowbrow either; distinctly lively; drawing on journalists as well as writers. The writers ranged from the famous to the little known, and that was one of the pleasures of working on the magazine – coming into contact with many relatively unsung writers who wanted to bring their particular sensibility and encounter with literature to paper in some form. It always seemed to me that this 'middle ground' gave the *Literary Review* freedom to run, for example, exhaustive interviews with writers that went at a serious ruminative pace, giving place to all kinds of unshowy detail that was nevertheless of literary interest.

Gradually, the *Literary Review* became a home for maverick columnists such as A. N. Wilson or Cosmo Landesman, where humorous or odder and more free-wheeling sentiments could be expressed in pieces that were short but piquant; later on, when Auberon Waugh became editor, this bent, the sense of the magazine's character as idiosyncratic, was to become more developed, as Auberon Waugh stamped his own exceedingly British and in some ways divinely eccentric personality on it.

There were three editors at the *Literary Review* during the period I worked there: Gillian Greenwood, Emma Soames and Auberon Waugh. I shall always be grateful to Gillian or Gilly for taking me on. Gilly had diplomacy, patience, sensitivity and an unerring feeling for whether or not a piece worked. We ran early pieces by David Sexton (two particularly good ones I still remember, one on Tolstoy's diaries, another on father and son in fiction, focusing on the Waughs), Paul Taylor and Andrew Graham-Dixon, and many others. The magazine was going from strength to strength when she left, to go to *The South Bank Show*, and a new editor was appointed, Emma Soames.

Emma was confident and instinctively clever in her judgements, and gifted with wit in abundance (certain jokes still make me laugh – '*TAXI!*'

to be shrieked when you want to get out of a situation). The magazine began to take off in new directions: we changed its typeface and logo, got in a very funny cartoon from Nick Newman and Ian Hislop, thought up the anonymous column 'Scrivener' (usually about the nefarious goings-on behind the scenes in newspapers); I persuaded Richard Curtis to do a television column, which was hilarious, and which he later passed on to Stephen Fry, who, perhaps less funny than Richard, was nevertheless an elegant, fluent and reliable contributor. In a relatively short time Emma had made her decisive mark as editor, and we had become great friends (we really did have a lot of laughs), but change was afoot again. Anna Wintour had come back from New York to edit *Vogue* and was claiming Emma as her features editor. Once more the editorship was vacant and this time Naim appointed Auberon Waugh.

I had met Bron, as he was universally known, at a *Spectator* lunch, but nevertheless his columns at the time, which could be so provocative, filled me with apprehension. The *Literary Review* was an extremely small ship. As deputy you sat about five feet away from the editor, and all day you shared an office, just the two of you in the one room; if one of you was on the telephone, for example, the other heard everything you said. In short, it was essential to get on.

However, when Bron did appear, wearing that memorable hat, I liked him immediately. It was in fact impossible not to. He was courteous, kind, considerate, but none of these words (though true) get what was fun about him, which was his drollery, his immensely discerning eye, his effortless dry intelligence – which he wore, almost as a point of honour, lightly. Nor was he ever affected. I couldn't imagine him ever adopting a sentiment that wasn't truly his. He had an original, interesting mind, and was without fail interesting to talk to.

I think Bron was grateful for my help because of course it was new to him, running a literary magazine. But it was clear to me that he viewed me sometimes as a sentimental leftie. We always tried to run a short story and we were inundated by short stories, most of which were, to put it bluntly, screamingly terrible. But I remember one on the slush pile depicting a mining community devastated by pit closure. It seemed to me a moving story, that felt authentic, even though the treatment of the subject was in no way surprising; and I showed it to Bron. He read it and was horrified by my suggestion that we run it, seeing it as predictable in the nth degree. I suspect we both had a bit of a case.

As a team, we had our comic moments. I remember that if I arrived and Bron had got there first, perhaps even just fractionally earlier than me, and was sitting ensconced at his desk, I would feel extremely guilty, as if his silent diligence were a reproach. Later, as we became more relaxed colleagues, it turned out that he experienced the identically persecuted sensation if I had preceded *his* arrival.

With such a small staff there was always a great deal to do. There were proofs to correct and re-correct, proofs to be sent out to authors, authors' corrections to transfer, 'shouts' on the cover to be decided, illustrations from publishers to be chased up, short stories to read, and so on; and it was characteristic of Bron that shortly after arriving he advertised for a 'slave' to work gratis in the *LR* office, on the grounds that this menial apprenticeship would be the gateway to future triumphs. I was sceptical if amused, but sure enough, the next month found Grub Smith, whose very name seemed to beggar belief, like some fantastic projection of a Dickensian imagination, sitting at an exceedingly small and low table, almost child-level, below the intercom phone near the door, our slave for the immediate future. Bron was proved right.

Auberon Waugh did to a degree re-mint the magazine in his own image, with his opening column 'From the Pulpit', and that was very good for the magazine's profile. At the same time the magazine became more hospitable to a strand of literary activity that was in some ways proudly anti-intellectual (I always remember him saying that Proust would have written a good book had he kept it to one volume), yet in other ways deeply committed to the concept of the literary, even if it came to that notion by ranging it against a partly exaggerated foe, the too-intellectual or the narrowly academic. Perhaps this battle too found its secret expression in Bron's commitment to placing, at all costs, the word 'sex' on the cover (no dry magazine this). Thus it became a running and well-known joke: even if this month's literary offerings refused to yield anything involving sex, there might be a piece by David Sexton, that would then get cover billing, as in – 'David SEXton on Kingsley Amis', and so on. And then obviously there followed all sorts of things like the 'Bad Sex' competition, all of which earned the *Literary Review* more publicity. But by this time I had followed Emma to Condé Nast, to edit the arts and books section of *Vogue*.

During all this time Naim was the kindest and most supportive of bosses. Although he sometimes got a mixed press, being often depicted as a very sexist employer, the truth is that Naim defied simple labelling. In the world of British publishing he always seemed to me to be something of an innocent who, like all essentially good-hearted people, expected the same in return – windfalls of goodwill. One has to remember certain things about Naim: that it was he who also owned and funded The Women's Press, and published an imprint [of foreign-language literary translations] like Quartet Encounters, run by Stephen Pickles – a less commercial, more riskily high-minded list would be hard to find.

When I came to leave the *Literary Review*, I helped Bron find a successor (pointing him in the direction of Kate Kellaway, for which he was always grateful). But before then various candidates came along, including the sadly late Linda Brandon. Linda – who was to die tragically young – was extremely intelligent, with an exceptional CV. She had also become a lesbian, and wore short hair and dungarees. Accordingly we had an interview: Naim, Bron, Linda and myself. Bron, who was usually utterly unlike the persona of his more extreme kind of column, behaved briefly like the said invented persona – as soon as Linda had gone, he dismissed her completely. Naim on the other hand was perplexed by the single-mindedness of Bron's response. All he could see was this incredibly impressive CV, and her pleasantness as a person. Naim and I argued for her, but Bron was resolute.

That was typical of Naim, who had a disinterested open-minded respect for achievement, and, at the risk of stating the obvious, an appreciation of women above and beyond their appearance.

Well, to be fair, he liked that, too. But then, to recycle that great last line in cinema, nobody's perfect.

※

A review of *Fulfilment and Betrayal*, written by Bron's son, Alexander Waugh, was published in the *Literary Review* in the May 2007 issue. The book managed to encapsulate the end of an era and provide a brief history of the tribulations and successes of belles-lettres publishing. The review is reprinted in full.

From Soho with Love

ALEXANDER WAUGH

At first glance *Fulfilment and Betrayal* might easily be mistaken for a James Bond thriller, with its jacket photo of a shadowy, handsome man (obviously a spy) glowering above a row of five voluptuous pouting belles. On the back cover there are more photos of luscious lovelies, one of a roaring tiger, and another of a dancer stretching her lissom arms high into the air to reveal, in profile, a pert, bare, well-benippled breast. *Dum, da, da, da* ... How do you stop that famous James Bond theme entering your head as you pull this hefty tome down from its shelf?

Actually the book has nothing to do with 007 and everything to do with the magazine you are presently reading, for the figure on the front cover is the author, producer, entrepreneur, photographer, philanthropist and publisher, Naim Attallah, who bought the *Literary Review* for £1 in 1980 and sold it twenty-one years later, for an undisclosed sum, to 'a most unpleasant character' called Christopher Ondaatje. These are his memoirs of the years 1975–1995. For want of illustrations inside the book, the girls on the jacket are, we may assume, a representative smattering of his glamorous friends and ex-employees (this is how *Private Eye* readers came to know of Attallah as 'Naim Attullah–Disgusting – the Hideous oily Monster with his Harem of lethal Nigellas'). The growling tiger is the author's lucky mascot, a stuffed head with the name of 'Kaiser'; as for the bare breast, that, I think, is intended to convey the author's lifelong passion for the female form – a theme, incidentally, that weaves itself in and out of this long and absorbing autobiography as lustily and at times grotesquely as the *idée fixe* of the Beloved in Berlioz's *Symphonie Fantastique*.

The enjoyment of an autobiography generally depends on how interesting the author is able to make himself. In this instance Attallah's self-confessed naivety, disgustingness, warmth, sensuality, exceptional energy, bossiness and diversity of enthusiasm certainly make him as colourful as anyone in Dickens or Powell, but the long-term value of *Fulfilment and Betrayal* will, I suspect, reside not in Attallah's self-portrait but in the riveting picture he gives of a vibrant literary world that has, in his view, all but vanished – a world invented in his fantasy and brought to life with the bounty of his purse – a crazy, hyped-up, uncommon little world that was centred on Soho, jewels, books, eccentric personalities, gossip columns, 'It' girls, parties, rifts and deep friendships. At its hub – and this is perhaps the oddest thing about it – lay Attallah's small, unassuming flagship title, the *Literary Review*.

Anyone who has been reading this magazine since its inception twenty-seven years ago will be interested to learn of its many vicissitudes. It was founded and first edited by a Scottish academic, Dr Anne Smith, who from the start succeeded in persuading famous writers to contribute 'for the love of it' to what was then a fortnightly magazine produced entirely by herself from her own small flat in Edinburgh. After six months the burden of the enterprise became intolerable to her. She had sunk her life savings and could no longer sustain the cost or the vast effort that the work entailed. Attallah came to the rescue, absorbing the title into his Namara Group of publications, which incorporated at various times Quartet Books, The Women's Press, and magazine titles like the *Wire* and the *Oldie*. Dr Smith continued as editor. In time the *Literary Review* merged with the short-lived *Quarto*, but despite a growing and fanatically loyal readership, the magazine continued to lose money. Dr Smith, according to Attallah's account, became aloof, restive and depressed, eventually tendering her resignation, which he promptly (and much to her surprise) accepted. There then ensued a very public and very bitter battle between the two that came to a head with Attallah threatening legal action against *Harpers & Queen* for publishing scurrilous extracts of Dr Smith's diary.

For the next three years *Literary Review* was edited by Gillian Greenwood, now a novelist and producer of the South Bank Show, under whose stewardship was printed an inflammatory review by Roald Dahl of a book [by Jonathan Dimbleby and published by Quartet] called *God Cried*. Viciously attacked by Zionists, the review remains notorious even today and Dahl continued to believe up until his death in 1990 that the reason he was never knighted was because of accusations of anti-Semitism that arose from it. When Greenwood left the magazine to pursue a career in television, Emma Soames took over and it was under her editorship that the magazine was threatened with annihilation by the 'petty, sensitive, unvulgar, ungreedy' Countess of Dudley, supposing herself libelled in an Ali Forbes review of Anne Somerset's *Ladies in Waiting*. [see pages 129–142]

The case trailed on, but it was only under the editorship of Auberon Waugh, which began in 1986, that it finally came to the High Court. The *Literary Review* lost and was ordered to pay costs and damages, which almost put it out of business. Despite the unfavourable result, Attallah's vivid account of these events is highly entertaining. My father enjoyed nothing more than the prospect of a court battle (I think he would have liked to be a judge), but in this instance both he and Attallah found the affair only 'dismal' and 'ludicrous'. In the end Attallah settled with the countess and the *Literary Review* was able to continue, but as his own fortunes diminished the magazine's future remained precarious.

Attallah has had in his life a great many female friends, some of whom have contributed fond memories to this book. His male friends have been few – a partnership with the jeweller John Asprey ended only in acrimony and betrayal – but he counted Auberon Waugh as his closest male companion. They shared a sense of humour, a sense of honour, a sociability, a belief in loyalty, a love of risk, and, above all, an abiding belief in the quality and purpose of the *Literary Review*, which, now freed from the Ondaatje grip, is in safe hands once again. But it will never be the same for Attallah, whose relinquishing of the title shortly after Auberon Waugh's death in 2001 marked for him the sorrowful end of an era. Despite 763 pages of extraordinary upbeat hurly-burly, the book ends in a tone of lament, which (for various reasons) struck me as warm, sincere and moving: 'The world suffered a tragic and irreparable loss with the death of Auberon Waugh five years ago. His memory is for me as sharp today as it ever was. His uniqueness as a person … whose eloquence drew on the music of words, stood supreme and unassailable. The years we worked together were the happiest I can remember. Soho is, as a result of his death, no longer a place I hanker to be. The void his departure created is too painful to bear … "Tout passe, tout casse, tout lasse," as the French say.'

Bron's own account in *Will This Do?* gives the flavour of the appeal the magazine had for him in a single sentence: 'Nobody looking for a small literary magazine to edit could have hoped for a pleasanter office.' After Kathy O'Shaughnessy left, she was succeeded as deputy editor by Kate Kellaway, 'straight from running the English department of a school for 1200 black children in Harare'.

By then we had been joined by Grub Smith, a boxer from Cambridge who turned out to be the grandson of a GP in Dulverton who had delivered me as a baby and, indeed, circumcised me with great cruelty three years later. A Downside boy, with down-to-earth views and a sense of humour which is best described as Rabelaisian, Grub was a strange part of the mix, but a successful one. I knew that Kate, who like Kathy, had won a brilliant first at Oxford, was the right person for the job when, in her first issue of the magazine, she printed a review by David Profumo of a book called *The Dictionary of Disgusting Facts*. It was so disgusting that I felt my few remaining hairs stand on end, but Kate rocked with laughter and hero-worshipped Profumo as a result.

Bron found Kate to be 'a person of limitless warmth, generosity and sense of fun, as well as of high intelligence', whose 'fatal organizing ability' would, he warned, unless she was careful, see her confined to dull jobs. Kate had other ideas though.

Unfortunately, her life's ambition was to work for the *Observer* and when a job came up she was off, remaining only as our esteemed theatre reviewer, like a lingering fragrance.

Next [as deputy editor] came Laura Cumming, also from Oxford, with valuable experience in the publishing world which brought a host of bright, left-wingers into the magazine. Laura, a blonde bombshell in every sense, stayed two and a half years, and effectively shaped the *Literary Review* as it eventually emerged under my editorship. She invented the 'Oppression' section, into which we tended to dump any books dealing with South Africa, South America, domestic politics, religion, marriage, education. A very strong character, given, like Grub, to occasional alarming mood-swings, she endowed the magazine with all the intense loyalty of her passionate nature, and while she was not holding secret meetings to aid the Polisario rebels in Morocco, made it her entire life.

It was during Laura's tenure that Robert Posner arrived to take over the business management of the magazine, and a whole new dimension of zaniness descended ... Robert had spent many years – we were never quite sure how many – as a fish farmer on an Israeli kibbutz and another long spell – we were not sure how long – in Afghanistan, no doubt studying the flora and fauna, between selling computers for Canon. When we met him, he was living in a squat and working as a motorbike delivery boy. He was the obvious man to rescue the subscription, advertising and office management of the *Literary Review*, all of which he did (except, perhaps, the advertising) with breath-taking panache.

Since we could offer him little in the way of money, we decided to award him an honorary doctorate, and it was as Dr Posner that he sat over his humming computer. Later, when we founded the Academy Club in the basement [of which more later], he became a key figure in that. Appointed secretary, he became Captain Posner, as I felt strongly that all club secretaries should have a military title, and anything above the rank of captain seemed rather to be chancing our luck. I liked to think that at weekends he stood in Oxford Street in a tall hat and frock-coat, offering to perform the three-card trick for the edification of tourists and visitors to London. In that role, he would have been known as Professor Posner. On his fortieth birthday, the Academy [Club] committee – Mepellu, Glendinning, Attallah, Cumming and Sophia Sackville-West – promoted him to Major.

In due course Laura Cumming departed, seeking her fortune as literary editor of the *Listener*, and Lola Bubbosh emerged as her successor, having 'arrived from Washington as an intern, or unpaid slave'.

We had several of these, among whom Elizabeth Daniels, from Tennessee, shone out in glory. There is a quality of benevolence and simple goodness among some young American women which their counterparts in the Old World seem to have lost. Lola, a Catholic of Armenian extraction, developed a devotion to the magazine which became almost alarming in its intensity. At other times, when nothing challenges her beloved chick [she was still at her post when Bron published his autobiography in 1991], she is the gentlest, kindest person imaginable, radiating a sweetness and joy which spreads throughout the entire building. If the magazine has an essential quality of niceness, as against the nastiness which people claimed to perceive in *Private Eye*, it came from her. By nature left-wing (like Laura) and vegetarian by adoption, reluctant to say a bad word for anyone, she shows her claws only when she sees the magazine threatened.

Sam Leith, today literary editor of the *Spectator*, once described how Bron took him on as one of the unpaid 'slaves' in the *Literary Review* office. Sam had written to a number of newspapers and magazines, looking for openings as a gap-year student. The only reply he received was from Bron, who told him, 'We would love to have you here as long as you are available. Unfortunately we have no money of any description. Would you be prepared to work as a slave for no wages?' Bron, Sam remembered, may have been sharp in print but was an exceptionally nice person. Having arranged to lodge rent-free with relatives in London, he then spent 'eight extremely happy months slaving at the *LR*'.

This involved reading proofs, helping with commissioning, running errands (one important duty was to scamper to Fortnum's to buy fruit cake when the Academy Club ran out), playing bridge in the office on Wednesday afternoons and, when he decided to treat the staff, going out for lunch with Bron.

I returned from one such lunch with my eighteen-year-old brain soused with claret and port and my eyes visibly rotating. The then deputy editor, Lola Bubbosh, directed me to a sofa to sleep it off. Bron himself slept off lunch in his own chair, his snoring rising in crescendo until it became unbearably loud – at which point he'd wake with a start and look round crossly to see who had disturbed him. My eventual leaving present to him was a pillow, stencilled with the magazine's logo.

Bron's genius was to charm big-name writers into contributing for peanuts; but he had to pay Julian Barnes in wine from his own cellar. There was visible pain on his face as he'd lift the telephone with the words: 'All right, Barnes. We're talking some serious claret ...'

A remark that, in Naim's view, was vintage Bron.

Bron's very first days at the *Literary Review* were overshadowed, however, by the cruel irony of a personal tragedy when his sister Margaret, who had first commended it to him, was run over by a car and killed outside an art gallery in north London. He had seen her as being a source of support in his new undertaking, and thought she could have made a better editor than he was likely to be. He therefore began with a dark period, but was to spend almost fifteen years editing the magazine. His first editorial had announced his intentions: 'So far as I have any revolutionary intention in becoming editor, it is to produce a magazine which will be enjoyed by intelligent, educated people who read books rather than flatter the socially and intellectually insecure by claiming some deeper meaning for whatever is obscure, muddled, incomprehensible or frankly meaningless.' By his second editorial, he declared that he would display the word 'SEX' prominently on every forthcoming cover in order to give uplift to the magazine's bookshop sales, a threat he finally did not keep, though under his editorship sales quadrupled in his first year and circulation doubled in his next.

His outlook in general, however, remained bleak.

Writers will have to confront the fact that nobody is much interested in them anymore. Literature is a minority interest, like budgerigar breeding, catered for by minority magazines, kept alive by small groups of enthusiasts at ill-attended meetings in small libraries and halls. When all its followers come to realize that there is no pot of gold at the end of the rainbow, they may become politer, friendlier people and lead happier lives as a result.

Bleak though he may have been in his outlook on life's realities, memories of working at the *Literary Review* under Bron's editorship do not sound bleak in the least. Jo Craven penned a sparkling account from her own memories:

Saved from Spiritual Death

JO CRAVEN

When I first walked through the door of the *Literary Review*'s Beak Street office in 1993, straight from university and fresh off the train from Yorkshire, I was amazed to be greeted like a long-lost friend by a beaming Bron Waugh, whose first words were, 'How long can you stay?' Never one to miss an opportunity, I dived in with, 'As long as you like.' 'Good,' he said in a very pleased way, looking around the room at the other two staring members of staff for confirmation. It would be some time before I would witness him wave vaguely at his own daughters and mistake many another stranger for an old friend. But it would never occur to him to go back on his word and I stayed for the next five years. Within weeks Bron had invited me to stay in his Brook Green flat, taking pity on my penniless state and constant flat-hopping. At that point I was working for free as 'a slave'. I couldn't have been luckier and quite enjoyed my friend's taunts about our 'special relationship'. My part of the deal was to make sure there was always plenty of loo roll and Bran Flakes, and occasionally arrange a party with food from Lidgates. Bron's son and girlfriend would also move in, his daughter for a period, and then my boyfriend, and then the deputy editor. It was open-house for the impoverished. In the overcrowded office I would package up books, type in copy, eventually commission reviewers and generally be in the same room, at the same lunch table as Bron, his other editors and some of the most fascinating figures in British literature. I've never been so drunk in all my life. I loved sharing a couple of bottles of wine over lunch – Bron always paid from his own pocket – and often in the afternoon, over a game of bridge, I could never remember the rules, probably because of the port we'd sip, and maybe thanks to lunch. Then there'd be more boozing after 6 p.m., downstairs in the Academy Club, from where I'd stagger back to the flat; and late at night in Brook Green, Bron would often suggest a nightcap of sweet gin, half gin and half red Martini. It was revolting, but I'd do anything to please this kind generous man for saving me from spiritual death in an ordinary office. By the following morning, I honestly thought no one noticed as I sat at my computer, nestling a can of Coke to cure the worst of my hangover. I always knew I was lucky to be part of this wonderfully ramshackle universe, so removed from the regular working world. I was one of the last in a long tradition of girls who either worked at Quartet Books, waitressed in the Academy Club or slaved on the magazine. Most had already gone off to find fame. Of course one day it would come to an end: the rickety buildings heated by plug-in radiators, doing every-thing by hand, paying only £25 for reviews – many writers framed the beautifully handwritten cheques rather than cash them – and top writers being paid with wine from Bron's cellar. It couldn't last. Every few months reality would come knocking. Naim Attallah, the endlessly benevolent owner, would apologetically announce that he just couldn't keep supplementing us while we failed to make any money. Bron would go into a spin. He most of all didn't want anything to change and was always the first to say how much we had to be grateful to Naim for. Naim in turn was hugely fond of Bron and was only doing what any rational person would when the debts kept coming. Selfishly the rest of us found it hard to understand that twenty-first-century accounting had a part in our lives. We were used to being paid terribly and produc-ing a brilliant magazine, and having so much fun that we didn't want anything to change. For me, the moment of departure came when I finally gave up on the notion that someone would head hunt me as a brilliant literary editor, and decided £7,000 a year could be improved on. Two years later Bron died, but the *Literary Review* lives on with its present proprietor, Nancy Sladek, who keeps Bron's flame burning ...

Economic realities, alas, were, by 1995, starting to impinge and becoming more pressing all the time. Though the *Literary Review* was doing well as a prestigious and highly readable literary magazine, it was continuing to cause a serious drain on Naim's resources. Bron, well aware of the accumulated losses suffered by Naim – which by that stage had topped the £2 million mark – was very concerned that he should be having to carry on single-handedly shouldering the magazine without the help of some other benefactors who might ease the burden by sharing some of those losses through annual contributions. He fired off a first shot in a campaign to gain support in his *Spectator* column, the truth of the matter being, he said, that 'the country is swimming in corporate money'.

This brings me to a rather delicate point. For fourteen years Britain's liveliest and most worthwhile literary magazine has been entirely paid for by one man, the great and noble philanthropist Naim Attallah. He not only houses it free of charge and encourages the various enterprises he is associated with to advertise in it, but has also been picking up the losses – currently about £120,000 a year.

Naim is a model proprietor who never interferes, never complains, but I do not think it is reasonable to expect him to go on paying this enormous sum out of his own income indefinitely. Is there any company or individual who will join in? Tiny Rowland, perhaps? The *Literary Review* is much cheaper than the £6 million a year the *Observer* was losing and I feel sure we could work in ways of encouraging African industry. I think I may have found one new benefactor; he talks of putting up £30,000 a year if two or three others will do the same. If any philanthropist is remotely interested, I would be most grateful if he would get in touch with me; I promise to protect his or her confidence with my life.

Once again the *Literary Review* was the subject of speculation in the press as to its chances of survival. The accumulated losses over the years of two million pounds represented the extent of Naim's cash losses, though the figure did not take into account some facilities enjoyed by the magazine as a member of the Namara Group. Out of the deep concern he felt at the way Naim was carrying this financial burden, Bron came up with the idea of forming a trust where like-minded people could join forces in allocating a yearly donation to the review, simply to spread the load of future losses. He started a campaign in the press to help him achieve this goal. The first fruits of his tireless efforts were reported in the *Daily Express* of 24 July 1995:

> Anonymous benefactors, I can reveal, have come to the rescue...
>
> 'Bron has been buttonholing millionaires and firing off letters in all directions,' says my man with the quill pen in Beak Street. 'Now it has paid off.'
>
> Bron tells me: 'There is no one millionaire ... But five or six people have given us cash and it should be enough to keep us going for the next two years.'

The team was thus to be spared the misery of watching the magazine wither and die. By October Bron was able to announce in 'From the Pulpit' in the *Literary Review* that the Charity Commissioners were considering an application to turn the trust into a charity. 'It is easy,' he wrote, 'to show that the magazine is a non-profit-making organization, and one which has no remote prospect of making a profit.' By November it became public knowledge that two of the world's richest men were among those who had rallied to the cause: John Paul Getty II and Lord Hanson. They had joined a distinguished list that already included Sir Tim Rice and the Duke of Devonshire. 'It may seem a little bizarre,' said Lord Hanson of his pledge of £25,000, 'but the *Literary Review* is well worth supporting. It is the good quality work that counts with me.'

This did not yet take the situation out of the wood, since the cover price of £2, with sales of 15,000 copies, was never going to cover production costs. The magazine was to stay on in its offices at 'what Mr Waugh calls Château Attallah, in Soho', said *The Times*, but was likely to have to pay for the privilege. Hitherto it had been there free of rates or rent. '"Naim has been an absolute angel," Mr Waugh said yesterday. "He has never got any advantage from owning the *Literary Review*."'

The appeal to the Charity Commissioners was, perhaps predictably, a non-starter but Naim, having been the proprietor of the *Literary Review* for many years, finally sold it only after Bron's untimely death. Christopher Ondaatje bought it in partnership with Nancy Sladek, who had been with the magazine a long time before assuming the editorship eighteen months before Bron died. Mr Ondaatje had made his fortune in Canada and gave Naim the impression he was trying to infiltrate the higher echelons of British society. 'Unfortunately,' said Naim, 'he turned out to be someone who took a cheese-paring approach and fussed about trifles in a way that I found dispiriting. As I feared, he proved the antithesis of what a good proprietor should be, lacking sympathetic qualities and being hard to get on with. To resort to more mundane phraseology, I would describe him as a most unpleasant character.'

Eventually Nancy Sladek managed to buy him out and she has continued happily as sole proprietor, successfully running the magazine to which she has dedicated so much attention, and maintaining its character with high consistency.

'Thinking back,' mused Naim in *Fulfilment & Betrayal*, 'there was an irony in the way I was accused by Anne Smith of having stolen the magazine from her, and then by her supporters, who kept on reviving the falsehood over a number of years.' The fact was that the *Literary Review* was never going to be a commercial proposition. Naim had become involved in it because, in his view, Anne Smith had shown great courage in founding it and he could not bear to see her efforts go to waste. The way she behaved subsequently did nothing to deter him from backing the magazine, especially as it had become so important to Bron, with his entire life revolving around it. For him it was a labour of love that was to endure in its intensity until his untimely death.

> He rang me ten days before he died, his voice quavering with weakness as he apologized profusely for his illness, which had prevented him from continuing to edit the magazine. He felt he had let me down. I was close to tears. This colossus of a man maintained his nobility to the very end. There was certainly no one else remotely like him.

There are those who have wondered how it came about that such a close friendship could have developed between Naim and Bron, the two of them coming from such vastly differing backgrounds. Sophia Waugh perhaps gives some clues in her recollections of what happened after Naim phoned her to sound her out about the possibility of Bron taking over the editorship of the *Literary Review*.

> I was not sure Papa would want to do it, but to my amazement he was more than interested in the idea. How odd it was that Papa had brokered my job with Naim, and then the tables were turned. I think Naim was too shy to ask Papa directly. And yet from that there came a real part- nership, a mutual admiration and trust and even, on my father's side certainly, and certainly on Naim's, even a love that lasted until Papa's death. Papa loved the *Literary Review* and the Academy Club, which Naim, with his characteristic energy, generosity and enthusiasm, backed. He would never hear the faintest criticism of Naim from anyone. They both shared loyalty, I think. Naim has often said to me that I was responsible for Papa taking the job – not true at all, but it warms me to think that, however erroneously, they both gave me the credit for such a successful partnership.

The hard work that Bron put in helped to ensure the survival of the *Literary Review* and laid the foundations for its future. Nancy Sladek's nurturing of it subsequently raised the circulation figure to a point where it reached almost 50,000 copies. Bron's invention of the 'From the Pulpit' feature provided over the years a platform for many independent spirits, questing, questioning and dissenting, to express considered points of view on the lives of writers and the complexities and oddities of the world of books in all its manifestations.

2

A DIFFERENT SORT OF CLUB
(THE PEOPLE THERE ARE CIVILIZED)

B RON ALWAYS GAVE PRIORITY TO MAKING LIFE AS CONGENIAL AS possible, not only for himself but also for those who lived and worked alongside him. The idea for the Academy Club was a case in point, first put to Naim by Bron and Victoria Glendinning during a casual meeting in his office. It was immediately clear it would mean requisitioning a basement downstairs in Beak Street, till then set aside as a recreation room with tables for snooker and table tennis. Earlier on Naim had used this space to indulge his weakness for table tennis especially, until such leisure activities became neglected as the pressure of work mounted with the expansion of his field of interests.

At first Naim was more than a little taken aback by the suggestion, not so much on the grounds that he was reluctant to give up the basement as because it seemed obvious there was just not enough space. For another thing, occupying the ground floor was the Academy Bookclub, a determinedly literary book club, created before the end of the Net Book Agreement and only open to subscribers to the *Literary Review*. It was a valiant attempt to imitate the success of the *New York Review of Books'* Readers Subscription Book Club, offering such inducements as editions of Joseph Conrad's letters or Richard Wagner's *Ring* diaries at significant savings, and was currently being run by Sophia Sackville-West, with her sister helping on a part-time basis. Then there was the *Literary Review* itself, which took up the first floor. The rest of the available space was utilized by the accounts department of the Namara Group.

In the end Naim was disarmed by the keenness shown by Bron and Victoria. They made it clear that no practical consideration was going to deter them from pursuing their objective. Naim finally went along with the idea, and without enquiring as to what it would cost or its commercial viability, simply said, 'Do it!' Work soon began on transforming the basement into a Soho club, and Bron's brother Septimus, an inspired carpenter, was commissioned to refit the place with solid wooden benches and tables as well as chairs to give it a simple but robust look.

Tracing her own part in its founding, Victoria Glendinning remembers how, in the mid-1970s and having four children, she needed work; after a time at the *New Statesman* she went to *The Times Literary Supplement* as an editorial assistant while continuing to write her books, and it was when she was there that Bron asked her to contribute to the *Literary Review*. She became socially friendly with the Waughs, and with her husband, Terence de Vere White, would go to stay at Combe Florey, where she discovered that the Bron of that time was intensely competitive at table tennis. Bron had been disappointed by the closure of the old French Club in St James's Place and Victoria was not happy about the manner in which the Groucho had been launched, so during a slight conversation at Combe Florey, she and Bron hatched the idea of creating a club connected to the *Literary Review*. One feature she remembers at the club's start was its expensive notepaper, another was the tomato-red paint they decided on for the basement walls.

In a 'Pulpit' announcement in the *Literary Review*, Bron described the projected club as 'primarily designed for writers who are too poor, too mean or too proud to join the Groucho'. Applicants were to submit a copy of what they considered to be their best book. This would join the club library once its author was deemed worthy of election by the club committee, consisting of Bron, his deputy editor Laura Cumming, Victoria Glendinning, Sophia Sackville-West, Robert Posner and Naim himself – to whom Bron always referred as 'the philanthropist'.

Applications began to flood in on this basis, but included many from *Literary Review* subscribers who, while they would have liked to join, did not qualify. This set Bron brooding on the matter and he amended his original concept.

> I decided that a club made up exclusively of writers was not a very good idea because (1) they are often quite unpleasant people, (2) they do not always want to meet each other, and (3) it would do them good to meet the nice, intelligent readers of the *Literary Review*. The problem is to devise a system which will deter all the bores, pigs and PR men who make the Groucho so disagreeable. What I have decided is a variant of the old 'cinema club' practice, whereby to see a dirty film you had to buy a ticket and return next day. Membership will be open to all who have been subscribers to the *LR* for two years – that is to say, who have renewed a one-year subscription before applying. They must also offer a published author as their reference, and submit a few lines of self-description in their letters of application. The club ... will be limited to 600 members, 30 present at any one moment. It will offer a club room, bar, good wine and light meals.

Naim became convinced that the basement was never going to be spacious enough in the long term, and it began to look inevitable that the ground floor would have to be sacrificed, and with it the Academy Bookclub, a decision that would inevitably upset Sophia Sackville-West deeply. She had nurtured her project with enthusiasm and dedication of a quality rarely equalled. The bookclub unfortunately did not attract enough customers to pay its way, though in ordinary circumstances Naim would have maintained it, if only because it meant so much to Sophia. When the axe fell a year later her disappointment was extreme, as was apparent from a piece she penned for the *Literary Review*, headed 'And So Farewell – In Memoriam: A Great Little Bookclub':

> Once upon a time there was a literary bookclub who lived in the middle of Soho. This bookclub often went hungry because his father, try as he might, had too many children to feed them all equally. But the little

bookclub, who was called the Academy Bookclub, had many friends and managed to grow quite well on the nourishing berries which came his way. But one day the father came to him and said, 'Great news. I have a son of unparalleled beauty and strength. And because you have always been a brave little sort I have named him The Academy Club and you will live together in peace and harmony.' But the Academy Bookclub was much afraid. His old friends soon forgot him as they rushed to worship at the paragon brother's shrine, and as the latter grew bigger and bigger the Academy Bookclub began to waste away. Until one day his father came to him and said, 'Academy Bookclub, although it breaks my heart to say this, now that you are so thin and your brother is so fat, you must give up your space in the house to him.' So the Academy Bookclub set off to seek his fortune. But without a roof to protect him from the driving rain, he soon sickened and died. THE END.

I hope that all Academy Bookclub members received a letter informing them of the Academy Bookclub's demise back in June. It tried hard but never quite made it through.

No flowers, please. Donations and offers of employment to: Sophia Sackville-West, c/o Knole, Sevenoaks, Kent.

According to Bron in *Will This Do?* the deciding impulse to found the Academy Club was triggered by an unfortunate episode at the Reform Club, where a party was thrown to celebrate the *Literary Review*'s tenth birthday:

The library at the Reform Club has often struck me as one of the loveliest rooms in London, and certainly one of the best to give a party in. If only the members were less dim, it would be a wonderful club to join.

I had to leave for China next day and was away for a full month, thereby missing the later developments. Apparently one of our guests – the daughter, as it happened, of a great friend – was caught short and could not find the ladies' lavatory, so she availed herself of the gentlemen's, where a member was so shocked to find her that he reported the matter to the committee. There are other, more lurid versions of the same story, but that is the one which seems most likely. At any rate, I returned from a month abroad to find a letter banning me and Naim from ever giving another party in the Reform Club, with no reasons given. I do not suppose I would ever have had occasion to give another party in the Reform Club (although Naim might well have wanted to), but it was the old problem of holding a cat by the tail. Suddenly, it seemed an appalling shame that such a beautiful building designed by Sir Charles Barry should be controlled by such bores.

Every club, I suppose, has its quota of bores and pompous oafs. It is only when they manage to take it over that the dimness really sets in, becoming eventually its dominant characteristic. I played with the idea of mounting a massive ten-year campaign, using initially the very few acquaintances I had among the members, to topple the committee, fill the club with Our Sort of People and establish unisex lavatories, such as you have in nearly all private homes. But then I decided there were too many things to do in life, and I simply did not have the time to do them all. Perhaps this decision was the first real acknowledgement of middle age. I simply did not have the energy to declare another great war and wage it to the bitter end.

Instead, we decided to found a smaller club of our own, a club where, God willing, there would be no pompous bores, or where, at least, they would never gain the upper hand. The actual inspiration for the Academy Club, or more properly the Academy … came from a weekend at Combe Florey when Victoria Glendinning and I were lamenting the old French Club, in St James's Place, to which we had both belonged. It had an informality, a friendliness and a lack of pretension which had passed by the Groucho. So Victoria and I decided to go it alone.

Where the incident in the Reform Club is concerned, Naim describes it in *Fulfilment & Betrayal* as the occasion when Richard Ingrams's daughter, Jubby, a free, anarchic spirit who was working on the event's organizational promotion, 'was discovered by a club official in the gentlemen's lavatories', relieving herself in one of the basins with the help of a fellow employee who, like herself, was somewhat on the wild side.

Jubby was certainly high on spirits in every sense, having had her share of the drinks available. She apologized at once to the Reform, saying she had been bursting for a pee and the ladies was too far off for her to make it in time. Nevertheless she was unceremoniously marched out of the club.

The Reform then declared a ban on any event to do with Bron or Naim or any organizations with which they were associated, without giving an explanation. Bron was utterly outraged and issued a warning that any lady who attended a reception at the Reform Club in the future should take a chamber pot with her.

Bron's editorial in the August 1989 edition of the *Literary Review* announced the opening of applications to become a member of a new London private members' club:

At long last we have received planning permission to turn our basement in Beak Street into a licensed club for literary folk and their friends. Applications for membership to the Academy Club should be sent to me at this address, accompanied by a returnable cheque for £50 from applicants outside the London postal area, £75 from those inside it.

Membership, which is limited to 600, is open to anyone who has written a book in English prose which, on being presented (unreturnably) to the committee, is found acceptable; to anyone who, having been a subscriber to the *Literary Review* for over a year, can propose a writer as referee who is known to the committee; to anyone who has reviewed in the magazine or contributed articles to it; finally, to anyone who is known to a member of the committee, whether as friend, acquaintance or relation ...

Facilities for chess, draughts and dominoes will be supplied, as well as reading, and there will be one bridge table but no gambling. The biggest snag is that only thirty members and guests are allowed on the premises at the same time, and it is just possible that in the early days members will have to be turned away by entry phone. However, they can always go round the corner to Andrew Edmund's Wine Bar in Lexington Street, where the food and wine are excellent, even if there are no games and there is slightly greater danger of meeting poets, architects, advertising executives, etc.

In the November edition he commented further:

> News of the Academy Club – more properly the Academy – is all good at the moment of going to press, except for some irritating suggestions in the newspapers to the effect that the club is hoping to be smart in the sense of fashionable and exclusive. Nothing could be further from our intention … The idea is to provide a friendly refuge in the West End for contributors and subscribers to the magazine, poor writers and other congenial people prepared to put up with them. Taki [the legendary *Spectator* author of its weekly column 'High Life'] may belong, if he wishes, but I swear that none of his worrying friends could possibly wish to join.

And his editorial for the last (December) edition of that year amounted to a fully-fledged advertisement for membership applications:

> One of my innovations on first becoming editor of this magazine three and a half years ago was a 'Literary Lonely Hearts' column in the classified advertisement section. Impressed by the extraordinary niceness of the readership I had inherited from my predecessor, Emma Soames – they were intelligent, well-read and humorous, too, but above all nice people – I felt concerned for them. I feared that in the general dispersal of intelligent society to such places as Brixton, Tottenham and the provinces beyond which has occurred with changing property values, many of the nicest people would feel isolated or lonely.

'Literary Lonely Hearts' was only a moderate success. Occasional advertisements trickled in, but they never took up the pages and pages and pages of self-revelatory appeals I had hoped for. Perhaps because amiable, intelligent people tend to be shy, perhaps because the wrong sort of people answered the advertisements, my idea never really took off.

Perhaps the Betjeman Society's *thé dansant* [an activity much favoured among events organized by the Betjeman Society] will eventually fill the gap. For the rest, we have the Academy, which, short of some unexpected disaster, will open its doors on Tuesday, 12 December, at 10.30 a.m.

The opening of the Academy Club was in fact an event temporarily marred by an oversight. Both Bron and Naim had forgotten to have the drinks licence rubber-stamped by Marylebone Road Magistrates' Court. Bron was therefore to be seen scampering to the court to get the formalities completed. In the absence meanwhile of both Bron and the licence, the barman, Jock Scott, and the club secretary, Robert Posner, were not allowed to charge for drinks. 'Any member can now get blottoed,' sighed Posner. But cheers were soon heard from across the road as Bron came into view triumphant and waving the approved licence. This signalled the start of what was to become the most talked-about dive in Soho of that era. In the weird chronicles of clubland tales, few could match the bizarre goings-on at the Academy. It established itself as a place where fame and notoriety intertwined, where cultural conversations were heard alongside juicy gossip, where social status counted for nothing; where, while boorish behaviour was frowned upon, decadence with style was accepted as quite the norm. The atmosphere of the club was merely the reflection of its rules as Bron had formulated them. Here is a sample of the eccentricities:

1. Dress shall be informal, but shoes must be worn.
2. Members are invited to make civilized conversation with other members, unless seeking solace behind a newspaper.

3. The Academy is a private club and nothing that is seen or heard in the club may be reported outside, on pain of instant expulsion without refund of membership fee.
4. Smoking is encouraged, but cigars and pipes are not allowed.
5. Poets are banned from the club.
6. Any member who has the misfortune of being sent to prison may take up the unused part of their membership upon release.

After a few weeks of the club's existence, Joseph Connolly of *The Times* 'Diary', phoned Robert Posner to see how it was doing, 'only to be told that it was policy not to talk to the press because it did not want any publicity – which is one of the funniest things I have heard in ages'. Later, *The Economist*, in a summary of the merits or otherwise of London's clubs under the heading 'Change and Decay in Clubland', put the Academy in the 'Fun' category (there was only one other).

> The Academy Club was founded by a cantankerous writer, Auberon Waugh, in a fit of fury at the stuffiness of the old clubs. The Reform had complained about a party he had held there: many turned up without ties and a woman was said to have relieved herself in the gentleman's lavatory. The Academy has only one rule – shoes must be worn – but members may be expelled for being boring.

Bron was the main attraction, in Naim's view; the club's life, its very soul. It took him back to his student days years before, when he joined a club in Paris in St-Germain-des-Prés, where Jean-Paul Sartre used to hold court, dispensing his Existentialist philosophy surrounded by his flock of adoring young men and women. Juliette Greco was often there, and at night would sing some of her melancholic ballads to an audience of left-wing intellectuals. Yet Sartre was in some ways a messenger of doom, whereas Bron was a purveyor of joy and wit. The similarity was only in the setting. Bron's following was usually made up of pretty young women with a high level of intelligence and a cheeky disregard for convention. They hovered around him with pure delight written on their faces. They sat at his table in the club, listening to every utterance, smoking, drinking and enjoying the whole ambiance. They would also berate him – which he liked – whenever he went overboard with an attack on feminism or a particular contrariness that made them shriek. But it was all done with great humour and no trace of malice. The club was Bron's haven and he took to it as if it were his natural habitat.

Victoria Glendinning recollected that the club 'crept into being' under Robert Posner and Matthew, her son, who worked there for four years. Matt recalled that when Bron came downstairs from the *Literary Review* at 5.30 or 6 p.m. every day, he would mix him a special martini which was basically all gin. Bron, Victoria remembered, made a special point of talking to people who were alone. He never stayed the whole evening.

Matthew Glendinning, kindly reporting from the coalface, confided in his mother that though he worked behind the bar for four years, the first two were the best. Bron chose all the wines, especially liking the Lebanese Château Musar, Côtes du Rhone, Colombard Chardonnay and Gewürztraminer. When Bron was not smoking, he liked breathing other people's smoke, and as the ventilation was poor, the air was often thick with cigarette fumes. Matthew maintained his own skin went green.

Bron was unfailingly very amiable, thought Matthew, though he found Naim's infrequent appearances rather grand, in response perhaps to the abundance of *Telegraph* journalists in three-piece suits and an increasing number of lawyers and solicitors. Last drinks were served at eleven, and the club was meant to close at midnight, but people sometimes stayed till 1.30 a.m. when Matthew had to close up. Once he found a drunken woman in the lavatory and had to call the police to get her out. The food provided was basically a salad of sliced avocado, sun-dried tomatoes, mozzarella and asparagus spears, with bread, the ingredients being bought from a deli round the corner.

Matt told his mother, 'It was never very hip' and had an 'eccentric mix, no great bloom of success.' And after the upstairs room was made into an extension, it never really worked in his opinion. His mother noted, however: 'He's ironic and amused about it now, but at the time it did a lot for him. He became familiar with a lot of people he wouldn't otherwise have known, learnt to listen to the crashing bores for hours, and picked up a great deal about life and the world.'

In taking on responsibility for choosing wines for the Academy, Bron was adding another layer of wish fulfilment to the whole pleasurable enterprise. His relationship with wine was essentially a sensuous one, as Naim had observed when he gave him a bottle of rare and prized Cheval Blanc 1947 as a present. The way Bron caressed the bottle with joy on his face, 'as if it were a beautiful woman', remained etched on Naim's memory. Back in January 1982, at the invitation of Tina Brown, he had become wine correspondent to *Tatler*, 'welcoming the discovery of a new art form'. Should he write it under his own name, he wondered in *Private Eye*, or 'pseudonymously as Crispin de St Crispian, which should be a pretty impenetrable disguise'? Subsequently, he said, he was amazed at his audacity in accepting the job, his only qualifications being that he had drunk wine all his life and bluffed his way through 'any conversation which threatened to become knowledgeable'. Nevertheless, when he fell out with a new editor at *Tatler*, he moved on to write the wine column for *Harpers/Queen* and travelled the world on the trail of old and new vintages; and in 1986 he published *Waugh on Wine*. None of this, however, meant that the ridiculous pretensions in the vocabulary of wine tasting would escape the sceptical thrust of his pen, as when he wrote:

> My own feeling, despite several unhappy experiences, is that wine-writing should be camped up: the writer should never like a wine, he should be in love with it; never find a wine disappointing but identify it as a mortal enemy, an attempt to poison him; sulphuric acid should be discovered where there is the faintest hint of sharpness. Bizarre

and improbable side-tastes should be proclaimed: mushrooms, rotting wood, black treacle, burned pencils, condensed milk, sewage, the smell of French railway stations or ladies' underwear – anything to get away from the accepted list of fruits and flowers ... I am not sure that it helps much, but it is more amusing to read.

All sorts of characters worked in the club. Jock Scott, the one-time barman, was a pub poet with whom the actress Anna Chancellor fell in love one night when seeing him perform in a London dungeon. The romance yielded a daughter named Poppy. In Naim's view, Jock, like many performance poets, had never written anything good after the age of eighteen, but he went on repeating his old act till he was forty-five. His tenure at the club was short-lived. Anna, on the other hand, was a club regular. She used to stretch out her beautiful body on the leather Chesterfield, commenting on any man who came down the stairs. Club members used to finding her there were surprised to see her on the screen as 'Duckface' in *Four Weddings and a Funeral*.

Lucy Cohn, a stunningly beautiful half-French actress, the sister of the former *Telegraph* columnist Will Cohn, worked behind the bar for several years when 'resting' between acting spots. She was to star later as Princess Margaret in a Channel 4 documentary drama about the life of the princess. In one scene she appeared naked, but she never took her clothes off during working hours at the club. Lucinda Galloway, another actress, was employed as a waitress for a couple of years. She was very beautiful and intelligent but away with the fairies much of the time. Robert Posner recalls her in the vivid recollections he has of his time at the club.

MEMORIES OF THE ACADEMY

ROBERT POSNER

Lucinda was in the Star Café in Soho, passionately kissing her boyfriend goodbye at the door, wearing the smallest red leather mini-skirt invented and an almost see-through top. A movie producer came up to her and asked if she would like a part in his latest film, which happened to be *Robin Hood – Prince of Thieves*, starring Kevin Costner, Morgan Freeman and the brilliant Alan Rickman as the evil Sheriff of Nottingham. Lucinda can be seen in the film, naked apart from a small bearskin rug, when Alan Rickman comes up to her and says, 'You – be in my bedroom at ten o'clock. And bring a friend.' I don't think she got any other parts. Remember the wretched Arnold Arnold, who was eased out from the club? The row started because he had reduced Lucinda to tears, shouting at her when she borrowed his dreadful book [possibly *Pictures and Stories from Forgotten Children's Books*] from the Academy shelves and forgot to return it in time for him to show off about it to one of his guests. When Arnold Arnold sent in his application for membership when the club first opened in 1989, he included a photograph of himself. Bron took one look at him and said no. I begged Bron to accept him because [to me] he looked like a big friendly bearded bear in great thick spectacles. Bron then said, 'All right, Posner – you can have him as a member – but on your own head be it.' Rather prescient of him, as it turned out.

Lucinda's boyfriend, James Richmond, was a lovely guy but suffered from severe manic depression and had to be permanently medicated with lithium to keep him on an even keel. Unwisely he stopped taking it on the advice of some friend and went completely nuts in the club one afternoon. Bron, unaware of his illness or his missing medication, wrote him a letter terminating his membership. A week later, we received a humble apology explaining his behaviour and begging to be allowed back. It was on the headed paper of a psychiatric clinic, so we invited him back.

Diana Rigg came to the club on the opening day as the guest of a film producer, Colin Campbell. She looked at the menu, but each time she chose something to eat, we had run out of that particular dish because we were so amateurish and disorganized during the first week. Eventually, she glumly settled for her fourth choice, a pork pie. She started to chew her way through it and stuck up her hand to ask if we had any mustard. Embarrassingly, we had to admit we had none. Ten minutes later, she stuck up her hand again and said, 'Do you have any toilets here? Or have you run out?'

Several months before the club was even fitted out, Bron wrote a letter which I sent to about 900 prospective members gathered from Naim's, his and the *Literary Review*'s address books. In his letter, he asked that anyone who wished to join should send a cheque for £75 together with a copy of their best book, in order to start filling the empty and, as yet unbuilt, bookshelves. Three hundred people responded with books and cheques, eight months before the club opened, such was Bron and Naim's reputation. By mistake, half the books that arrived in the post were immediately put on the reviewing shelves of the *Literary Review* and duly disappeared off to the second-hand bookshop in Charing Cross Road. We used to empty the shelves every month to clear the way for the next 500 books from publishers seeking reviews of their latest output. We received a telephone call from the puzzled bookshop several days later. They couldn't understand why several dozen books contained £75 cheques made out to something called 'The Academy Club'. Unfortunately, many books, possibly containing similar cheques, had already been bought by their customers. The fate of those cheques was never resolved.

David Irving, who lived in Mayfair, applied for membership. The membership committee – Naim, Bron, Laura Cumming, Sophia Sackville-West and me – considered his application, but apart from me, the only Jewish member, were absolutely against electing him. I lost the argument. Naim and the others were right, as it turned out. I thought that although he was a neo-Nazi sympathizer, he was the leading expert on modern German history and would make an interesting member. Whoops!

Regarding Rule 6 [the one that stated any member receiving a prison sentence should have his membership put on ice and the unexpired portion restored on release], I received a letter from Dr Roger Cooper from his prison cell in Teheran in April 1990. He had been arrested by the Ayatollah's regime for spying (he probably was a sort of spy, being a member of Chatham House). He had been sentenced to sixteen years in the infamous Evin Prison and for some strange reason he was denied any publications apart from the *Spectator*, in which Bron had announced the birth of the Academy and printed the rules as well. Roger Cooper's imprisonment was the subject of a lot of activity by human-rights activists at the time. He was not allowed to write or receive any letters from the UK, but for some mysterious and bizarre reason had been allowed to write a single letter to me at the club address in Beak Street. In this letter he wrote, *inter alia*:

2 APRIL 1990

Dear Captain Posner – I have just read Auberon Waugh's article about the Academy in the *Spectator* and would like to apply for membership. It sounds an ideal club for people like myself … You will note from my address that I would not at present be able to utilize my membership and indeed have been sentenced to sixteen years' imprisonment, expiring on 4 July 2003, but I am an incurable optimist and membership of the Academy would be most useful to me if I am set free at an earlier date. It would also be comforting to imagine myself there from time to time, even if this is not possible at present …

Unfortunately, they let him out a couple of years later and he often came to the club, where in the opinion of certain other regulars he nearly bored them all to death. Perhaps that was the reason the Iranians let him out.

There was a well-known *Daily Telegraph* correspondent who used to drink himself senseless in the club several nights a week and could sometimes be found sitting on the pavement outside the club doors at 1 a.m., weeping and declaring his love for Victoria Glendinning's beautiful son, Matthew, who used to manage the bar most evenings. I was very concerned and asked Bron if there was anything we should do to modify his drinking. Bron's reply was that there was nothing we could do and that, in any event, it was our job to serve him drinks. I know this journalist very well. He has not had a drink since 1994 and thinks this is the funniest story he has ever heard about himself.

Michael Bywater, a brilliant columnist and diarist, was the last member to leave the club on the last night, having concealed himself from the staff by hiding under the stairs. He wrote for the *Independent on Sunday* a wonderful article on the club after it closed down in Beak Street, 'The End of Life as I Know It'. 'A hole has opened up in my life,' he announced. 'Do you want to hear about it?'

So you shall. It's a deep yawning hole. A deep yawning black hole. What you'd call a pit of melancholy, a chasm of accidie, a gulf of gloom. Do you begin to get the picture? Good.

I have had holes like this before. They can be caused by debt, women, deadlines or foreclosure ... But this hole is different. This hole has been brought on neither by financial defalcation nor by sexual incontinence. This hole has been dug by others. And how have they dug it?

They have closed my club...

There are other sorts of clubs, it's true ... But the Academy Club was different. The people there were civilized. Nobody ever gained or sought advantage by being a member of it, because all that being a member of the Academy said about you was that you were a member of the Academy. It was just sort of ... there. The rules were few and enlightened. Members were obliged to wear shoes. Cigarette smoking was encouraged. Members who had the misfortune to be sent to prison could claim the unexpired portion of their subscription on their release. Members were expected to talk to each other, unless hiding behind a newspaper (or engaged in intense rapid conversation, in which case they were not to be homed in on). The best rule was: no poets.

The application of the rules was capricious. One man was barred for several months for the offence of coming to the club too often. 'He's down here every evening, drinking brandy-and-ginger and beaming at people,' said the barman, petitioning for a ban.

It was, in short, a haven for amiable, civilized misfits who wouldn't have liked it anywhere else, and now that haven has been closed off I feel at sea. Where can I go? Where can I go where I don't have to contend with ballripping music, surly barmen, barking yuppies, stinking microwaved food and the sense that I am enriching some filthy coterie of brewery executives? Where can I go, on the off chance, and be reasonably sure of bumping into someone affable? Where there's nobody on the make, nobody trying to impress, nobody who even owns a cellular telephone, nobody dressed in black. Where people say 'Hello' and mean it? Where nobody laughs at my hat? Where nobody will hit us if we burst into song?

There is talk of reviving the club at some unspecified time, in some unspecified place. But you can't go back. No; it's over. The best thing to do is climb into my pit and pull the rotting boards over my head. Don't bother to call; from now on, I'm staying in.

One person who evidently held out against being charmed by the Academy was Richard Ingrams. The reason, he told an interviewer from the *Sunday Times*, was that, 'It's a bit too spartan for me. I've complained to Bron that it should have cushions on the seats.' He preferred the Groucho, he said, despite having been disparaging about it when it first opened. The man from the *Sunday Times* wrote he could only conclude it must have to do with the fact that Ingrams at the Groucho and Waugh at the Academy inevitably became surrounded by bevies of lovelies, and if they frequented the same premises an unavoidable competition would develop over who was attracting the most nubiles.

∾

In fact the Academy Club (inevitably altered to some degree) continued under new management, Bron's view of it being:

> The end-product is not exactly as it was conceived. In effect, it has become a smaller, slightly bohemian version of Pratt's, somewhere between an ordinary luncheon and dinner club, a Viennese café, a wine bar with spirits and a Soho drinking dive.

The closing of Beak Street allowed the Academy Club to rebirth itself in Lexington Street, under the auspices of Andrew Edmunds, in a room on the first floor above his Soho restaurant and adjacent to the new offices of the *Literary Review*. Those who wish to eat there can order from the menu of the restaurant below and the wines have a good reputation. Bron was not able to be there as often as he had before. Increasing ill health and finally his death in 2001 saw the end to a unique association, though his role as founder is fully acknowledged. A more recent glimpse of the Academy is given in an article by Joy Lo Dico in a piece in the *Evening Standard* (19 July 2013):

> [The] Academy: a motley collection of writers, art dealers, academics, military top brass and ne'er-do-wells – the heirs to Hazlitt, who dine from Edmunds's kitchen and drink from his cellar, in a front room decorated with Hogarth prints. I had been going for several years on my

nights out and found something that I could not find in West London: a camaraderie of itinerant but intelligent souls.

It sounds not so far removed in character from the Soho dives visited and described by Arthur Ransome in *Bohemia in London*, the book he wrote for Bron's grandfather, Arthur Waugh of Chapman & Hall, over a hundred years ago, with which this account began.

3

Words from the Pulpit, 1986–2001

WHAT FOLLOWS IS A SELECTION OF BRON'S MUSINGS COMPILED mostly from his monthly essay which greeted the reader even before the list of contents – 'From the Pulpit'. We begin with the very first:

LITERARY REVIEW, APRIL 1986
Lord Gnaim Writes: Not a Manifesto

For the first time in its brief but distinguished history the *Literary Review* has a male editor. Many will see this as a retrograde step, and for my own part I will have no objection if correspondents wish to continue addressing the editorial chair as 'Dear Madam' – whether in deference to the shades of the three staunch women who created the magazine in its present form, or because they prefer to address themselves to the deputy editor, Kathy O'Shaughnessy, whose continued presence in the Beak Street office affords a measure of reassurance not only to readers and contributors, but to the editor as he struggles to learn his new trade.

My greatest debt is to the editor immediately before me, Emma Soames, who invigorated the magazine with her own energy and illuminated it with her charm. All that remains for me to do is to find some more readers. This has always been the problem. The history of small literary reviews is strewn with the wreckage of new brooms and manifestoes.

When I deny that I have any intention of acting as a new broom in the Augean stables of the London literary establishment, this is not because

I am unaware of all the filth and futility to be found there. Affectation, mediocrity and pretentiousness swarm like dung flies around a cow pat wherever the State milch-cow lifts its tail. But the worst charge against State patronage of literature is surely that it encourages would-be state pensioners to turn their backs on the public whom they should be addressing and address only dispensers of patronage. Hence the idleness, self-indulgence, and even sheer stupidity of literary intellectualism, where it aspires to the highbrow.

My point is that the dunghill may be vast and it may stink to heaven, but the best thing is to ignore it. We on the *Literary Review* did not make the mess, and it is not our job to clear it away. So far as I have any revolutionary intention in becoming a literary editor, it is to produce a magazine which will be enjoyed by intelligent, educated people who read books, rather than flatter the socially and intellectually insecure by claiming some deeper meaning for whatever is obscure, muddled, incomprehensible or frankly meaningless. The cult of the 'difficult' in literature may be assailed from time to time, but without too much reference to its supporting structure of academic idlers, journalistic pseuds and Arts Council scroungers.

As anyone who reads books will be aware, the great wealth of English literature is to be found in its back-lists. Although good work is being done in most fields, it is swamped by the rubbish pouring out of every publishing house, week after week. Obviously, we will continue the struggle to identify whatever is worthwhile in this great flood, but I should also like to pay slightly more attention to reprints and new editions of rediscovered old favourites. At present the reviewing establishment tends to ignore them; the classics and old favourites are mentioned, if they are mentioned at all, only in the context of some drivelling new book of criticism, or trivial academic research. Yet these reprints are likely to be of greater interest to book-lovers than, for instance, the latest novel or book of verse from Lisa St Aubin de Teran. Even as I write these words, the *Literary Review*'s deputy editor – a veteran of Oxford's English Literature course, from which she emerged with a First – is sitting at the desk next to mine sobbing quietly over a beautiful new illustrated edition of *The Secret Garden* which Michael Joseph is bringing out on 14 April. This month we also review the classic anthology *Weekend Wodehouse*, reissued by Hutchinson; in future months there will be opportunities to celebrate the glorious revival of E. F. Benson...

Poetry undoubtedly presents a problem. Traditionally, anyone has been free to send in stuff and we have always guaranteed at least to read it. However the trickle has now turned into a torrent. A problem of 'free verse' is that it requires considerable effort and concentration to separate the wheat from the chaff, let alone to identify those very few offerings which might be marked by some incidental felicity of expression, originality of thought or depth of feeling. My own impression is that the Free Verse movement has run its course. Many more people wish to write it than wish to read it. Our poetry editor, Carol Rumens, on whom the task of reading all this drivel falls, takes a more sanguine view, however, and will continue to produce her selections of modern poetry to delight its dwindling band of enthusiasts. But she is hopelessly overstocked with material awaiting publication and requests that no more unsolicited material be submitted until further notice.

To keep the nation's would-be-poets happy, however, I have decided to institute a Verse Competition which will differ from the usual run of such competitions in soliciting straight verse, rather than pastiche or parody. Each month it will occupy a full page of the magazine, with prizes which will be lavish by our standards, starting with a £50 first prize, £20 second prize and further prizes of £10 for any entries printed. Subsequent competitions may embrace the *haiku* and *ottava rima*, but for the first I would like a simple English sonnet (fourteen lines, iambic pentameters, ABABCDCDEFEFGG) on the theme of spring. It need not be funny and should not be a parody or pastiche – just the best original sonnet you can do. My ambition is to have all schoolteachers and librarians in the country writing their milk-orders in heroic couplets.

Like all small magazines unsubsidized by the State, the *Literary Review* pays its contributors peanuts. They write for us chiefly because they enjoy it. The next task is to find as many readers as possible to share their enjoyment. I have to learn more about the readers, and would welcome letters for publication or otherwise, containing criticism, praise or suggestions. I have various ideas for increasing the circulation, the first of which is to declare a standard subscription rate of £10 per annum. This is cheaper than the cover price of 95p a time, let alone cover price plus postage and packing – and much more convenient. I apologize to those who have recently re-ordered at the old price of £14, and can only congratulate those who took advantage of the special £9.35 offer. These anomalies will not recur. The standard price is now £10 a year, payable as easily with a £10 note as by cheque or postal order...

The *Literary Review* cannot survive, let alone improve, unless it increases its circulation. Please encourage friends and relations to subscribe, as well as your local libraries, schools, dentist's waiting-rooms. Our only purpose is to spread happiness, light, common sense and joy in the language we share.

LITERARY REVIEW, AUGUST 1986

Reasons for Not Reviewing Jeffrey Archer

A furious article on the Books Page of the *Mail on Sunday*, signed by the newspaper's editor, Mr Stewart Steven, recently took the entire literary world to task for not paying enough attention to the novels of Mr Jeffrey Archer. 'Literary critics ... cannot speak of him without a well-bred sneer', we read. Mr Steven suggested that the 'literary establishment' finds Mr Archer's commercial success 'unforgiveable'. Writing about the most recent addition to the Archer *oeuvre* (see how my well-bred sneers trip out) he continues:

> *A Matter of Honour* is not literature neither is it the best thing Archer has written. But it stands in the long and noble tradition of the British adventure story.

He proceeds to list the names of other writers in this long and noble tradition: Buchan, Sapper, R. L. Stevenson, C. S. Forester and Rider Haggard. I am not a close student of Jeffrey Archer's writings and must confess that on the few occasions I have looked into them, they struck me as pretty good piffle, several points below any of the authors mentioned.

But I would not quibble with Mr Steven's article, written partly in the assumed voice of the Common Man mimicking the outrage of literary élitists, 'How dare he write books which ordinary people can enjoy? How dare he be so unfashionable as to manage an entire novel without any steamy sex?' – if there was not an important kernel of truth in all this Paul Johnson-style populism, the dreaded voice of the English saloon bar talking to itself. It is only partly where he talks of the 'literary establishment' – a safely vague group – as having become 'incestuous, precious and removed from the world at large'. The greater truth, as usual, is to be found in specific instances:

> Funny, isn't it, how these names (Buchan, Sapper, etc.) and their books still trip so lightly off the tongue when the name of Keri Hulme, author of *The Bone People* which won the Booker Prize last year, is about as familiar to most of us as is the formula for making a nuclear weapon.

In the matter of Jeffrey Archer's *A Matter of Honour* (Hodder & Stoughton) I can easily explain why no review has appeared in these pages. I had asked for a review from Frank Johnson of *The Times*. He agreed to do it, but when I asked Hodder to send him an advance proof, I was told that all copies were being kept under lock and key – like some new design for a nuclear weapon – until the last minute before publication. This would have meant that our review appeared at least a month too late.

One does not need to subscribe to the Jeffrey Archer Admiration Society to agree that Mr Steven has a valid point when he complains about the damage which has been done to English literature by such bodies as the Booker Committee, the Arts Council's Department of Literature and other award-granting bodies. Bad writers do no harm in themselves, except by default. It is only when they start appointing each other to committees and controlling the few sources of literary patronage that one can reasonably complain of their activities.

Another reason why we are often disappointed by the results of Booker and other awards – Keri Hulme's almost unreadable novel is only one example – is the shortage of clearly identifiable literary talent. Once again, with this issue, we have failed to find a short story which was considered good enough to print – despite having searched conscientiously through about forty or fifty sent in. It is true we don't pay much, but practically nobody else prints them at all, and the general standard is frankly appalling.

With this issue we welcome Kate Kellaway as the new deputy editor. Miss Kellaway, after the usual First Class Honours in English at Lady Margaret Hall, Oxford, went to teach in Zimbabwe, eventually becoming head of the English Department at a 2,500-pupil [*sic*; see page 156] school in Harare. I feel her experience in keeping all those little black children under control may prove useful in dealing with short-story writers, as well as with reviewers who are late with their copy. She has reviewed in these pages before, and reintroduces herself in this issue interviewing Vikram Seth. His novel in fourteen-line rhyming tetrameters *The Golden Gate* struck us both independently as revealing one of the wittiest and most engaging talents to have emerged for a long time. He is unquestionably the Literary Discovery of the summer. I feel sure that Mr Stewart Steven will enjoy the book as much as we both did, if he will give it a try. It requires little more effort to read than Clive James's dismally unfunny verse sequences – *Felicity Fark*, *Peregrine Prykke* or (worst of all) *Charles Charming*.

Finally, the next Prose Competition. I have often observed that although food and wine provide two of life's greatest pleasures, very few writers can describe a meal without making the reader feel sick. Elizabeth David can do it, but Clement Freud can't, nor can Bernard Levin. His gloating descriptions of food usually strike me as particularly disgusting. Competitors are asked to describe a meal in such a way as to sharpen the reader's appetite. This is much, much harder than people may imagine. I would suggest that the meal should be part of some other narrative – whether thriller, love story or seduction scene – on which the reader must be left to speculate, since the absolute limit is 220 words. No parody, no pastiche.

Those who wish to examine the contrary technique – how to be as disgusting as possible in the fewest words – should turn to David Profumo's excellently dense review [of *The Dictionary of Disgusting Facts*]. I promise not to visit many of these shocks on readers. I had thought that obscene graffiti and talentless modern writing generally might have undermined the power of mere words to shock, and was vaguely encouraged to discover that in the hands of a good writer they still can. But readers with weak stomachs are advised to skip Mr Profumo's offering on this occasion...

LITERARY REVIEW, SEPTEMBER 1986
Ways of Persecuting Writers

Writers are peculiarly prone to persecution mania, in fact the whole literary world is riddled with it. Many novelists look to something called the Critics' Circle, which undoubtedly exists, although in twenty years of reviewing books I have never met anyone who claimed to belong to it. Perhaps its members communicate by finger signs and take hideous oaths of secrecy, but there are few novelists, in my experience, who have not entertained conspiracy theories about this or some other sinister group of reviewers. The conspiracies are usually inspired by some political allegiance, whether of the left or right, but sometimes just by personal spite. Their purpose is always to ensure that the novelist concerned is ignored although a fiendishly ingenious refinement is to review his or her earth-shaking product in four or five lines of faint praise.

It was only when I became a reviewer, and experienced the extraordinarily chaotic conditions under which most literary editors work, that

I appreciated the untruth of this and every other conspiracy theory. A book's critical reception depends on too many haphazard circumstances in too many places to be explained by anything except a combination of luck and merit.

So the next focus for their resentment is the bookseller. They see it as an act of deliberate spite that certain booksellers neglect to stock their brilliantly self-revealing novels, about how a female novelist decides not to have an affair with her sensitive publisher who never gets round to suggesting it in any case, or about how a male novelist nearly comes to terms with the chilling fact that he has nothing to say until, in an uncharacteristically happy end, he is struck with the idea of writing a novel about his predicament. It is true that many booksellers are wary of the literary novel nowadays. On recent form, one can scarcely blame them. Under the malign influence of the book prizes – which attract far too much publicity, and encourage writers to write for their peers rather than for the wider market of intelligent readers – every sort of self-indulgence has been allowed to creep in, every sort of exhibitionism and affectation has been encouraged. Seriously excellent writers like Martin Amis and Russell Hoban have allowed themselves to be seduced into the opaque self-importance of Delphic priestesses. Worse than this, they have been praised for it. In America there is a 'campus' market for any sort of incomprehensible quasi-prophetic rubbish, but in Britain there simply isn't. It falls to booksellers to break the news to the nation's writers. They certainly could not learn it from reading the review pages or studying the Booker short-list.

Having said all of this, I must admit that the greatest single frustration in the editorship of the *Literary Review* is to be stopped wherever I go – by strangers as well as by friends, at railway stations, in restaurants and on the street – and informed that the magazine is nowhere for sale. They have tried in four bookshops and eight newsagents. The newsagents have either denied all knowledge of it, or instructed them to search among 800 magazines devoted to the care of budgerigars and making model aeroplanes. Booksellers have scowled horribly at mention of the word 'Literary' and shown them the door. There are one or two bright spots. W. H. Smith in Taunton, which never stocked either the *Spectator* or the *New Statesman* in all the years I worked for them, now stocks the *Literary Review*, although this will be vehemently denied by most of the sales staff. One by one, the better bookshops are reluctantly accepting a few copies on sale-or-return basis, but even when they have sold out and turned away prospective customers they absolutely refuse to re-order. Perhaps it is all part of some national death-wish that we are allowed to read about nothing but the Princess of Wales's hairstyles. If only she would write a book, I could put a picture of her on the cover of the *Literary Review*. Perhaps she would let me write one for her.

No. That way madness lies. There must be simpler ways to sell the magazine. At present we rely on word-of-mouth recommendation from happy readers. A regular subscription, which costs only £10, is easily the best, as well as the cheapest way to be sure of this life-enhancing experience… But reading is by definition a lonely business, and it takes a long time for the word to spread. Literary folk seldom congregate, but they will be doing so for the Cheltenham Literary Festival from 5th to 17th of October and the *Literary Review* has decided to stage a desperate attempt to draw attention to itself there.

On Sunday, 12 October, Kate Kellaway, the deputy editor, and I will be holding a great debate on the future of literary magazines – what they should have in them, at whom they should aim – with the help of a distinguished panel of *Literary Review* contributors and friends: Peter Cook, William Donaldson (aka Henry Root), Anna Ford, Keith Waterhouse, William Rushton, Paul Theroux. The whole world is invited to come to Cheltenham and join in. I hope that copies of the magazine will be sold by beautiful, nobly-born young Quartettes in *Literary Review* sashes and fishnet stockings, but that suggestion may founder on the rocks of sexism, ageism or simple good taste at committee stage…

LITERARY REVIEW MARCH 1987

Time to Unscramble Some Eggs

A fifteen-page 'consultative document' which has arrived on my desk, explains that it has been produced by the Arts Council's Advisory Panel on Literature. Its Acting Director writes that she is 'currently seeking views on it from a number of organizations and individuals' and would welcome my comments:

> although I should emphasize that the paper is at present a working document on which the Council wishes to enter into a debate with other bodies including its partners (the Regional Arts Association, for example) and potential papers. It will not have the status of the Council's formal policy for Literature until the consultation process has taken place and it is published in its final form...

My first comment is that if the Advisory Panel supposes anyone else has time to read its turgid, fifteen-page document it must be barking mad. It is a document produced by committee persons for other committee persons whose only real purpose is to give committee persons something to do. Although it claims to interest itself in Literature, the vast bulk of its pages might have been lifted, *mutatis mutandis*, from the hallowed archives of the late lamented Egg Marketing Board:

> 3. The objectives of the Council's policy for Literature / Eggs are:
> 3.1 To initiate discussions with all national bodies who have an interest in Literature / Eggs and to facilitate communication between them.
> 3.2 To work in Partnership with Regional Arts / Eggs Associations in planning and implementing national support for Literature / Eggs.
> 3.3 To devise, carry out and monitor pilot schemes and to promote at a national level through conferences, reports and other appropriate means, examples of successful projects and initiatives.
> 3.4 To implement the Literature / Eggs and Education policy...

My own single recommendation is that the Council for Literature should be closed down, its employees encouraged to find more useful occupations elsewhere, its panellists sent home. Some years ago the then minister, Sir Keith Joseph, canvassed opinions on the subject at a *Spectator* lunch – admittedly this was in the bad old days of Osborne and the Australia mafia [to quote from Osborne's obituary in the *Guardian*, 18 October 2017: 'As literature director of the Arts Council of Great Britain during one of its most turbulent periods, Charles Osborne, who has died aged eighty-nine, will be remembered by many for his coruscatingly witty memoranda and public responses to criticism of his often controversial policies'] – and we all gave him the same advice. He left with the air of someone who intended to do something about it.

But still this wretched organization survives, if in reduced form. The kindest thing that can be said about it is that its bureaucratic activities have nothing to do with Literature, past or present, and it therefore does no real harm to English letters: it provides employment for a small number of people who might have difficulty in finding employment elsewhere. If only it could shift its interest to Eggs, and seek (through consultation with the appropriate bodies) to encourage the appointment of Egg Eaters-in-Residence in every town hall, I would be happy to applaud its continued existence. But so long as its word-processors spew out the word 'literature' where 'eggs' would be more appropriate, it will remain an irritation to all those who genuinely labour in the vineyard of English letters.

Literary Review, July 1987
Let's Get Gay and Regional

A recent report from that venerable 'think tank' which resides in Westminster, the Adam Smith Institute, called for an end to all state subsidy of the arts and public funding of cultural activities on the grounds that such payments alienate writers and artists from the public they should be seeking to please. Far from making 'the Arts' more popular, as Melvyn

Bragg would believe, public subsidy encourages idleness and affectation in artists, as well as fostering a sense of superiority, not to say arrogance, among the patronage-dispensing classes. The result is to antagonize all but the most uncritical.

This has long been a favourite theme of mine. It would be absurd to pretend that all state subsidy has a deleterious effect. I do not feel that the *London Magazine*, for instance, has suffered much from receiving its £34,000 annual subsidy, which survives as a relic of Charles Osborne's days as literary director of the Arts Council. His other great enthusiasm, the *New Review*, mercifully sank without trace, carrying with it many hundreds of thousands of pounds of government money, when people refused to buy it at any price. Nobody has ever taken me up on my offer to swap a (nearly) complete run of this magazine for an equivalent number of Mars Bars.

Its collateral descendant, the *London Review of Books*, continues to propagate the same sort of cliquish, affected writing, with an annual subsidy of £32,000 from the government. No doubt this huge sum of money pleases the editor and his [*sic*] friends; I suppose the magazine may bring comfort to a number of the intellectually or socially insecure, assuring them that they are somehow superior persons for being prepared to read the self-conscious posturing which has replaced what used to be called 'fine writing' in the same market.

But such a function belongs to the DHSS vote, and should not be taken from pitiful sums made available to protect our cultural vitality. Earlier this year Lord Wyatt of Weeford, as my friend Woodrow Wyatt nowadays likes to be known, was so shocked when I told him that the *Literary Review* has never received a farthing from the Arts Council or any other body, that he tabled a question in the House of Lords to ask the government just what magazines it did support and why.

The minister's answer listed 123 publications, and assistance totalling £678,033. Allocations were made according to literary merit, we learned, taking into account 'relevance to the regions, local documentary or oral traditions and the need to foster new writers'. Nobody can have a better record of fostering new writers than we have with all our university and school-leavers, but I suppose we may fall down on regional relevance.

Perhaps it was lack of regional relevance that explains why *Books and Bookmen*, our only serious rival and a most excellent magazine in its time, was allowed to die without a halfpenny of support while the precious *London Review of Books* continues to have its pitiful inadequacies swaddled by government intervention. Perhaps London is seen as a region, like Tyneside, in need of special help. The money would surely be better spent preserving a few old buildings in London, or fighting the jackals of the Royal Institute of British Architects in their disgusting plans to 'rejuvenate' our inner cities, just as they have 'rejuvenated' Wapping and the Isle of Dogs.

But if, as I say, we cannot qualify for the regional hand-outs, a further group of beneficiaries catches my eye. The Only Women Press received £14,575 of government money in the year under review, although I cannot remember that the magazine *Men Only* ever benefitted. The Gay Men's Press received £7,970. The *Women's Review* received £4,000 although *Woman's Own* struggled for years without such help. None of these sums would do much to off-set the frightful depredations of Lady Dudley [see pages 124–137 above], but an idea has occurred to me which might explain this long moan. I hope readers will not be too upset if in the coming months we suddenly appear under the banner, the *Gay London Literary Review*. The antithesis will, of course, be with 'boring London' and 'gloomy London' as in the *London Review of Books*. But I rather feel that in these difficult times we must all bend to the prevailing winds.

Librarians at the Bodleian have been trying to raise the scare of American libraries who buy up the papers of British authors, thereby denying British academics the chance of new research into the endlessly fascinating question of W. B. Yeats's laundry bills. They point out that Texas alone has already bought the major manuscripts of Evelyn Waugh, Grahame Greene, Samuel Beckett and Siegfried Sassoon, not to mention the D. H. Lawrence and N. R. Foggis archives. V. S. Naipaul is next on the list, said to be offering his papers to whoever is prepared to pay around £400,000 for them. Even John Braine's papers are expected to fetch £25,000.

As one who played a minor part in selling the Evelyn Waugh papers to Texas twenty years ago, I should like to put an oar in. Authors are treated abominably in Britain, as a result of our politicians' abiding hatred of anyone who might be thought cleverer or more admirable than themselves. When an author dies, his widow and orphans are charged for estate duty as if any future, putative income from his books represented a capital sum, despite the fact that such receipts are taxed as income and there might easily be no savings with which to meet the estate duty bill. In other words, an author's widow has no choice but to sell her husband's manuscripts, if anybody is interested in buying them, and British universities have never shown the slightest interest.

I think they are right to be uninterested. Appreciation of a finished book is very little increased by studying the various drafts and corrections involved in writing it. Our academics in the Eng. Lit. departments have shown themselves marvellously resourceful in the search for things to keep themselves occupied and amused: phonetics, structuralism, Marxian analysis, *Sunday Times*-style graphics, charts and doodles. Even in the sacred interests of job creation, there is no case for spending further government money on acquiring author's manuscripts.

LITERARY REVIEW, NOVEMBER 1987
Further Endowments Needed

At this time of year many literary editors find themselves gloomily looking at children's books for a special Christmas feature. Although it is usually possible to find one or two books which show some spark of originality or imagination, the general standard is so abysmal that this year we have decided not even to try to find a children's hospital or similar charity to take them away. Instead, we are putting them all straight into the dustbin, as they arrive. There can be no virtue in assisting what seems to be a concerted effort to hobble and stultify the nation's children. To persecute those who are ill, or poor, or in some other way underprivileged, seems even more wicked.

What has happened is that even quite respectable publishing houses have allowed themselves to be persuaded that their children's departments should be run by people with degrees in social and child psychology, rather than by people with any interest in literature or imagination. Hence the rising ride of twee, patronizing rubbish, which is calculated to turn our children – sorry 'kiddies' – into listless, apathetic stuffed dolls until such time as their imaginations can be stirred by a horror movie.

Enough has been written about Ladybird's New Brit version of *Peter Rabbit*, with its bland, condescending text and its repulsively ugly colour photographs of toy rabbits to replace Potter's delightful watercolours. In a sense, Frederick Warne and Ladybird have done us a service. By giving us the two to compare, we are allowed to see just how it is that the new breed of conceited mediocre social scientists hopes to produce a race of near-morons for themselves to patronize and instruct. It won't work, of course. From the sanitized version of *Peter Rabbit* to the mindless thrills of *Rambo* is an obvious step, as inevitable as the connection between *Rambo* and Michael Ryan, the Hungerford mass murderer.

The purpose of children's literature is to stimulate their brains, widen their horizons and stretch their imaginations. Pandering to their naturally idle appetites is one of the more contemptible forms of child abuse, which should not escape punishment just because there is no law against it. If senior publishers refuse to apply some sort of dilation test to the child abusers on their staff, we will simply have to single out the bosses for individual chastisement until they do.

LITERARY REVIEW APRIL 1988

[Bron wrote most of this month's *From the Pulpit* about a new
sponsor for the poetry prize and new guidelines for entering, but his last item took off into other realms...]

One disadvantage with the young reviewers who come to us straight
from university is that they tend to discuss new novels in the perspective
of English literature. These errors are easy to correct with an editorial
blue pencil. The virtues of the young are a freshness of approach, and an
excitement about the whole idea of being in print.

I gave up writing novels (after publishing my fifth, in 1971) for various
reasons. One of them was undoubtedly depression at the appalling standard
of reviewers, who were and remain a novelist's chief contact with his reading
public. In those days – seventeen years ago – the critical orthodoxy was that
novels should concern themselves with the struggle and ancient disabilities
of the working class. It was a waste of time to suggest that the vast majority of novels, since the form was invented, had been written by the middle
classes about the middle classes for the middle classes to enjoy. Anything
written by, about or for the middle classes was obscurely judged 'escapist'.

Having given up the struggle myself, I follow the fate of novels written
by friends and relations with a certain wry pleasure. In one of the Sunday
newspapers recently a reviewer started her review of three novels – two
of them by first novelists, thus:

> Middle-class women writing about white, college-educated middle-class
> women ... Bad luck if you come from Wigan, or you studied sciences,
> or you were born in Jamaica, or you sweep the streets.

After banging on about the characters' 'socio-economic factors', living in
areas where it is 'de rigueur to be middle class', the reviewer concluded:

> Where a prevailing notion can be one of unthreatened (and unthreat-
> ening) capability the authorial view is blinkered.

Reviewers' blinkers seem more alarming. I know nothing about this reviewer, or her socio-economic problems, nor have I any great desire to learn. There is a grand old literary tradition of class warfare, but I suggest that a less boring way to keep the struggle going might be if the two camps emptied jugs of orange juice over each other and their socio-economic problems at publishers' parties.

LITERARY REVIEW, MARCH 1989

The Joke Needs Changing

This issue of the *Literary Review* is my thirty-sixth. In my second, for May 1986, I rashly promised to put the word SEX in capital letters on the cover of every issue of the magazine under my editorship, regardless of the actual contents. I hoped that regular readers would not be offended, or potential readers discouraged. My purpose, as I explained, was to embolden booksellers who seemed reluctant to put the magazine on show. The only alternative, as I saw it, was to decorate the cover with pictures of the Princess of Wales, but I did not suppose we could really do that until she had either written a book, or been persuaded to join our panel of reviewers, just as the Prince of Wales used to review occasionally in *Books and Bookmen*.

Three years later there is no sign of either development, and it is apparent that the *Literary Review*'s decision to feature SEX on the cover of every issue has had a deplorable effect on the rest of the British Press. Whole sections of it, from the pioneering *Sun* through the slavishly imitative *Daily Star* and *People* to Murdoch's stinking *News of the World*, now devote most of their pages to describing the alleged sexual behaviour of pop and television stars, usually in tones of disapproval. I am not saying that sex has become a dirty word, but that interest in other people's sexual activity must have receded.

In any case, even if the whole country had not been surfeited with information on the subject, even if the activity had not been called into question by the two plagues of feminism and AIDS, the joke has surely gone on long enough. The magazine is still a very long way from covering its costs but the time has come for it to set a good example to the Murdochs, the Maxwells and the Stevenses of this world. Whatever filth may creep into the pages, it will not (outside exceptional circumstances) be advertised on the cover.

∾

Having decided to set a good example, perhaps we can now afford to take a high line about developments in the lower reaches of the tabloid press. For many years I defended the right of newspapers to throw as much mud around as they liked, always within the bounds set by our extraordinarily savage libel laws, on the grounds that if newspapers really behaved badly in exposing the sexual peccadilloes of private citizens to the merciless gaze of neighbours and public, then it would rebound to their own discredit.

The *Sun* claims to have lost circulation during its vicious pursuit of Elton John with the lies it had bought from a former rent boy and homosexual pimp, but I take leave to doubt whether that is normal. The experience of the tabloid press, as it follows the *Sun* down that particular road, is that the new British reading public has lost any quality of fairmindedness and actually revels in the suffering caused by these revelations.

I am not saying that such publications should be banned, merely that if the British public has this taste for intruding into the privacy and destroying the domestic tranquillity of its fellow citizens, it must expect to pay rather more expensively for it. Whether or not Elton John ever received the £1m., which the *Sun* claims to have paid him, that figure should be the norm for privacy settlements where malice can be shown. Before long the *Sun* would be a more expensive newspaper to buy than the *Independent*, the *Telegraph* or the *Guardian*, and possibly even more expensive than the new, squeaky-clean *Literary Review*.

LITERARY REVIEW, APRIL 1989
Should Woolf be Cornered?

The unveiling of a plaque to Matthew Arnold in Poets' Corner was attended by a crowd of nearly three hundred *Literary Review* readers, who heard an address by Oxford's Professor of Poetry, Peter Levi, in the presence of the Dean of Westminster, Michael Mayne, with a sprinkling of bishops and other clerical dignitaries. It was a most joyful occasion. Many of those present were able to come round to the Westminster Arms afterwards to receive whatever modest hospitality the magazine could offer.

I do not propose to publish a list of those who attended, since such lists invite speculation about the reasons for absence of those who did not. Where were Anthony Burgess, Karl Miller, C. P. Snow, even the egregious Martin Seymour-Smith? Not all can have boycotted the event, like the *Review*'s deputy editor, in protest against High Church tendencies discerned in some of Arnold's early writing. One might have been ill, another too old, another dead. Perhaps Mr Seymour-Smith reckoned that as he was unlikely to find evidence of homosexual activity among the congregation, his presence would be a waste of time. [Martin Seymour-Smith is now a somewhat forgotten literary critic who, at the time of Bron's writing this comment, had recently written a controversial biography of Rudyard Kipling, implying homosexual tendencies in the great writer's personality.]

But attendance, as I say, was most impressive, and the standard of hymn singing was a credit to the magazine. We owe a huge vote of thanks to Dean Mayne. What a relief and pleasure it is to find an intelligent, conscientious and literate incumbent once again in the Westminster Deanery. The Arnold plaque will eventually be balanced by one to John Clare – the poor, mad peasant poet who died in a Nottingham asylum 125 years ago.

The Dean is at present considering the proposal for a memorial to Virginia Woolf in Poets' Corner. I feel vaguely disqualified from giving advice, since it was a kinsman of mine, called Duckworth, who sexually abused Woolf when she was a child, although I suppose it is taking liberal guilt too far if I therefore accept blame for any rubbish which might have poured out of her in later life. But anyone who has relevant information about Woolf's attitude to religion, or any intelligent opinion on the subject, might care to address it to the Deanery, Westminster, SW1.

LITERARY REVIEW, MAY 1989

May 1989 saw the magazine reach its tenth anniversary edition. All four editors contributed to the Pulpit.

Anne Smith, Founding Editor, 1979–1981, remembered why she had started the ball rolling: 'What kept me going was an idealistic sense of gratitude to all the writers of all the good books which one way and another had enriched my life; I wanted to give something back. Book reviewing seemed to have become a mere academic or political exercise or even worse, an outlet for the vanity of the reviewer; the book pages were a refuge for the self-interested... At the same time, publishing itself seemed to have developed schizophrenia. On the one hand there were the literary novels and on the other were the trashy best-sellers. No one had the courage, or it might be the perception, to say that Iris Murdoch's novels all seem much the same, being about trivial navel-gazing people for whom no one but another trivial navel-gazing person would give a damn and that in respect of repetitiveness there is little to be drawn between her and Harold Robbins, for example. No one said, or saw, that *The Magus* is a piece of posturing vacuity. Everyone followed the fashion; no one dared refuse to take the literary novelists on any estimation but their own, or the junk novelists seriously. The middle ground was pretty much ignored.

'I thought that there were still a lot of people who read for every reason under the sun except to gain yuppie-points at cocktail parties. Like me they had probably long ago given up looking to book reviewers for guidance, they would rely on chance and recommendations of like-minded friends. They are the real readers, but they were also the outsiders, and it was to them I tried to address the *Literary Review...*

'Even though the *Literary Review* cost me everything I had and left me exhausted, I would do it all over again. If anything, the need for an eccentric literary magazine that refuses to kow-tow to trends and speaks to the intelligent reader is greater than ever now that publishing has shrunk to a tiny number of impersonal conglomerates hell-bent on quantity over quality, while which books will be reviewed by whom and what they will say is as stultifyingly predictable as it was ten years ago.

'Fortunately I do not have to, for the *Literary Review* is still here, still struggling, and still upholding the principle of its conception, that it is better to light a penny candle than to curse the dark.'

Gillian Greenwood, Second Editor, 1981–4, lacking 'Anne's high academic background or network of scholar-contributors', decided 'to adopt a policy whereby books would be reviewed by writers, journalists, politicians (all parties) and young hopefuls, with an occasional academic or theatrical, and an emphasis on cultivating a wide range of views and keeping up a high standard of prose.

'The joy of a literary magazine is that writers who otherwise might be confined to eight hundred words in a Sunday review supplement can be allowed to write at length on subjects dear to them… Certain books and the space to express their sympathy, fury, spleen or praise can be powerful bait for even the grandest Man or Woman of Letters.'

Emma Soames, Third Editor, 1984–6 came 'from a background that does not exactly bristle with academic, literary or indeed many cultural references at all [so] I realized that it would be foolhardy to try to emulate the *TLS* or to beat the *LRB* at its own game. So I could try to produce a magazine that I would read myself… Essentially I would never read a highly specialized literary magazine, so the *Literary Review* began to include such profane subjects as a gossip column about newspapers, book reviews of cookery books, style bibles and a much more extensive arts coverage. The problems of running a lively magazine were compounded by the magazine being monthly. This meant either that our reviews were appearing fifteenth in line after the dailies and weeklies or that we were jumping the gun on the publication date – an agreeable pursuit, but one that does not endear the title to publishers. So the problem of getting the right chemical explosion between reviewer and title became central.

'As a result the work in the office turned into something of an after dinner party game ("The most unlikely…") as we toyed with unexpected names for obvious books, and just as importantly tried to lure big, obvious names to review for the magazine using unexpected books as bait. The secret, if there was one, was cross-dressing: politicians on fiction, novelists on cookery, biographers on photography…

'Since leaving the magazine I have had larger budgets to play with and more money to fling at writers. Yes, I know they've got to live but it doesn't actually make a lot of difference to the quality of the finished product. Largely due to this important insight I speedily sussed out that, from an editor's point of view, literary agents are little more than a parasitic pain. The next lesson to be taken on board was never to waste time asking anyone with a novel due to appear in the next year to review anybody else's fiction. As one reviewer finally confessed to me when I rebuked him for failing to take a definite line on a novel, "But I *can't*. I want *him* to review *my* novel next spring."'

And finally, **Auberon Waugh, Fourth Editor, 1986 –** : 'More observant readers may have spotted that for its tenth-anniversary appearance this month the magazine has been completely redesigned from front to back. Those who failed to notice should not be dismayed. The new design is intended to appeal to advertisers, who are thought to be very sensitive about the design of the magazine in which their adverts appear. They like everything to be nice and modern and above all to be *designed* – belonging to the nice, modern, designed life-style which their advertisements project.

'Personally, I remain sceptical. The reason the *Literary Review* cannot attract more advertisements, I feel, is that with a limited circulation it can charge only £450 a page (£690 for a page in full colour). Advertising agents, who are human beings like everyone else (i.e. avaricious, lazy and with an eye to the main chance) are simply not prepared to interest themselves in such small accounts. Never mind that our readers are among the loveliest, cleverest and most influential in the country, if not the world. But perhaps the exciting new design will attract advertisers, like wasps to a jam jar.

'For my own part, I loved the old design (or lack of it) and imagine it will take at least another three years before I feel the same affection for any replacement. The new design has been valiantly undertaken by Lucy Ward in the face of almost overwhelming gloom from the editor. She deserves our thanks for her tenacity as well as congratulations on the result.

'From Emma Soames I inherited a magazine which, while still faithful to the philosophy of its founding editor, Anne Smith, and continuing Gillian Greenwood's policy of maximum variety, had acquired a new panache through her journalistic connections, and was already required reading for anyone in the communications industry with ambitions to be thought smart. My chief concern has been to broaden the readership by finding people to whom the existing formula would appeal, and for this I have relied heavily on readers' help. But the main burden of the work – and the labour has been rather coarsely compared to that of producing a baby every month – has fallen overwhelmingly on the three deputy editors: first Kathy O'Shaughnessy, then Kate Kellaway and now, triumphantly for the past two years, Laura Cumming. As an editor who works only three days a week, and is sometimes less than totally in command of things after luncheon, I am painfully aware that without the organization and hard work – not to mention intelligence and charm – of an enthusiastic deputy editor, no magazine would ever appear.

'My two causes for self-congratulation are in having taught the staff to play bridge, to the extent that at the end of a hard day's work we can now field a respectable team, and in the Grand Poetry Competition, which I honestly believe may be helping to put the English back on the path of poetry which rhymes, scans and makes sense…'

A Scribbler in Soho

LITERARY REVIEW, NOVEMBER 1989

From the Pulpit – [untitled sermon]

The height of the literary-prize season, when everybody – or nearly everybody – is talking about books, might, perhaps, be a good time to talk about politics instead. In six years as a political correspondent – first for the *Spectator*, then for *Private Eye* – the only useful thing I learned was that even fewer people are interested in politics than are interested in books. But a magazine which tries to cover the field must also take account of the minority interests. Current efforts being made to re-politicize the novel from the left – however sad and hopeless the effort may seem – offer an opportunity to examine the subject anew.

A briefly fashionable young book reviewer was urging readers of the *Independent* last September that literary prizes are a danger to the health of British novels. Oddly enough, this is a burden I have been singing for nearly twenty years on the grounds that such prizes encourage affectation and esoteric dilettantism. But the new objection to literary prizes, I learn, is that by their nature they discourage political commitment. Thatcher. The bomb. Fundamentalist Islam. The single European market. These are the subjects which novelists are discouraged from addressing – possibly because the judges are as bored by these subjects as everyone else.

I feel I scarcely need to re-state my conviction that to encourage novelists to take an interest in these dismal subjects would be the worst possible service to the English novel. When the Booker shortlist was published last September, it was generally observed that many front-runners had been excluded: Amis mi, Barnes, Brookner, Drabble, Faulks, Frayn, Golding, Thubron, Weldon. To these I would add my own particular list of Forster, Lively, Mantel, Massie. But Amis mi seems a particularly pointed exclusion, rather like the exclusion of Graham Greene, year after year, from the ponderous deliberations of the Nobel Committee. It has been suggested that Amis was excluded from the list on the insistence of the two women on the committee, who felt that his disregard for feminist sensibilities made him politically unacceptable. One hears that Amis mi has had similar difficulties with his novels in New York. I see no point at all in worrying about Islamic fundamentalists, whose literary surveillance is necessarily limited to their own bizarre concerns, if we are to accept this blanket censorship on one of the gigantic struggles of our time.

After which it is good to report that the Tilling Society, dedicated to celebrating the memory of E. F. Benson, the Rye social satirist, is planning a huge ball at the Reform Club on 19 May to commemorate the fiftieth anniversary of his death. I understand the choice of the Reform Club, since its magnificent Barry design makes it one of the finest buildings in club-land.

However, I must warn them about our experience after the *Literary Review*'s tenth anniversary party [see also pages 165–167], an occasion much enjoyed by nearly all who attended it. A female guest, caught short and confused by the club's inadequate arrangements, was forced to avail herself of the gentlemen's lavatory. Now the club's administration has banned the magazine and its saintly proprietor from giving a party there ever again. Tickets for the Tilling Society Ball (from Martello Bookshop, 26 High Street, Rye, East Sussex) cost a cool £57.50 per person. Female guests are advised to bring a chamber pot.

Literary Review, February 1990
Public Lending Right as an Insult

February is the month when the Public Lending Right computers eventually produce the sums they have been mulling over since June. The result is that 17,594 registered authors share between them the sum of £3,072,000. This should give the authors an average of £174.61 each, to compensate them for the free gift of their work to the nation, but in point of fact over 75 per cent of them – 13,254 out of 17,594 – earn less than £100 a year.

My purpose in producing all these figures – many readers will already have decided to skip the rest of the piece – is certainly not to urge that the money should be shared out more equally, or according to some insane yardstick of 'literary merit' as determined by a Committee composed of Mr Seymour-Smith [see page 197], Professor Miller [presumably the critic Karl, co-founder of the *LRB*] and Lady Rachel Billington [the daughter of Elizabeth Longford and sister of Lady Antonia Fraser, a prolific author who seemed to symbolize a particular 'type' of writer for Bron – successful but mediocre. When attacking the award of the Nobel Prize for Literature to William Golding in his *Spectator* column during 1983 he took another swipe at writers he considered mediocre, however successful: 'By whatever process the Swedish Academy decided that Pearl Buck made the most significant contribution to literature of all authors living in 1938, the choice had a strangely liberating effect on the whole prize system. There was always something odious in the idea that a group of Swedes sitting in solemn conclave was in a position to decide who was the best writer of English, or the most worthy to be honoured. After Pearl Buck one saw it as a lottery. If she could win it, anyone could...'] No, my purpose is to ask whether the whole apparatus is not an entire waste of time, whether authors would not be better off nursing a grudge over the State's expropriation of their labour rather than accepting these derisory sums in settlement.

By any normal reckoning, £100 is better than the proverbial slap in the belly with a wet fish, but nobody is yet threatening authors with this form of assault. The question is really whether £100 – and 75 per cent of registered authors earn less than that – is better than nothing. I should have said it was worse than nothing. It is both an act of piracy, since the author has no choice in the exchange, and an insult, since the valuation is so low. The idea that a senior author's income should cut off at £6,000 – half the sum paid to a trained children's nurse – might suggest that the purpose of the whole scheme is to punish authors, rather than compensate them for the enforced loss of their livelihood.

Perhaps 10p per estimated borrowing (against the present rate of 1.39 pence) with no ceiling for more successful authors like Catherine

Cookson, would be fair. The cost to the Exchequer – about £25 million a year – would still be chicken-feed in the context of government expenditure of £165 billion, amounting to a sixty-sixth part of one per cent of government expenditure, dedicated to feeding the minds of the citizenry.

Of course it could be argued that a reform which increased Miss Catherine Cookson's PLR receipts from £6,000 to approximately £250,000 might be very nice for Miss Cookson but would do little to feed the minds of her admirers, since they already benefit from the same nourishment at a much cheaper rate.

It is a genuinely humbling fact that of the hundred adult books listed by PLR as having been the most-issued in 1989, very, very few were reviewed in this magazine. This is not the result of intellectual snobbishness on our part. I would love to cover the whole literary scene, reviewing the Catherine Cooksons, Victoria Holts and Danielle Steeles as well as the Salman Rushdies and the Lisa St Aubin de Teráns. Alone among literary magazines, we have the space and the young reviewers waiting to cut their teeth on whatever they may be given. By and large, the Cooksons and Holts do not send us their books to review. But I remain convinced that it is only by the intelligent reviewing of unpretentious books, and by the insensitive reviewing of pretentious ones, that we can eventually make sense of a library readership which is as keen as anybody else to be guided towards new discoveries, new delights.

The purpose of a magazine such as this one is not so much to encourage Catherine Cookson to stretch herself a little more, although that might be a useful side-effect. In present circumstances there is no need for Cookson or Holt/Plaidy to try any harder. She is doing very well. But we might persuade the Coriolanus figures on our literary stage – the Burgesses, the Ackroyds, the endless circus of Booker short-listeds – to make more effort to ingratiate themselves with the huge market of library borrowers. They are human beings, after all.

LITERARY REVIEW, APRIL 1990
Time to Stand Up and be Discounted

Like Dr Leavis, I was never much impressed by C. P. Snow's warnings about the Two Cultures because I doubted then – and still doubt – whether any such thing can be said to exist as a scientific culture which embraces such disparate and unconnected disciplines as botany and mathematics (to name only two sciences of which I had vaguely heard). There was one high culture, that of classical studies: philosophy, literature, the arts, history... everything else, like the Second Law of Thermodynamics, was esoteric technical jargon.

Determined efforts have been made in the universities to reduce the study of language and literature to the same levels of esotericism, but I do not think anyone would claim that the humane culture of our bourgeois society has been much influenced by these efforts. Perhaps there has been a weakening at the top, where the social and intellectual insecurities of academic life have driven otherwise intelligent men and women to take refuge in their own forms of incomprehensibility. But the chief characteristic of the past ten years has surely been the development of a robust and assertive popular culture which could scarcely be described as being in opposition to the old, high culture since it had virtually no point of contact with it.

At its clearest, the low culture can be seen daily in the pages of the *Sun* newspaper, which provides, with television, the chief source of information and intellectual nourishment for the majority of our fellow citizens. People learn how to think and behave from it when anxious to learn how to confront the perplexities of modern life.

So far as there can be said to be a predominant culture of our times, it is surely the popular culture of the *Sun*. It is neither humane nor bourgeois, nor is it particularly intelligent or well-informed. In many ways it is rather loathsome, holding loud, moronic opinions on many subjects from the European Community and foreigners generally to the punishment of offenders, with a tortured attitude to sex, or bonking, whereby although it approves of the activity in theory and provides endless photographs of naked women to assist its male readers' jaded masturbatory fantasies, it reserves the right to expose, humiliate and possibly destroy anyone whom it suspects of actually bonking. In its favour it can be said to reflect a certain cocky good nature in other fields, to have preserved a humorous scepticism about most things and to have done something to restore the self-respect of the British worker after generations of whingeing welfare-ism and patronage from the Left.

But I am not sure that this new breed of self-respecting Briton presents a very amiable front to the world, and I am certain that few readers of the *Literary Review* wish to belong to a culture which is dominated by the New Brit philistine triumphalism of the *Sun* newspaper. Hatred of books, or learning, or anything which smacked of the liberal bourgeois establishment which has ruled Britain for most of this century, has always simmered under the surface of working-class radicalism in its more farouche manifestations. For the first time, under the leadership of Thatcher and with the active support of Murdoch, these ancient resentments are in the ascendant and have been harnessed to create a brutal, ignorant guiding force in our society such as makes the old NUM under Arthur Scargill seem positively mild. At least Scargill was forced to employ the gentler rhetoric of English Labourism alongside the Marxist rhetoric of the class war. Neither Mr Andrew Neil, editor of the *Sunday Times* and self-appointed herald of the New Dawn, nor Mr Peter Morgan, the garrulous new director general of the Institute of Directors, is under any such constraint. As spokesmen for the new Thatcherite 'enterprise culture', which is rapidly devastating what little remains of beauty or charm in the country or its people, they choose to use the educated professional classes as their scapegoat. The cry that Britain was being throttled by its old school ties was bold and to a very large extent true, when we first heard it from Cambridge and, later, from the red-brick universities in the mid-1950s. Today it is neither brave nor true, nor does it provide an excuse for the abomination of desolation which these New Britons are creating around us.

When I became editor of the *Literary Review* four years ago I vowed that I would eschew politics entirely, partly fearing that my own prejudices would be repugnant to the existing readership, but chiefly because I was aware, after six years as a political correspondent, that most intelligent and civilized people are thoroughly bored by the subject. I had also watched our colleagues on the *London Review of Books* make tremendous fools of themselves, as I thought, by pontificating on the political issues of the day.

But the new popular or 'low' culture which threatens to overwhelm the liberal bourgeois culture cannot be ignored. When the New Britons start putting on their war-paint and issuing war cries, it is time for the rest of us to take our weapons down from the wall. Previously, the challenge has come from the left and has been contained within the left with a bit of help from others. Now it comes from the right, but shows no signs of being contained within the right. Those old school ties might as well have strangled their wearers, leaving the field open for the new barbarians of the Murdoch press and the Institute of Directors.

LITERARY REVIEW, MAY 1990

Save Us from the Palumbo Millennium

Many expressed misgivings at the time of Peter Palumbo's appointment to be chairman of the Arts Council in succession to the mild and benign figure of Lord Rees-Mogg. This was not merely because all his ideas about art seemed stale and discredited. It was more that despite his proclaimed enthusiasm for the work of Mies van der Rohe, the Dutch [sic] architect whose functionalist absurdities will continue to clutter several continents for at least the next twenty years, he seemed essentially a man of Mrs Thatcher's 'enterprise culture': a businessman to whom any consideration of beauty, however defective his perception of it, would always be subordinate to the business at hand.

Now, we learn, he plans to extend the activities of the Arts Council to embrace the care of old buildings, including cathedrals. Perhaps we should be grateful for any initiative that reduces the Council's residual interest in literature. If he took away the Poetry Society's entire subsidy of £129,600 and gave it to the Dean of Westminster for a marble statue of John Betjeman as winged cherub, flying to Heaven in the rococo manner, English letters would have every reason to be grateful to him.

But I am not sure that this is what was meant by his recent manifesto in *The Times*, illustrated with a photograph of himself squatting in front of Henry Moore's twee-triumphalist 'altar' in the City church of St Stephen Walbrook. This is what he wrote, in the unspeakable English of our new masters:

> The stock of buildings that constitute the cultural fabric of the nation, including cathedrals, leave [*sic*] much to be desired in terms of their [*sic*] structural condition and essential artistic facilities. The council will quantify necessary repair and building projects to construct a policy for the cultural fabric of the nation for completion by the millennium.

The poor old Church of England may be in a bad way with its strange plans to build public toilets in every parish church, where much larger congregations than todays have done without them for many centuries. But heaven protect us all from Palumbo's millennium.

Literary Review, June 1990

What Price a Pair of Ted Hughes's Underpants?

As we approach the publishing desert of the summer months, I am delighted to observe that the Booker Prize panel for 1990 includes two of the *Literary Review*'s star contributors: Hilary Mantel and Kate Saunders. I hope the other three judges – Sir Denis Forman, of Granada Television, Susannah Clapp and an American academic – pay attention to what they have to say.

I look forward to the day when fledglings from Beak Street have made their nests on all the literary pages and control all the literary prizes. When one looks at Booker's list of rotten choices, there can be no doubt that they are sorely needed.

One caution, however, might be sounded. Although, as I say, we are proud and happy to see our reviewers taken up by the mighty Sunday newspapers and magazines, many of which pay ten or twenty times our standard fee for a review, the new rivalry between them has produced a tendency to demand exclusive agreements from their reviewers. This means they can no longer appear in the *Literary Review*.

It seems a scurvy way to treat the only literary magazine in England which operates an 'open door' policy, allowing anybody remotely promising to come in from the street and try a hand at reviewing. The policy involves immense amounts of work from me, Rosemary and the rest of the staff, sifting material which comes in, encouraging some and discouraging others as appropriate.

We keep the whole industry supplied with new reviewing talent, and nobody can really pretend that this magazine represents a threat to any of them in their circulation wars. The least they can do is to allow our own reviewers to continue to appear in these pages.

H. Bradley Martin, the Manhattan millionaire book-collector who died in 1988, had the genial idea that when he died his collection should be broken up and sold, so that the individual items might continue to give that fierce pleasure of ownership which only collectors know. So many collectors, in a last act of spite or greed or self-glorification, arrange for their collections to be preserved for all time as a monument to themselves, or presented to a nation which has seldom, if ever, done anything to deserve such a gift, and which derives only the most academic of pleasures from contemplating its possessions.

Like many people who work on literary magazines, I find myself consumed by a deep and burning hatred of books, and never wish to own more than are absolutely necessary for reference purposes. However, reading through the list of Bradley Martin's sale, my eye was caught by a volume of poems written by Sir Stephen Spender as a young man: *Nine Experiments by SHS being poems written at the age of eighteen, 1928*. The volume, which included two unpublished poems in manuscript, was expected to fetch £10,000–£15,000.

When one thinks what the old boy *did* manage to get published in the course of eighty years, the mind boggles at the thought of an unpublished Spender poem. Similarly, as one examines the products of Spender's maturity, it is not easy to think what a fair price for his juvenile experiments might be. But £10,000–£15,000 is serious money by anyone's reckoning. Obviously there are madmen around prepared to pay higher sums for even odder goods, and competing whims can always produce a freak result, but here we had a sober state-of-the-market estimate. If anybody still trusts the market principle to bring good sense into the regulation of human affairs, let him brood on this. It is as if all the ingenuity and effort which went into the invention of waste-paper baskets has been in vain.

Literary Review, December 1990

For Whom the Bells Jingle

It may be a pious act for friends and relations to respect a dead person's wishes, but even that charitable exercise would seem to require some sort of belief in the survival of intelligence after death, if not in the immortality of the soul, or superstitious dread of being haunted by the ghost of the departed. If death involves obliteration of the awareness, as many people, on balance, believe, then there can be no logical reason for them to take an interest in whatever may happen to their literary estates after death.

Nobody, it would appear, could have been more convinced than Philip Larkin of the finality of death. He left a small canon of fairly good poems – very good indeed, by the dismal standards of the period through which we have lived – with instructions that all unpublished material should be destroyed. Such instructions from the grave, unenforceable in law, have a peculiarly vapid quality, yet a certain feeling of decency, whether derived from residual superstition or from genuine gratitude and affection or from inarticulate sentimentality, makes us reluctant to see them disregarded.

There are good reasons why the dead should not be allowed to dictate the future conduct of the living. We can sympathize with Larkin's desire, having published a small amount of fairly good poetry, not to have the waters muddied by second-rate work which he had judged substandard, or by biographical information which he wished to suppress. But the obvious course of action for anyone whose wishes in this respect are sincere is to destroy the material himself. I suspect that in everybody who preserves things – indiscreet diaries, second-rate poems, unfinished novels – there is a secret, unacknowledged hope that they will, indeed, be published one day.

Mr John Whitehead, the lawyer and Larkin enthusiast, regards the question of whether Larkin's wishes should be respected as a moral point. When lawyers start invoking morality, one is bound to take notice, as when politicians start drawing attention to their patriotism. To which system of morality does he refer? Thomist Christianity offers little guidance on the subject of obedience to the dead, as does traditional Judaism, although I suspect that within the enormous diversity of the Koranic tradition there may be some useful precepts. But perhaps he refers to some specific voodoo ethic, flourishing in one corner or another of the sun-kissed Caribbean.

I fear Messrs Thwaite and Motion will achieve little more than to add to the sum of general boredom, as they pile on information about a minor poet who lived an extraordinarily uninteresting life. But that is no reason to suppress their efforts on the bogus grounds of good taste. Since the publication of *The Literary Review Anthology of Real Poetry* (Ashford, Buchan & Enright) this month, there is hope of a New Dawn. We can afford to be generous to the scavengers.

Mention of Christmas has been reduced to two reviews in this issue. I hope that genuinely religious people will forgive me, but they must find their joys and their sorrows elsewhere. I decided that this year the magazine should serve as a refuge for those who wish to forget about the whole thing.

Before October was out, I found the first beautiful woman sitting alone in the Academy [Club], weeping at the prospect of having her mother to stay. I think the best way to get through Christmas is to sit alone nibbling at a fruit cake, sipping a glass of wood port, and meditating about the poor. Least of all does one want to read about it. There will be no Christmas decorations in the Academy and we will be shut on Christmas Day. Those feeling Yuletidish can go to a disgusting pub next door. But I sincerely wish everyone a happy Christmas.

I hope that *Literary Review* readers who have no interest or desire to join the Academy will forgive me if I continue to use the Pulpit as a club notice-board, but it is a traditional function of pulpits to advertise parish events.

Since the excellently successful party given by Fourth Estate and Craig Brown to launch *The Agreeable World of Wallace Arnold* [by Craig Brown, with illustrations by Willie Rushton] it has been decided to encourage members to use the club for small book launch parties. One condition is that no member of the club can be excluded. This applies even if they confine themselves to Sophia's Book Club upstairs. [For the Academy Book Club, see page 167.] It would be intolerable if members had to be turned away. The usual 'no poets' rule continues to apply, and we may impose a quota on pin-stripe suits. Otherwise it all seems to work quite well. Sophia's room will be open by the time this appears, with a magnificent new fireplace and Rangoon-style overhead fans, as a place of quiet meditation and decorous card games for members who wish to escape the turmoil of the main club room downstairs.

Long Shadow of the Jenkins Clan

Attentive readers of this magazine will be aware that last month saw the publication of a slim volume which heralded a revolution in this country no less remarkable, for all its smaller scale, than the similar revolutions which have been occurring in the Soviet Union, Poland, Hungary, Czechoslovakia, Romania, Bulgaria and wherever else intelligent, well-disposed people have started having doubts about the benefits of socialism.

The revolutionary event of which *Literary Review* readers will be aware was, of course, the publication by Ashford, Buchan & Enright of the first *Literary Review Anthology of Real Poetry*, edited and introduced by me, at the extraordinarily reasonable price of £6.95. But while I am reasonably confident that most readers of the *Literary Review* will be aware of this event, it is hard to judge exactly how far the news has spread outside.

One review appeared in *Private Eye*. It was written by D. J. Taylor, Young Turk of the 1950s Conservation Movement in literature – he believes that all fiction, to be truly valid, must be written by members of the working class about themselves. While obviously well intended, it was also painfully facetious, and might well have puzzled some of the less sophisticated and younger readers of the *Eye*, even if it provided a good quotation: 'It is this that gives the anthology its status as one of the decade's great exercises in literary subversion.'

Quite how subversive it is may be judged from the fact that at the time of writing, a full month after publication, it has not received a single other review in any publication. BBC Radio and Independent Television, both notorious hotbeds of subversives, have been happy to devote programmes to it. In a few gossip columns – similarly, the traditional refuge of the outlaw – it has received a friendly mention. But in no other of the country's myriad newspapers and magazines – from *Budgerigar Breeder's Gazette* to the *Independent*, through *Women's World* to what you will – was it judged worthy of notice.

I am not arguing for a moment that any fame or notoriety I may have acquired in thirty years of diligent scribbling might have earned the book a little notice, however brief or unfavourable. Nor would I stoop to the odious device of drawing attention to some of the books that were judged worthy of attention. Least of all would I suggest that the literary editors of all these struggling publications have a duty to promote their deadly rival, the *Literary Review*. But I am slightly shocked at their disregard of the ancient tradition, based on nothing more sinister than self-interest, whereby literary editors have always treated each other's drivelling offerings as important literary events. If Alan Jenkins, poetry editor of the *TLS*, chooses to ignore *Literary Review's Anthology of Real Poetry*, who on earth is going to notice Alan Jenkins's next match-book of dead maggots?

As the editor of a literary magazine, I am also well aware that many authors, finding their books unreviewed, assume that they are the victims of a conspiracy to do them down. In my own days as a struggling novelist, I used to pin my suspicious fantasies on a mysterious body called the Critics' Circle. Twenty-five years later, after twenty years as a book reviewer, I still know nothing about this shadowy organization, or even whether it still exists. Is it left-wing in its orientation, as I originally assumed, dedicated to the overthrow of the liberal bourgeois society we know and love? Or is it dominated by crypto-fascists of the extreme right, and funded by South Africa, as many others have averred? I do not know. All I know is that in nearly five years as editor of the *Literary Review*, I have never been approached by anyone suggesting I should ignore a particular book or author. When books are not reviewed it usually means that the idle publishers have failed to send a copy for review, or failed to send it in good time.

So I see no conspiracy in the fact that 250 literary editors have simultaneously reached the independent decision to ignore the first anthology of real contemporary poetry which has appeared since the war. I attribute the phenomenon to the fact that they are all bored stiff with 'poetry' and handed the book over to their 'poetry' editors or 'poetry' experts. The reaction of that splendid corps of conservatives is best summed up by

Alan Jenkins, 'poetry' editor of the *TLS*, as reported by Peterborough of the *Daily Telegraph*:

> It's terribly damaging to allow people to think that these absurd little ditties are poems. Waugh's taste in poetry obviously stops short at nursery rhymes. He's encouraging appalling ignorance by implying that everyone has been writing in vain for the past seventy years. It's a joke that's just not funny.

One day I shall write a treatise on the baneful influence of all these unrelated people called Jenkins: Peter, Alan, Roy, Clive, Simon... I wonder what the second syllable of D. J. Taylor's name represents. But first I must congratulate my old colleague Ferdinand Mount on his appointment as editor of the *Times Literary Supplement*. Mount has already made his mark as the greatest political commentator of our time, as well as having been head of Mrs Thatcher's Policy Unit. Just as in politics he avoided the siren voice of Enoch, I hope that at the *TLS* he will be able to avoid the critical examples of his uncle Anthony Powell [see page 50], for thirty-five years chief book reviewer of the *Daily Telegraph* and creator of the most monstrous Jenkins of them all in the faceless narrator of *Dance to the Music of Time*. It is time that we all grew out of these Jenkinses, who have been squatting like giant toads over the last twenty years of our history.

LITERARY REVIEW FEBRUARY 1991
An Area of Vitality and Hope for the Future

... There is an uncharacteristic atmosphere of impending struggle in Beak Street as we await the arrival of Rupert Murdoch's new conservative *Times Literary Supplement* under the formidable editorship of Ferdinand Mount, who was at one time head of Mrs Thatcher's Policy Unit at Downing Street. Are we, perhaps, about to be eclipsed by a publication which, for all its many merits, has hitherto shown little sign of spoiling the market?

Both Mount and I are members, at any rate in a chronological sense, of the generation which Lord Rees-Mogg is trying to exclude from exerting any influence on television. The beginning of that dreadful decade [the sixties] found us at Oxford together; in the years which followed, when he worked for the *Daily Sketch* and I for the *Daily Telegraph*, we would meet for lunch and discuss with horror the way the world was going.

Where do we stand now, thirty years later? Dr Spock is discredited, even Dr Kinsey is under attack, the *Sun* (always Murdoch's trail-blazer) has come out strongly against permissiveness in any form. 'They sneered at morality and decency and family life,' it declared recently of these Children of the Sixties. 'Today we can see the results of "civilization" with record numbers of illegitimate babies, broken marriages and drug addicts.'

Will Mount put more filth in the *TLS*, or less? For myself, I have not yet sorted out my ideas on this subject. Should we have more filth or less? Be sure, we will be watching the *TLS* very closely.

LITERARY REVIEW, MARCH 1991

Elected Silence – the Music that We Care to Hear

One of the more agreeable aspects of the Gulf War, which is still raging as I write, is that no publisher has yet had the idea of producing an opportunistic volume in imitation of [those on] Spain and Vietnam: *Authors Take Sides on the Gulf War*. Quite why no publisher has had this bright idea is another matter. Perhaps it is yet another blessing of the recession. Probably, by the time this appears, half a dozen rival volumes will be in the process of collation, creating a terrible agony of mind among our more fashionable literati on the point of which to support.

The fact that they have been so slow off the mark may reflect no more than that sales of the last effort – *Authors Take Sides on Vietnam* – were disappointing. But the temptations of such a book are obvious. It writes itself; it costs nothing, since authors are always so flattered to be asked for their opinions that they treat it as charitable work; and it is bound to score a mention in all the up-market gossip columns of the quality press.

Perhaps there is a general feeling, even among authors, that there is no more to be said. Their views are no more or less fatuous than those of everyone else; they have access to exactly the same sources of information and misinformation as the general public.

On this occasion, they have confined themselves to a round robin, printed in the *Independent*, drawing attention to the atrocious treatment of a Palestinian writer, interned without any right of appeal in a London prison. It is exactly the sort of issue which British authors should feel concerned about. Nobody, I fear, or practically nobody, is much interested in their views on the wider issue, whether judicious and responsible, or exhibitionist and partisan. But in the general atmosphere of boredom and irritation with writers, largely the product, as I would argue, of literary festivals, 'poetry' bangs and the heavily subsidized cult of the 'difficult' in contemporary letters, the most useful thing writers can do is to support each other. Nobody else is going to support them.

I was distressed, a few months ago, to read in my *Daily Telegraph* how Martin Amis had had a Granada Television interview cancelled as a result, according to the newspaper's columnist Peterborough, of 'widespread public apathy'.

The producers of a programme called *This Morning* got cold feet when someone suggested that nobody up North had ever heard of Martin Amis. They conducted a telephone poll which revealed that only three per cent of viewers had heard of him, and promptly cancelled the interview.

It did not, apparently, occur to Granada producers that this might have been a good opportunity to introduce this brilliant young novelist to their grunting, apathetic, largely unemployable viewers. And so the great north-south divide yawns ever wider. When told of the three per cent who had heard of him, Amis commented wearily: 'I'm not bothered. It's not likely to be much more unless you're Charles Dickens.'

At least they have heard of Dickens. I wonder if any northern reader would be interested in an appeal for the Dickens Museum, situated in his former home at 48 Doughty Street, WC1. For some years the interior and furnishings have decayed. Send money, DHSS vouchers and messages of support to Troy, at Susan Llewellyn Associates, 101 Barkston Gardens, London SW5 OEU.

LITERARY REVIEW, APRIL 1991

A Gulf which is Growing Between Us and Our Masters

From this pulpit in March I congratulated the nation's publishers and editors for having resisted the temptation to solicit contributions for a volume entitled *Authors Take Sides on the Gulf War*. No sooner had March's magazine left the printers, than a letter dropped through my postbox signed by Jean Moorcroft Wilson and Cecil Woolf headed 'Authors Take Sides on the Gulf War'.

This time the questions read:

'Are you for or against the use of armed force in liberating Kuwait?'

'How, in your opinion, can lasting peace and stability be restored in the Middle East?'

Within a day or two of the letter's arrival, the Gulf War was over. While it might have been a matter for idle literary curiosity to know what particular authors thought about the war before it started, the idea that authors, as such, have any useful contribution to make to a settlement involving all the warring factions of Kurds, Palestinians, Jews, Ba'athists, Sunni and Shiite Muslims, all the rival nationalisms and major international oil interests involved is laughable. I do not think I will be contributing to the symposium on this occasion.

From a purely literary point of view I would not judge that the eventual outcome of the Mother of Battles, which lasted only a hundred hours, was entirely beneficial. Whatever the rights and wrongs of Iraq's occupation of Kuwait – and I do not feel I know enough about it to give any certain judgement – the defeat of Iraq was above all a victory for superior technology. Its result will be to give the Americans a renewed confidence in the superiority of their technological culture which it may not entirely deserve. Although American military technology is undoubtedly superior to that of any other nation – the Japanese scarcely compete in that field – the social, economic and financial culture which it protects would seem increasingly neurotic and irrational, if not in the process of disintegration.

The Falklands victory had a similarly unwholesome effect on British self-regard – and one that may explain our involvement in the Gulf War. But the likely result of a sudden, massive injection of self-esteem into an America which already seemed poised to reject everything which 'dead, white European males' have taught it cannot be an entirely welcome development for the rest of the world. The economic collapse and gradual disintegration of the Soviet Union leaves the United States unchallenged top dog for the present. The immediate prospect would appear to be that of a world led by semi-literate technicians. One result must be a certain closing of the ranks among the older countries of Europe. For some time, I have been thinking that we devote too much space on this magazine to the reviewing of American fiction. Few of our readers seem very much interested in it.

People may have been puzzled to notice that there was no review of Kingsley Amis's *Memoirs* (Hutchinson) in the March edition of the *Literary Review*; nor is there one this month. Whether or not readers share my view that it is the most entertaining book yet published this year (however disgusting in many respects), it has certainly proved the publishing sensation to date.

The reason for its absence is that the publisher – Hutchinson – refused to send out review copies until the week before publication. This would have meant reviewing it a month late, after every newspaper in the country had had its say, usually at enormous length. Hutchinson was prevented from sending out early review copies by the *Sunday Times*, which had bought first serial rights. I thought the *Sunday Times* made a rotten job of them, too. Nearly every Sunday newspaper did better. But I hope that authors who are faced with serialization offers from more than one newspaper will remember the damage caused by this crass, dog-in-the-manger attitude of the *Sunday Times*.

LITERARY REVIEW, MAY 1991
Stop Publishing and be Saved

We are told there was once a time when book publishing was an efficient industry in Britain: as soon as a first printing was sold out booksellers reordered, and subsequent impressions could be rushed through at a few days' notice; it seldom took more than six weeks to prepare a manuscript for press and print it, while allowing literary editors to receive their early editions, post them to reviewers and receive their reviews, beautifully written in copperplate, by return of post.

Perhaps these conditions applied in my grandfather's day – he spent forty-one years at Chapman & Hall, never failing to answer a letter on the day he received it. However, they have certainly never applied in my lifetime. By the time I arrived on the literary scene in 1960, publishers were amiable people who always got drunk at luncheon, never answered letters and preferred to talk of other things than books. As a profession, it attracted pleasant, idle, incompetent young men and over-educated, idealistic young women, always kept in subordinate positions because they had not been to a public school for boys and did not have the right connections.

In the publishing revolution of the 1970s and 1980s nearly all these pleasant, idle, incompetents were pushed out; their places were taken, as we now see, by unpleasant incompetents who manage to hide their idleness in occasional bursts of officious activity. As an outsider on the publishing scene, listening occasionally to its gossip but avoiding its main celebrations, I am aware of an atmosphere which is not so different from that of a Las Vegas fruit-machine saloon, except that the players are so busy watching each other's scores that they have no time to study their own.

Perhaps the same is true of many British industries at the present time. The concentration on hitting a jackpot precludes any interest in ways of making smaller, surer sums of money. Perhaps we are becoming a nation of wide boys, spivs and quick-money merchants. The only trouble is that we don't appear to be very good at it.

Quite suddenly, it would appear, the British have stopped buying books. What has really happened, I imagine, is that publishers have stopped lying to each other about how many books they were selling. The piles of unsold Dickens and Shaw biographies [Peter Ackroyd's Dickens biography and Michael Holroyd's multi-volume biography of Bernard Shaw were both over-hyped blockbuster items, as a consequence of receiving record-breaking advances and massive media coverage] in every bookshop have become too obvious to ignore. Even the huge sums of 'investment' money to be extracted by pressing the right button on a Video Display Unit and converting some phantom, electronic digits into paper are now drying up, and the time has come to sack staff.

The publishing recession is no skin off our nose at the *Literary Review*, except in so far as it affects a few friends. Practically none of the publishers ever advertised with us, much preferring to spend vast sums advertising their wares to people who had no interest in books and never bought them, like the ignorant and half-witted readers of the *Sunday Times*, rather than spending small sums advertising them to people who are concerned about books and buy them in huge quantities, like the gentle, well-educated readers of the *Literary Review*. The explanation for this phenomenon, which I have often written about on this page, is not to be found so much in the malice of publishers' advertising departments, or in some sort of New Brit proletarian triumphalism, as in their idleness. It takes just as much work to prepare copy for a £300 advertisement in the *Literary Review* as it does to prepare a £10,000 advertisement in the *Sunday Times*. Never mind that the £300 advertisement will probably sell as many copies of the book. By blowing their budget on a *Sunday Times* advertisement, they can impress booksellers, satisfy their masters that they are once again going for the Big One – and take the rest of the week off.

Now, in the recession, there is practically no book advertising for anyone, the *Sunday Times* books section has shrunk out of sight and book pages in many review sections are disappearing behind the Cooking Hints and Budgerigar Club news.

Only *Literary Review*, the *TLS* and the *London Review of Books* continue to cater for the small but by no means inconsiderable number of people who are still interested in books. But the recession in the book trade comes as a blessing for us. Fewer may not mean better and probably won't, but at least we will be able to give more attention to those which seem to possess some interest for the intelligent general reader.

This copy of the magazine was just being pasted up when we heard the news of Graham Greene's death. Our choice was between scrapping two or three pages and coming out a week late, or seeming to ignore a major milestone in English letters. Greene was the last of the literary giants, a good friend to this magazine although never, alas, a contributor, and a good friend to its editor. By the time of our June issue, hundreds of thousands of words will have been written, and there will be little to add. Greene's fierce intelligence burned to the end, but by the end it was possible to guess what his reaction would be to most events, and he must have been happy to see many people carrying his torch. The flame still burns.

The 'Farewell Thatcher' Grand Poetry Competition was a disaster. The debris may be inspected [not reproduced here], along with details of the new competition (results in July) which is for poems which rhyme, scan and make sense on the subject of LOVE IN AN ENGLISH GARDEN. The garden may be metaphysical, but its Englishness is absolute.

LITERARY REVIEW, JULY 1991

Not Street but World Credibility at Risk

One of the great advantages of having so few advertisements in this magazine is that we are under no pressure from advertisers to adjust the editorial content to their liking. I imagine it was pressure from advertisers which brought that harmless old British institution, *Punch*, to its present sad state, but one sees evidence of the same pressure on almost every newspaper and magazine in the land.

There used to be a cruel joke that those who could not make the grade as creative writers became book reviewers or critics; those who could not make the grade as book reviewers or critics became teachers of English literature at university. I do not think it is true; in an age when practically no 'creative' writers make any sort of grade, it might be truer to say that it is chiefly those who are plainly unemployable as primary school teachers, or local government health inspectors, or British Rail booking clerks, who decide they have a vocation to write creatively sometimes novels, more often short stories or what politeness requires us to call poetry.

Even so, there might be a case for explaining the present state of the advertising industry in terms of the people it recruits; those who cannot make the grade as journalists (and when one looks at those who do, it may seem inconceivable that there are such people), become advertisement copy writers; those who have lost even the ability to write copy for advertisements become advertising directors.

If advertising directors, as I suspect, share the same general level of creative intelligence and originality as BR booking clerks, this may explain why the entire industry is dedicated to wasting its clients' money on its own 1960s obsession with the youth culture and with what the thirty-two-year-old editor of *Punch* chooses to call, in the language of Berkeley Square, its 'streetwise credibility'. [A legendary weekly magazine and revered institution for over 150 years, *Punch* had three editors appointed in a desperate attempt to keep the magazine viable in the three years before 1992, when it finally closed. Despite an attempt by Mohamed Al Fayed to relaunch it in 1996, it ceased publication and now resides as a website selling its satirical products as stationary items or illustrative resources for general media exploitation.]

The simple truth of our present state is that the young have no money and there is no youth culture worth talking about. The people with money to spend are those whose children have grown up, whose mortgages are paid off and who are earning more than ever before in their last fifteen or twenty years of working. The fact that the advertising industry chooses to ignore this large and growing market and concentrate on the hopeless fantasies of the young is something we may reasonably leave it to sort out with its clients. The tragedy is that these advertising moguls do not just control the advertisements which appear in our newspapers and magazines, on our screens and on hoardings, and which, accumulatively, account for a large part of our country's self-image. They also determine, to an ever-greater extent, the presentation and substance of newspapers, magazines and television programmes which will be awarded the prize of carrying their advertisements. In this way, they influence what we read and see to a greater extent than any proprietor. Editors and programme controllers become their reluctant tools in the promotion of Britain as a nation of imbeciles.

The stereotype to which we must conform derives in part from an inaccurate nostalgia for the 1960s – when, briefly, the young were comparatively rich and carefree, before rents and housing costs adjusted to a 'double-income-no-kids' norm – and partly from the widely promoted idea of yuppies in the City, earning hundreds of thousands a year with no commitments, no kids. There may have been a few thousand of these at one time, but their chief function, as a focus for the envy and resentment of everyone else, has become confused in the advertisers' mind with the notion of an established and significant socio-economic group. No wonder so many firms, encouraged to cater for this virtually non-existent market, are going broke. No wonder so many magazines, designed to be read by yuppies, have difficulty in finding any readers. But the worst casualty of our incompetent, reactionary and imitative advertising industry is the effect it has on the rest of the press. For years I have been fulminating against the stupidity and idleness of publishers' advertising departments which refuse to place their advertisements in the *Literary Review*, whose readers buy hardbacks at an astonishing rate, and place them instead in the *Sunday Times*, few of whose readers even open a book from one year's end to the next. But that is not the worst part of the story: it is what newspapers are prepared to do to attract these imbecile advertisements. The *Sunday Times*, apart from its comment section, has been unreadable for almost as long as I can remember. It is when serious newspapers like the *Guardian* and the *Telegraph* start adopting the same idiotic affectations that we must start to worry about our world credibility. Is it not time that serious advertisers started looking more critically at the advice of their advertising experts?

LITERARY REVIEW, AUGUST 1991

Time for a Bit of Class Domination

Any government which is prepared to spend £21 million employing 150 'experts' full-time for two years to produce a report on the teaching of Language within the National Curriculum deserves to have a practical joke played on it. At the time of writing, it appears that Kenneth Clarke, the Education Secretary, has foolishly decided to suppress the report, even to the extent of claiming Crown copyright against attempts to quote from leaked copies of it. By refusing to let the rest of us share the joke, Clarke aggravates the situation and highlights the waste of public money involved.

If he had allowed free debate, he would have found his arm was strengthened by public reaction to the document, whose general tenor may be gauged by the remark attributed to Professor 'Ron' Carter, of Nottingham University, to the effect that the lyrics of Kylie Minogue were as worthy of study as anything within the canon of English literature, or by the suggestion apparently contained in the unpublishable report, that the novels of Barbara Cartland and Thomas Hardy should be studied on an equal footing.

The new doctrine was spelled out at a weekend conference for some 400 'left-wing' English teachers, held at Ruskin College at the end of June. It divided into two schools. According to one speaker: 'There's stuff in the national curriculum that can be used very positively. You can't talk about Standard English without talking about the power structures of society. That's the way to empower the kids.'

Another was not so sure: 'Literacy can be a means of social control. Instead of making children more powerful, it makes them feel less intelligent because they realize that some read better than others.'

And so it went on. One speaker complained that schools are 'fixated' on book culture, ignoring what children know about television. Most seemed to be united in the belief that great literature, correct grammar and spelling, are 'instruments of class domination' – as, by extension, is any attempt to teach anyone anything.

The sadness is that these buffoons – among whom Oxford's new Warton Professor of English [Terry Eagleton was the controversial appointee] is only the most extreme example – should choose to dump their half-baked opinions on the teaching of English, rather than on the rubbishy pseudo disciplines of sociology, politics and peace studies, where they belong. It might be melodramatic to claim that our entire liberal, humane, bourgeois culture is under threat from the stranglehold these people have established on the teaching of English – through the teacher-training colleges and institutes of education – but it is obviously true that their inability to teach English language and their refusal to teach English literature, threaten this one corner of it.

The reason why English faculties have fallen to these people, while there is no immediate threat of a Marxist mathematics or a Marxist Greek composition, is simply that the study of English literature attracts mild, pleasant and tolerant people who are easily imposed upon by bullies.

One way for academic standards to be restored would be to re-impose a bit of class domination. I do not honestly think that it would do English literature, or the English language, any harm if all university English faculties closed down while the present generation of be-jeaned, sweat-shirted and leather-jacketed pseudo-proletarian jokers is winkled out. Those who are on speaking terms with the new Warton Professor of English at Oxford might tell the Dauphin his jest will savour of but shallow wit, when thousands weep more than did laugh at it.

LITERARY REVIEW, JANUARY 1992

So I Suppose We Might as Well Honour Ourselves

At Graham Greene's Memorial Service in Westminster Cathedral the congregation heard various hollow suggestions about which writer might be considered suitable to inherit the OM awarded to Greene in a rare moment of magnanimity by the Queen in 1986. Even at the time, the thought crossed my mind that a motive for Greene's award might have been to annoy Mrs Thatcher (as she then was) as much as to honour the writer who had such a powerful and salutary influence on the English novel, transforming, in many respects, the way Englishmen have looked at each other ever since.

In the event, however, the vacancy in the Order of Merit has not been filled by a writer, so we are left once again with only one writer on that somewhat gloomy list of elderly scientists and academics. The one writer left on the list is Dame Veronica Wedgwood, the historian, who was the merest slip of a girl of fifty-nine when awarded the OM in 1969 but has now achieved the venerable age of eighty-one.

There need be no element of disparagement, nor even of jealousy, in asking why Dame Veronica should have been singled out in particular for this greatest honour which a country can bestow. She writes well, but not earth-shatteringly so. Her histories are readable and well researched, but they have scarcely overturned our understanding of the world we live in. My own explanation may be thought unworthy. The Queen does not read much, nor does she come from a family which is particularly noted for its interest in literature. But if one found oneself, as a virtuous and unaggressive German housewife interested chiefly in horses and dogs, thrust upon the throne of England, the first book one might be tempted to read would be C. V. Wedgwood's *Trial of King Charles I* (1964). Dame Veronica now resumes her solitary perch as Britain's one writer of officially recognized merit.

The rarity and reluctance with which writers are honoured in Britain – despite the truth that literature is the only art at which we have ever excelled, and the English language is unquestionably our finest gift to the world – must be explained by the curious relationship between rulers and ruled in this country. I do not think it is connected with the strange fact that in more than two and a half centuries our royal line has been composed exclusively of Germans who chose to marry Germans, until the arrival of the Queen Mother in 1923 and, more recently, the Princess of Wales in 1981.

Never having tasted revolution – at any rate, since 1649 – our rulers are extraordinarily jealous of anything which seems to detract from their own importance. The idea that writers or philosophers might have some alternative perception or vision of society is deeply repugnant to them, and the idea that people might prefer the alternative vision is a constant nightmare. The worst form of subversion is flippancy, and the true spirit of England has always been incurably flippant. No wonder that Wodehouse was projected by Churchill and his political crony, Cooper, as a hate-figure on a par with Hitler in 1941.

So English writers, resigned to being excluded from official honours and any sort of place at the top table, have chosen to honour themselves.

The title 'Companion of Literature' has no place in the official honours system of the country. The CLits, as they call themselves, are not, like Companions of the Bath, or Companions of the Most Distinguished Order of St Michael and St George, thought to be companions of the monarch. In fact, it is hard to see whose companions they are – scarcely of each other, since few English writers have ever been able to stand each other's company for long. They are appointed by the Council of the Royal Society of Literature which is a dim and slightly dotty but amiable body of 430 members, united by the feeling that literature is vaguely a good cause.

In December the Council announced its newest appointments to the Companionship, limited in number to ten. They fill the gaps left by Greene, Samuel Beckett, Sir Angus Wilson and Rosamund Lehmann, to join the surviving six of Sir Stephen Spender, eighty-two, Sir Steven Runciman, eighty-eight, Dame Iris Murdoch, seventy-one, Sir William Golding, eighty, Sir Victor Pritchett, ninety, and Miss Ruth Pitter, eighty-eight, who is described as a poetess.

It is plainly an excellent idea that honour should attach to old age. Nothing could be more odious than the suggestion that writers should nominate each other for honours on the strength of merit alone. But a study of the names reveals that other considerations than those of merit and age must apply. Certain writers collect honours, others don't. Old age is not enough.

The new Companions, chosen by the Council, are to be Anthony Burgess, seventy-four, Patrick Leigh Fermor, seventy-six, Muriel Spark, at whose age I would not be prepared to guess and Seamus Heaney, a child of fifty-two. On this occasion, they do not even have old age in common, although Heaney's presence may be explained by Kathleen Raine's refusal at eighty-three. Perhaps the odd man out is Leigh Fermor whose books, while attracting innumerable prizes and giving great pleasure to a certain class of English person, are far removed from the academic syllabuses which cast such a baneful spell on the enjoyment of contemporary litera-ture. For that reason, his inclusion is to be welcomed, although I personally find his work affected and irritatingly boastful. But if we writers do not honour each other, nobody else is going to honour us.

LITERARY REVIEW, FEBRUARY 1992

Lead, Kindly Light, Amid the Encircling Gloom

There is much to be gloomy about which might justify the choice of Hell as this month's subject for the David Bayliss Grand Poetry Competition. [The *Literary Review*'s competition established by Bron, see page 189.] No millionaire or international combine has come forward to help with the enormous annual loss of £120,000 which this dear little magazine has been sustaining for several years. One begins to lose confidence in the rich. How on earth do they see their role or purpose in life if not to support exactly such a cause as the *Literary Review*? They cannot derive much satisfaction from stuffing themselves with £120,000 worth of extra food – *marrons glacés*, no doubt, and *duck á l'orange*. Ugh! But if anyone who reads this knows of a millionaire or international combine, I beg them to telephone the millionaire or combine concerned, as nothing seems to change, and I can't go on printing these appeals like the old *Daily Worker/Morning Star* [the Communist newspaper's Fighting Fund still continues and Bron did not live to see the *Guardian*'s constant plea for 'supporters'] or the maga-zine will become boring and people will stop reading it.

One of the gloomiest prospects on the literary scene is that of Lady Thatcher's memoirs, which have been bought by Rupert Murdoch (to no one's surprise) for his HarperCollins imprint at a reported price of £3 million, being considerably more than anyone else was prepared to pay for them. We may ask ourselves why Murdoch was prepared to pay so much over the odds for what is bound to be one of the dullest and most distressing books imaginable, particularly since the Thatcher camp has announced it will contain no gossip or matters of a personal nature. The Japanese are apparently willing to add £750,000 to Lady Thatcher's loot, but we may imagine that their generosity derives from some sort of war-guilt to which Murdoch, being only eight years old at the outbreak of war, should not be susceptible.

Those of us who remember the dreadful autobiographies of Wilson and Heath can only groan at what is in store for the book trade when HarperCollins try to justify this advance. We may be sure that not a penny of the advertising bonanza will reach the *Literary Review*, whose readers are too intelligent to be impressed by this tripe. Of all the political memoirs which have cluttered up the literary scene in the last ten years or so, only those of Denis Healey and Roy Jenkins were worth a second glance. Perhaps Nigel Lawson's will tell us something about those Thatcher years. At least he can write English.

So few of them can that there is something faintly unsavoury about the readiness of certain publishers to pay them vast sums of money for their dishonest and unreadable reminiscences, almost as if other considerations than literary commerce might be involved. [Mrs Thatcher's readiness to allow engagement of brutal police tactics in the bitter strike when *The Times* moved to Wapping was maybe such a consideration.] Perhaps political salaries should be treated as an advance on royalties, to be repaid if and when a publisher antes up.

As more and more county libraries dispose of their remarkable book collections by various processes of dumping, and as the new British Library proceeds with its fatuous scheme for a £450 million 1950s-style monstrosity in St Pancras, we read of a deal between W. H. Smith and leading publishers to phase out the hardback novel.

This will have a bad effect on the literary novel, but the sad truth is that far too many literary novels have been published, most of them are a complete waste of time, and the form now seems to have lost all vitality and relevance. It is time for writers to find new ways of pleasing.

Perhaps the literary novel will survive as an adjunct of the literary prize industry. Later this month, we will learn further and better particulars of Booker's new £10,000 Russian novel prize, to be judged and awarded in Moscow. [Nothing came of this.] No doubt the initiative is well intended. There should be plenty of good material for novelists during the next few years, while the rest of the world averts its eyes from what must happen inside Russia while that huge and hopeless country struggles to free itself from the physical and intellectual shackles of nearly seventy-five years.

But I am not sure Booker is the ideal teacher. If Russian writers are encouraged to indulge themselves in one half of the intellectual confusion, the arrogance, the obscurantist self-absorption and plain, wrong-headedness which characterize this year's prizewinner [Ben Okri for *The Famished Road*], it would be better to encourage them to tell their stories in cartoon-strip form.

LITERARY REVIEW, APRIL 1992

Some Useful Things To Do with Books

Bibliophobia, or terrified aversion from books, should be seen as an illness rather than as a crime, sin or character defect. It is liable to visit book reviewers, librarians, publishers and editors of literary magazines in a particularly virulent form. In milder form, it visits every householder who discovers that all available spaces in the house are full of books which are of no further interest, but which are protected from being thrown away by some quasi-religious dread.

Sharper eyes than mine spotted an element of bibliophobia in the enthusiasm which greeted Tim Waterstone's Book Aid appeal for Russia and the new Republics at the beginning of this year. The various branches of Waterstone's were overwhelmed as hundreds of thousands of books poured in, week after week. At last we had found something useful to do with our unwanted books. A slave empire of 280 million souls had been denied access to anything but historical lies and dismal socialist propaganda for the past seventy-five years. What a feast awaited those able to read English fluently – most of whom will have learned it in the language schools run by the KGB.

When Graham Greene announced, nearly thirty years ago, that he would sooner be a writer in the Soviet Union than in the United States of America, many decided that he was simply baiting the Americans. In those days, no Soviet writer of the slightest honesty could hope to be published in the Soviet Union, and if he was published abroad, he was locked up. What on earth was the point of being a writer if nothing you wrote was ever read? Greene replied that in Russia, at least, the authorities were frightened of writers. In America, where only a tiny proportion of households would ever buy a book from one year's end to the next, nobody paid the slightest bit of attention to them.

It is true that a vast number of middle-class homes in the United States – possibly a majority – would have no more than two or three books in them, one of which would be a medical dictionary, another a guide to slimming and the third some incomprehensible work of prophetic cosmology. The American culture, if one can call it that, has long since passed beyond the literate phase. Information is to be stored and conveyed electronically, subject to perpetual revision, while the imagination, or what passes for it, is stimulated and fed by short video sequences.

I began to fear that the same thing was happening over here when it appeared that many books sold in this country were being bought for other reasons than to be read. My first intimation of this was from a book by Edward Heath about sailing. It sold, as I remember, over 30,000 copies, many of them signed by the author. It occurred to me that they might have been bought as an investment, to be wrapped in heavy duty cellophane and kept in the freezer until they matured. Next came Tolkien's *Silmarillion*, which sold over 220,000 copies in hardback. Consisting of occasional jottings from the great man's pen, it made no sense at all, and was completely unreadable. This book was presumably bought out of brand loyalty to *The Hobbit* and *Lord of the Rings*, with no thought for the contents. Finally, there came Stephen Hawking's *A Brief History of Time* which apparently sold eight million copies worldwide, half a million in this country. Yet the name Hawking does not feature among the 104 authors with library loans over 300,000, let alone among the 66 with loans over 500,000 or the 14 with loans over a million. One may doubt whether five per cent of those who bought Hawking's book actually read it. They bought it for other reasons.

The time may come when people will borrow books from the library for other reasons than to read them, but I do not think it has happened yet. All over the country, public libraries are shedding books as librarians become exhausted by the effort of storing them. Fewer and fewer books are being bought by libraries, even where the choice of books is not controlled by monomaniac censors. A hatred of books is spreading among the educated classes much faster than among those who make up the greatest group of borrowers, and for whom the library is an essential refuge from the inanities of television.

If a magazine like the *Literary Review* can do anything to reverse this tide of bibliophobia, it is doing something useful. I wish I could be confident that our two rivals in the same field were pulling their weight.

LITERARY REVIEW, JANUARY 1993
Save the Children from these Drips

The start of a new year is traditionally a time for looking ahead, making predictions and resolutions, etc., but perhaps understandably in the present state of the country I feel reluctant to do this, preferring to look back over the past year and wonder where we all went wrong. It was foolish, for instance, to forget to put a Christmas present subscription offer in the last issue. Often, we catch a hundred or so new readers that way, but this year I was so disgusted by the approach of Christmas and by the uncertainty about whether Lola Bubbosh, the *Literary Review*'s beloved deputy editor, would be allowed to stay in England that I forgot, so there it is. Anyone wishing to give a year's subscription to the magazine as a belated present for Christmas or for any other reason may telephone or send in an order at the ludicrously reduced price of £18 for a year's supply (the normal rate is £20).

One thing which I do not regret in the least was that we failed to review Andrew Morton's distressing book about the Princess of Wales (*Diana, Her True Story*) through not being sent a copy in good time. If our reviewer had liked it, I should feel truly mortified, since the book, used by the *Sunday Times* as part of the Murdoch newspapers' single-minded campaign to destroy the marriage of the Prince and Princess of Wales, seems to have started the great movement which culminated in over 62,000 fellow Britons telephoning the *Sun* to demand that the Queen find the £60m required to restore Windsor Castle as a property of the State.

The Brits, it seems to me, have become an extraordinarily unpleasant race: mean, envious, full of rancour, hatred and bogus self-righteousness. Or perhaps it is just that these characteristics are dominant at the moment, largely thanks to Murdoch and his hirelings.

But the fact remains that we are left with a very unpleasant population, or at any rate a population among whom only those with unpleasant and rancorous opinions feel encouraged to express them. What is odd about it all is that such a society should have emerged after so many years of intensive propaganda to make us nicer.

Christmas is a time when many of us, whether we like it or not, find ourselves looking at children's books. Enough jokes have been made about the Politically Correct influence of child psychologists on children's publishing – how Dad has to be shown arranging the flowers, washing up and baking cakes in an apron, Mum, in track suit, as a miracle at mending Hoovers and changing tyres – for people to know what I am talking about.

What is most depressing is the unrelentingness of the propaganda. Perhaps all these causes being espoused are worthy ones – anti-racism, acceptance of homosexual situations as normal, deliberate blurring of sexual roles – although I am not sure. The suggestion that children can only 'relate' to economic and social circumstances with which they are familiar is obviously false. The purpose of all literature is to stimulate the imagination. By showing them nothing but working-class single-parent families you do no service whatever to that proportion of the population which lives in those circumstances. I suppose it might stimulate the imagination in middle-class, secure, well-married families a bit, but that is scarcely the purpose of the exercise. The point I am trying to emphasize is that all this unrelenting propaganda directed towards making us unselfish, socially adjusted, good citizens has had precisely the opposite effect. We are nastier than ever. I wish some underground children's publisher would start producing books showing cruelty, terror, malice, horrible animals and evil humans, kings, queens, millionaires, murderers ... all the things children are really interested in.

LITERARY REVIEW, FEBRUARY 1993

Joe Public is Not Worth the Trouble to Please

Guidelines sent to all six hundred churches in the Lichfield diocese draw attention to the traditional form of church noticeboards, described by the diocesan authorities as 'prime advertising sites': 'Words like matins are mumbo-jumbo to most people. Joe Public needs to understand what the noticeboard is saying.'

Clergymen have also been told not to put letters after their names – DD, MA, etc. – on the grounds that these qualifications are of interest to no one and merely help to feed their own egos. As the Venerable Dennis Ede, Archdeacon of Stoke-on-Trent and main author of the guidelines, put it: 'Academic qualifications have nothing to do with the priesthood and might cause people who do not have them to feel inferior.'

There was a time, as others have pointed out, when people might have been proud that their parish priest was a scholar as well as being capable of performing the divine office and ministering spiritually to his flock. Now we must beware in case Joe Public is made to feel inferior by not having such qualifications himself.

It would be easy to conclude from this that what Joe Public needs is not so much a specially simple form of address attuned to his ignorance and sensitivities as a kick up what the *Sun* delights to call his anus horribilis. The English word 'matins' has been in use to describe a particular morning service since the thirteenth century, and to describe the exact service it now describes since the sixteenth. If Joe Public does not know what the word means, that can only be because he has no interest in the subject. How on earth does Archdeacon Ede suppose that Joe Public will cope with words like Eucharist?

But of course there is no such person as Joe Public. He is an abstraction. Every participating member of the Church of England knows perfectly well what is meant by matins. What the archdeacon is really saying is everyone must be treated as an abstraction, dragged down to the same level of ignorance as the most ignorant people in the country. By changing the name of the service to 'Ten o'clock Ding-Dong', or whatever, he will not be adding to the clarity of the Church's message or broadening its appeal – if anything, he will probably reduce its appeal by antagonizing a proportion of its existing members.

The only effect of the archdeacon's initiative – he is Chairman of Communications in his diocese – will be to make one further contribution to the *trahison des clercs* which, in our time, takes the form of an abject surrender by the educated classes to the forces of illiteracy and ignorance. The greatest popular journalists, like Sir William Connor ('Cassandra' of the *Daily Mirror*) and Keith Waterhouse of the *Daily Mail*, have never written down to their readers. They sprinkle their writing from time to time with unusual and beautiful words, just as Beatrix Potter will suddenly introduce a word like 'soporific' in the hope that children are sufficiently interested to ask what it means and learn something as a result.

This acceptance of minimalist English by the Church, as well as by the tabloid press, may be seen as a gesture of despair: the humane, liberal bourgeois society in which we grew up has had its day; a newly-enriched proletariat, just beginning to flex its muscles in the market, is never going to allow itself to be educated again. I do not think it necessarily means that we are heading for the brutal, vindictive proletarian society we see conjured up every day in the *Sun*, where careless drivers will be locked up for ten years, child murderers beaten up in prison every day for the rest of their lives. It may not even mean the end of pluralizing – few societies could be more pluralistic than the United States, where the average vocabulary (unless you count words like POW! and OOFF!) is eight hundred words, of which Joe Public can usually spell about two hundred and fifty.

Nevertheless, I feel we should regret this surrender. It would have been a wonderful thing – and not just for writers or editors of minority-interest literary magazines – if we could have kept to the ideal of a literate population rejoicing in the language which is our greatest gift to the human race. The archdeacon's crime is to seem to welcome this reduction, to hasten its progress, like the accursed Moloch of Wapping to whom Mrs Thatcher has sacrificed our future and the future of our children, as well as our monarchy and our beautiful class system which was once the glory and the envy of the world. If the archdeacon is guilty of what I accuse him, I feel he should be forbidden to utter again until he has read and passed an examination in the Venerable Bede's *Ecclesiastical History of the English People.*

LITERARY REVIEW, JUNE 1993

Good News or Bad: These Publishers Will Die

A great row started by the TV presenter Martyn Lewis, angrily rebutted by Polly Toynbee, the BBC's dreaded 'social affairs' editor, and by Peter Sissons, has been convulsing the BBC. The issue is whether undue emphasis is given to bad news, and how we can identify the good from the bad.

It was good news when Robert Harris made a small fortune with his best-seller *Fatherland* after it had been favourably reviewed in this magazine, but what are we to make of the news that David Mason, a new writer, has made nearly £1 million from his first novel, a thriller about the assassination of Saddam Hussein, before it has been published, let alone reviewed?

Mason's success, at the time of writing, rests upon a publisher's gamble. While we may rejoice with any author who manages to squeeze a decent sum out of Bloomsbury, it is bad news to see another publisher succumb to this doomed emphasis on best sellers. It is a relic of the get-rich-quick ethos of the 1980s, and it is doomed because in their frenetic search for jam these publishers are not looking after their bread and butter.

Some may have noticed that more and more books reviewed in these pages come from small, specialist or academic publishers, although it is certainly not the result of any editorial policy on my part. The explanation is that among the greatly reduced output from the mainstream publishers, fewer and fewer books are worth reviewing. Even when they produce worthwhile books, they seldom send them for review in time. Now one mainstream publisher has announced that it will no longer supply finished, bound copies for review. When I tell my reviewers that they will receive only the scrappy, uncorrected sheet proofs from which to work, I doubt whether many of them will choose to review another book from this particular publisher. Yet the readers of this magazine alone, each averaging a stupendous thirty-five hardback purchases a year, could easily keep the entire firm in Twiglets and undrinkable white wine for the rest of its miserable (and probably short) life.

Whatever moves our reviewers to write for this magazine, it certainly isn't money. If one looks at the reviewers in this issue alone, one sees many names of extremely distinguished writers who can and do write elsewhere for enormous sums: John Mortimer, Dirk Bogarde, Lynn Barber, Wallace Arnold... Next month I hope we shall be able to show David Attenborough on pandas and Norman Lewis on the war in Italy in 1942–5. Others are well paid and esteemed members of a profession which does not always look kindly on bad payers: Matthew Parris, Martyn Harris, Edward Pearce, Hugh Massingberd, Henry Porter... I could go through the entire list of reviewers, attributing motives to each: some might enjoy practising a skill, others are happy to exercise a greater freedom of expression than might be allowed elsewhere. Some, young and struggling, are in desperate need of money, but even they are not deterred by the rates we pay. The only thing they all have in common (apart from something to say and an ability to express themselves) is a benevolence towards English literature and towards the human race which translates into the kindness and effort required to get their copy to Beak Street on time.

Our rates of pay will remain contemptible for as long as publishers refuse to advertise in the *Literary Review*, preferring to spend their entire budgets pushing trashy 'best sellers' in trashy newspapers. But it is not only the *Literary Review* which will disappear if this get-rich-quick policy is pursued. So will the entire supporting structure of British publishing. It will be reduced to a few flashy men and women sitting in a few flashy offices making ever more unrealistic bids to each other over the telephone. Never mind about the disappearance of English literature. No serious publisher gives a fig for that. It is the publishing houses themselves that will disappear, the office parties, the romances, the lovely Circes and sensitive young editors called Julian. Only the chairperson will be left talking to himself on the telephone.

LITERARY REVIEW, JULY 1993

At Last, We Have a Proper Sermon

Shortly after the collapse of socialism and the disintegration of the Soviet Union, this magazine was asked to support a Books for Russia campaign organized, as I remember, by Waterstone's. I was happy to do so through this column, and it was with some excitement that my eye fell on a new press handout from the Book Trust announcing Books for Balmoral.

It has long been a source of complaint in the literary world that the one branch of the arts at which this country has always excelled should receive so very little encouragement from the Fount of all Honour in our society. Even the Prince of Wales, having declined for three years running to present the magnificent prize at our annual £5,000 Grand Poetry Award, sponsored by the *Mail on Sunday*, must now sadly resign himself to the fact that he will never be asked again. The idea that we should all empty our houses of their unwanted books and send them to Balmoral seemed rather a drastic remedy, however.

In fact Books for Balmoral turns out to be an agreeably goofy scheme, financed by the Book Trust itself. A committee, made up of the ubiquitous Martyn Goff, the beautiful and gifted Valerie Grove (of *The Times*, the *Oldie* and the *Literary Review*), John Coldstream (handsome, strong and wise, of the *Telegraph*) and a Chelsea bookseller, chooses a list of thirty books for the Balmoral summer reading and then presents it, no doubt on bended knee, as one might present a sturgeon or other large fish if one were a fisherman.

So at least I need not ask the *Literary Review* readers to put their hands in their pockets for this scheme. All my memory of church and sermons from the earliest years – in the ill-favoured small industrial town of Dursley, Gloucestershire, home of Lister diesel engines – is of demands for money from the pulpit, usually delivered straight at my unfortunate father as the only rich man in the congregation, by an Irish priest called Father Murtough. I hope readers will forgive me if on this occasion I take a leaf from Father Murtough's book.

At the end of a memorable sermon just after the war, demanding money for a new harmonium or something of the sort, Father Murtough fixed the Waugh family with a terrible stare and said that if the money was not going to come from his parishioners, he would be forced to go to the Jews for it. I suppose this was his disagreeable way of saying that he would have to ask the manager of his local Barclays Bank for a loan, but the threat created quite an impression on my young mind, unattuned, at that stage, to the horrors of racism and ethnic prejudice. The only equivalent threat which occurs to me – that if the magazine does not find some new sponsors, I shall be forced to go to the Arts Council for it – has unfortunately been pre-empted. Much against my wishes, an approach was made to the Arts Council last year for help to launch a circulation drive. The response of that worthless, idle body was to send dozens of pages of forms with instructions on how to fill them in (knowing they would take endless hours to complete) and then refuse to help in any way. Our position is that we lose about £120,000 a year, all of it borne by one man, our saintly benefactor, Naim Attallah. No literary magazine in the history of the world has ever failed to lose money.

In fact, I launched [an appeal] a few weeks ago in the *Spectator*, reckoning that their readers might be richer than ours. It produced various helpful suggestions for people to whom I might apply, but no offers of help. We have one philanthropist prepared to chip in if two others do so, and I am awaiting replies from various people whose names were suggested. But the truth is that although these are hard times for some, the country is still swimming in corporate money. Wherever the *LR's* money goes, it certainly does not go on wages (which are Spartan), nor on contributors' fees (which are a disgrace), nor on entertaining expenses (which are non-existent).

The *Literary Review* is a lovely little corner of our contemporary scene, but it can't survive without help. If any captain of industry, or chairman of some important company, thinks his or her enterprise may be able to help, I promise to treat the approach in the greatest confidence. Second best would be to push some advertising our way. We have the capacity for full colour on every page, but, alas, we seldom seem to be asked for it. Third best – but by no means to be despised – would be further suggestions for people to whom I might write. Everything will be treated with tomb-like discretion.

LITERARY REVIEW, AUGUST 1993
Let Us Have Some More Literary Prizes

Sir William Golding's death in June at the age of eighty-one was adequately remarked by the nation's obituarists, who are taking over from novelists and travel writers as the best current practitioners of writing in English. He will not be much missed on the London literary scene, because he had the good sense to avoid it throughout his literary life, emerging from the privacy of the West Country only to receive honours and awards in London. But he should be remembered by the world of letters as possibly the last Englishman prepared to act out the part of the Great Writer, with his straggly grey beard and wispy hair, his general appearance of the Ancient Mariner and his refusal to join public causes or draw attention to himself by anything except his writing.

It might be said that he was extravagantly rewarded for this performance but I do not wish to be drawn into the argument. People must decide for themselves whether he was any good. Those who knew him, loved him. His greatest achievement in the recognition stakes was not that he was knighted in 1988, received the curious accolade of CLit in 1984, the James Tait Black Memorial Prize in 1980, the Booker Prize in 1980 or the CBE in 1966. It is that he was chosen as the only British writer born this century to win the Nobel Prize for Literature – in 1983.

On the principle that it was Buggins's turn for a Briton to win the Nobel, this award could only be seen as a deliberate insult to Graham Greene, a senior writer who towered over Golding as Golding towered over Enid Blyton. Among literary politicians of the time, it was said that the dim and humourless Swedes who form the Nobel Committee included a particularly dim, humourless and wrong-headed Swede who had made it his life's ambition to insult Mr Greene in this way. I do not know. Nor do I think we can reasonably blame Mr Golding (as he then was) for accepting it. Even the greatest writers can be excused for not turning up their noses at a tax-free £125,000 (or whatever the Nobel was then worth). But this disgraceful incident might well contribute to the belief which seems to be growing among novel-readers in particular, that literary prizes do nothing but harm.

I think I would dispute it. Although there is certainly a case for arguing that the Booker Prize has done nothing but harm – it has chosen too many duds and disappointed too many expectations – this is largely the result of its predominance in the field. If less publicity attended its dingy selections, it would be entirely benign in its operation, representing no more than a lucky windfall for whatever novelist came out on top. Nobody can possibly claim that the *Sunday Express* Book Prize – rather more valuable, in most years, than the Booker – has done any harm, or caused anything but pleasure. The same is true of the Whitbread. I do not think that our own £5,000 annual Grand Poetry Prize, sponsored by the *Mail on Sunday*, has done anything but good by helping to keep alive the tradition of formal poetry at a time when the neo-modernist barbarians control every other source of patronage.

In fact I would advance in defence of prizes for novels that they sometimes do good even beyond the windfalls they represent for novelists. When this year's Hawthornden Committee chose Andrew Barrow's *The Tapdancer* (Duckworth) for this year's prize, the book was little known. It is unusual, old-fashioned and very funny. The more people who read it the happier the country will be. No doubt some people feel the same about Ben Okri's *The Famished Road* (Jonathan Cape, 1991).

My conclusion is that the more literary prizes the merrier, but it also occurs to me that novelists already receive as much encouragement as they can reasonably expect in a country where practically nobody wishes to read their novels. What they also need is a little admonishment and guidance. Many novels are ruined by bad sex scenes – perfunctorily introduced, charmlessly described. My purpose in instituting the *Literary Review* Bad Sex Prize, to be announced next month, will not be to reward tasteless or unskilful writing, but to discourage it. If the author chooses to turn up for the prize-giving, he or she will be given some appropriate token, probably a piece of modern sculpture devised by Professor R. M. Posner [the magazine's business manager, see page 180] representing Sexual Intercourse in the 1950s. But the main prize will go to the reader (or reviewer) who sends in the most remarkable example of bad sexual description taken from any novel published this year. Details to be announced next month, when the prize will be launched on the literary scene.

On the Baseness and Ingratitude of Poets

When the Academy was first proposed as an inexpensive club of vaguely literary associations to occupy the ground floor and basement of the *Literary Review*'s offices in Beak Street, earnest discussions followed about the sort of person we should let into it.

It has been said that the purpose of forming a club is as much to exclude the Wrong Sort of Person as it is to provide a haven for Our Sort, the Right Sort. I do not think anybody involved had snobbish motives or exclusive intentions, but it is true that one or two seriously unpleasant members can ruin an entire club, and our purpose was to add to the sensual enjoyment and spiritual happiness of members, rather than create a new area of dejection. Various inappropriate suggestions were made – that we should exclude all male Americans, all lawyers, all architects, all Welshmen, all men in jeans and women in power suits with padded shoulders.

All of these exclusions seemed objectionable, exceptions could be found in every case. When it fell to me to draw up a draft Constitution and set of rules, only one exclusion remained, but that was absolute: under no circumstances would any poet be considered for membership, nor would members be permitted to bring poets onto the premises as their guests.

In the country which produced William Shakespeare, such a prohibition may seem incomprehensible. John Betjeman, too, was a lovely man: funny, wise, affectionate, kind and infinitely poignant. The trouble with Shakespeare and Betjeman is that they are both dead, as are all the other poets we can think of.

But that is not really the point. Just as the nature of what is called poetry has changed, so a different sort of person has stepped forward to satisfy the demand. It was – and remains – my experience of life that anybody who describes his vocation as poet, purveying the modern style of formless verse, is invariably among the meanest and most despicable in the land: vain, empty, conceited, dishonest, dirty, often flea-ridden and infected by venereal disease, greedy, parasitical, drunken, untruthful, arrogant ... all these repulsive qualities, and also irresistibly attractive to women. We certainly did not want them in the Academy.

So the rule that no 'poets' should be admitted was promulgated and remains in the Constitution of the club along with such sensible injunctions that shoes must be worn. As the Grand Poetry Prize went from strength to strength, it occurred to me that we were being too strict. Should we also exclude from our society those amiable ladies and gentlemen whose poems rhymed, scanned and made sense with sufficient skill to find a place in the magazine? It seemed unlikely that they would be as base, or as able to attract the women, as the bogus poets.

I should have been warned. About once every three or four months I receive a letter from one or another of these poets complaining about a misprint, a word changed or line left out which makes nonsense of their poem. My inclination is to be only fairly sympathetic, partly because of the querulous tone which so many of them adopt, partly because their poems are seldom more than fairly good, and I think it may be salutary to have them accidentally reduced to nonsense in this way, just as it is good for the immortal soul of a man wearing Gucci shoes if he steps in a dog mess on the pavement.

It is said that there are fourteen misprints and errors of arrangement in the new *Literary Review* anthology, *A Burning Candle*, edited by Dariane Pictet (Poetry Now, 1993). In a volume of over a hundred poems by sixty-six poets, I feel that is not bad at all. They rather add to its charm, challenging readers to stay on their toes and spot the mistakes.

Most hilarious of all these errors (although I was too polite to say so when the poet wrote a pompous letter of complaint) concerned a bad poem on John Betjeman which had lost twenty-two lines. Since poems are theoretically limited to thirty lines, the poet was lucky to be printed at all, but he wrote a second letter: '... is it not an insult, not to say a fraud, on the buying public, for you to proceed with its sale? ... I am baffled that you should be prepared to put your reputation at stake in this way. The loss should be stood by whomever (*sic*) is responsible ... and the present edition quietly pulped and replaced by a proof-read version. Then, and only then, should it be put on the market.'

[An Interview with John Osborne]

The most relentless preacher must abandon his pulpit sometimes to find out what is happening in the world. This week I decided to make a pilgrimage to distant Shropshire to sit at the feet of John Osborne and discuss his new collection of journalism and occasional writings, *Damn You, England* (Faber & Faber, 1994), which I read with as much pleasure as I can remember receiving from any book since the second volume of his autobiography, *Almost a Gentleman* (Faber & Faber, 1991). Another reason for my pilgrimage was to try and persuade him to give us another volume of autobiography.

His new book is particularly admirable and instructive in that it covers the whole range of his spiritual odyssey since 1957, from 'We socialists are not going to achieve anything by being polite', to the present time. Thus, in 1961, he was pleased to describe the monarchy as 'the gold-filling in a mouthful of decay'. Thirty-three years later, he writes in the *Spectator*:

> I can only cry: God Save the Queen and confusion to her enemies, for they are mine, too. May God rot the tyrannies of equality, stream-lining, updating; the deranged dreams of chimerical classlessness and most of all, absurd, irrelevant relevance. And God help the Prince of Wales.

My plan had been not so much to interview this magnificent, plain-spoken man as to hold a general conversation with him (what I called a *conversazione*, knowing his penchant for foreign words), in which we could discuss his book and the way the world was going generally. It was not even a dialogue I had in mind so much as a *koinonia*, rather as the Greek poet Callimachus claimed to have held with the philosopher Heraclitus when they tired the sun with talking and sent him down the sky.

I have always been puzzled to know how they achieved this, as Heraclitus died about two hundred years before Callimachus was born. Different impediments to the marriage of true minds emerged in my *conversazione* with Osborne.

My welcome could not have been kinder. The ogre of an Angry Young Man, now more often portrayed as some heartless, reactionary, squirearchical Blimp, seemed scarcely able to contain the warmth and benevolence that flowed out of him. Perhaps it was too much to hope that we would awaken the nightingales on a first meeting. It could be that our anxiety to agree with each other was also a trifle self-defeating. Another problem may have been that we are both a little deaf, and Osborne was suffering from a temporary speech defect as the result of a huge dental programme at enormous cost. Both of us suffer from bad memories for names, and words, and events.

But we admitted none of these impediments. In welcoming me to Shropshire, Osborne mentioned various mutual friends who had settled in the Ludlow area, including Pat Kavanagh, my agent at A. D. Peters for about thirty years. I expressed surprise at this.

'You mean to say she comes down here at weekends with her nice young husband – you know, Julian, Julian…'

'Bristol?'

'No, Barnes, the novelist Julian Barnes?'

'Yes, that's right, absolutely, Julian Barnes.'

We proceeded to discuss their personal life at some length, at the end of which we were joined by Osborne's fifth wife, Helen – clever, easy-going, humorous Helen Dawson, the former arts editor at the *Observer* – who said, no, it was not Pat Kavanagh who had moved into the neighbourhood, it was Deborah Rogers, an equally distinguished literary agent, with her gifted young husband, the composer Michael Berkeley.

'Yes, that's absolutely right,' said Osborne, whom I was now beginning to think of as 'John'. 'Deborah Rogers.' He seemed full of enthusiasm for this new woman in the neighbourhood.

Osborne's first break came when the late Kenneth Tynan reviewed *Look Back in Anger* in the *Observer*. 'I doubt if I could love someone who did not wish to see *Look Back in Anger*,' he wrote. Oddly enough, in 1956, quite a lot of people wanted to be loved by Kenneth Tynan. Thirty-five years later, Osborne writes about 'Clarence Peacock Tynan' at the National Theatre:

> His confrontational method of promoting dubious one-sex productions of Shakespeare, worthless offerings of agit-prop like *Soldiers* (by Rolf Hochhuth) or *Tyger* (by Adrian Mitchell and Mike Westbrook) or his foreign obsessions and flights of fancy with fork-lifts and phalluses, was a model of radical crassness and ineptitude.

My point in drawing attention to this apparent anomaly is not to suggest that John is an ungrateful beast, merely to point out that all along he has nearly always been absolutely right. Tynan was an abominable fraud. *Look Back in Anger* is a thoroughly good play. Perhaps critical fashion will eventually catch up with the fact that its chief drive is humorous, that Osborne is essentially a funny fellow with passions, rather than an embittered revolutionary. He was right to attack the Tories for their unreliability and philistinism and greed (to which catalogue I would add cowardice) and he is right now to identify the pursuit of power as the chief motivation on the Left, the chief destructive force in our culture. In fact, he has been pretty well right all along.

'I don't think I'm a reactionary. I think I'm exactly the same as I was when I was seventeen,' he explains, in a sudden burst of self-approval.

'A rebel,' suggests Helen helpfully.

'Absolutely. Quite right,' we all say.

Many of his anxieties settle on the false image of English life given by the press and television:

JO: English life seems to me to be played out in the provinces. Most people who write and appear on television programmes have nothing to do with it at all.

AW: This may be true, but you can't say there is such a thing as English life rather than 50 million English lives. There is no such thing as an English life to generalize about. Can you think of any particular moment when people decided you were politically incorrect?

JO: I remember exactly. A play called *Hotel in Amsterdam* in 1968. They all objected because the characters in it are professional and fairly rich and successful. They said ah-ha, he's not writing about people on building sites. The whole thing about class is absolutely ludicrous. I've never had any particular trouble.

AW: The truth is that you have been a celebrity since an early age and we both live at the comfortable end of the class system. We can't get away from that, but what interests me is that the pace is now being set by a new class of people, quite philistine and quite aggressive, who are suddenly richer than they have ever been before. They are setting the cultural and political agenda of the country, and the tone of political debate.

JO: They are absolutely intransigent. Quite unchangeable, I am afraid.

AW: Do you ever see the *Sun*?

JO: Quite honestly, I think I've only read it once. Really, I'm not being affected, but no.

Why should Mr Osborne ever read the *Sun*? It is abominable to think he should. Approaching sixty-five, he is a friendly, fulfilled private citizen, with a better sense of humour than most, and a particular talent for writing.

A final obstacle to our conversation about his book was that he had not actually read it. The book was put together by Helen and an editor at Faber & Faber.

AW: I find it very grand and admirable that you haven't actually read the book. Is it idleness or ...

JO: No, it isn't just idleness, em ...

AW: Embarrassment?

JO: Yes.

AW: Can you see a certain grandeur and nobility in not exercising any control over what they chose?

JO: Yes. I haven't even read the proof.

Helen: You never read the proof of anything. They were hanging around the house, darling.

JO: I'm not complaining, my sweetheart, you know, I...

Sometime before, on the subject of class, Osborne mentioned an earlier difficulty: 'Until I was about thirty, I really did think there were two kinds of language, the one you wrote or read and the one you spoke. I was very uneasy and inarticulate in company. I couldn't put a sentence together, as I could when I was writing something. It took me a long time to overcome. Even using certain words, I used to think that wasn't a word you used in company.'

Despite the charm and warmth of his company, Osborne is still essentially a writer rather than a verbal communicator on his own behalf. He is also, of course, a dedicated actor. As I left, I asked him whether we were ever going to see a third volume of the autobiography, as I sincerely hoped we would:

'Funny you should say that. I had decided not to do a third volume for all sorts of reasons. And then about a week ago I thought ... perhaps I will after all ...'

[Bron is not being entirely frank, or perhaps he had simply forgotten a thirteen-year-old review he once wrote, and was unaware of placing himself in danger of exposing the opportunistic waywardness of the reviewer's trade. In an article in *Literary Review*, six years before Bron assumed its editorship, Susan Marling put together a round-up of comments from reviews of John Osborne's first volume of autobiography, *A Better Class of Person* (Faber & Faber, 1981). Though she doesn't give the source of it, she quotes from a review 'by Auberon Waugh'. It is not appreciative: 'The worn look of what the second-hand garment trade calls a dead man's overcoat. Worse than this it is dirty and has a distinctly sour smell... Perhaps this unpleasant book should be seen as Mr Osborne's revenge on the world for an unhappy childhood. But it tells us little about Jimmy Porter which we could not have guessed.' Osborne never did write another volume of autobiography, but died on Christmas Eve, 1994.]

LITERARY REVIEW, JUNE 1994

Time for the 'Poets' to Take off their Clothes

One of the more demanding duties of the noble profession to which I belong is that when there is no news for us to report or comment on, we have to invent it. A duck crossing the road will suddenly become the most important event of the week. Another ploy is to use the existence of instant mass communication to create an event and declare it significant. How many of us were aware that last month was ushered in by a national Take Our Daughter to Work Day, sponsored by the Equal Opportunities Commission?

Only slightly less irritating than the promotion of non-events like National Take Your Daughter to the Office Day, is the despairing features editor's ploy of drawing up lists to define who or what is considered smart – 'in', and what is to be thought of as unsmart – 'out'. This convention allows my noble profession unlimited opportunity to reward friends and pay off old scores, but must bore everyone else most terribly.

Probably very few readers of the *Literary Review* still see the *Sunday Times*, but those who do will have been puzzled by the news story about a major poetic revival that appeared at about the same time as National Take Our Daughters to Work Day. '*New generation reclaims poetry*: Not since the Romantics quoted couplets at each other on Hampstead Heath has poetry been quite so fashionable,' began Rebecca Fowler, the newspaper's arts correspondent. I wonder when exactly it was that Romantics quoted couplets at each other on Hampstead Heath? 'A generation of youthful converts has pulled the art form out of its ivory tower and claimed it as the latest cult. The nation's poets ... have suddenly found their works selling in the thousands. They are being invited on to Radio 1 and even to model clothes in fashion magazines.'

And so it continues through about 700 words of tabloid-style hype until the end, where a poet of unrevealed gender, thirty-three-year-old W. N. Herbert, is quoted as saying: 'If you're like a pop star you have to go along with it, and we'll roll over and squeak if we need to. We're good for television, we're good for radio and some of us are even good-looking.'

It is true that *Vogue* had the amusing idea of dressing up some poets in designer clothes to promote their work, and it is true that Radio 1 ran a week of poetry readings, rather as the *Independent* has been providing a regular poetry slot for some time, presumably on the general principle that modem poetry is a good cause. But nothing heard on Radio1, and nothing I have yet seen in the *Independent*, supports the theory of a poetic renaissance. Perhaps it is true that some of these new poets are even good-looking. In that case, I would be happy to publish nude studies of them in the *Literary Review*. But where is the poetry?

I am afraid that this new enthusiasm for poetry among the young, if it exists, has another, sadder explanation: they have lost the ability to communicate in prose. This does not mean, of course, that they have found the ability to communicate in verse, or 'poetry' as they prefer to call it. The fragmented presentation of free verse allows the illusion of making a statement, of receiving a message, which is preferable to the bald admission of an inability to communicate. Few of the generation of semi-literate unemployables created by the new teaching methods can string a proper sentence together. If you ask them what an apostrophe is, they will tell you, after much thought, that it describes the end of the world, whether by ecological collapse or nuclear holocaust. Good subject for a poem, perhaps.

Let them think so, and let them put the word in their little poems if it will make them any happier. Recently, at a conference of the Chester Business Club held at the Moat House International Hotel, the mother of Britain's new education system, Shirley Williams, now sixty-three years old and called Baroness Williams of Crosby, was described as 'weeping'. The *Chester Herald and Post* reported her as saying: 'I weep for the problems of our youngsters who we must educate more highly.' Some of us might have preferred to say 'whom we must educate to a higher standard', but Lady Williams continued:

> We must never let our heritage slip away because that is the greatest thing we can bring to bear. That contribution could transform our sense of what the twenty-first century could be like.

Lady Williams is not an evil or a wicked woman, although the damage she has done is enormous, but for their intelligence, inner logic and felicity of expression those three sentences are fit only to be read on Radio 1 or printed in the *Independent* as an example of the new renaissance in modern poetry.

Literary Review, July 1994
Perils of Talking to the Press

There is no dignity, let alone grandeur, in the English world of letters. Some may regret this, thinking we should honour our great writers as the French have done by naming streets and squares after them, particularly since it is only in its language and literature that the English culture has ever excelled. But there is much to be said against revering writers in their own lifetime. A dreadful pomposity is liable to take over those who think they are taken seriously.

However, one or two British authors continue to live their lives as if theirs was a respectable and honourable profession of which they might reasonably be proud. Prominent among them for the last forty years has been V. S. Naipaul, who, according to the *Sunday Times*, is 'often cited as Britain's finest living writer'. Throughout his life he has seldom allowed himself to be interviewed and never engaged in any of the self-publicizing stunts which many authors find necessary. The *Daily Telegraph* put it tartly that he was 'notorious for his impatience, peevishness and intellectual arrogance'.

Perhaps it was to escape from this image that he decided to submit to an extended three-day interview with the *New Yorker*. As he put it, 'People think that one is a very serious, dour, gloomy man, but one is full of humour.' I have some advice for him. There are three cardinal rules for being interviewed: do not discuss your sex life; do not discuss your earnings; and avoid use of the impersonal third person. One always looks a fool.

In fact, Naipaul scarcely mentioned his sex life in the course of the long interview. But what he said was enough to swamp all coverage of the event – how he once developed 'a kind of tremendous sexual *soif*, very unfulfilled' and became 'a great prostitute man', although he was also kind enough to pass on the benefit of his experience that this was the most unsatisfactory form of sex. 'Terrible. There's nothing in it. It's nothing. It's worthless.'

Despite a reduction of his libido – 'With age, women have sunk in my esteem ... One has lost this excitement about women' – he reveals the existence of an Anglo-Argentinian mistress, married with three children, ten years his junior and several inches higher, who came into his life in the 1970s:

> I feel that a lot of my creative energy has come from that. I'm most grateful. Yes, I'm delighted to have had it. It would have been terrible to have died before that.

I do not enquire about the effect of Naipaul's revelations on his wife, Pat, because it seems to me that it is none of my – our – business. But then I would not have expected to be told about Vidia Naipaul's sex life, as it seems to have slipped out on this occasion. It is the sort of thing we may gossip about behind a friend's back, but not the sort of thing we expect to be handed on a plate. Perhaps I am wrong: understanding and appreciation of an artist may indeed require knowledge of his or her sex life. We like to know these things about people we admire.

In that case, Naipaul, far from succumbing to some regrettable, quasi-senile urge to expose himself, is performing a public service, helping to explain (or 'explicate', as they say) his work to generations of

English-literature students yet unborn. I do not know. The whole relationship between sex and literature – or sex and anything for that matter – is bedevilled by neuroses, compunctions, prejudices. In this magazine we have a long tradition, dating from before my editorship, of glancing occasionally towards the darker corners and the dirtier shores of the human imagination, but I have noticed increasing sales resistance on the part of the punters. An excellent piece by Tony Parsons on Johnny Rotten and the Sex Pistols in particular seems to have excited a large number of peevish letters, mostly from abroad.

I don't care. Sex provides a dimension in most people's lives, even if it is only a small one, and a large one in many people's imaginations. I would no sooner ban it from the magazine than I would ban all mention of politics, which many would prefer to see banned. For next month, Fiona Pitt-Kethley has suggested she might provide a round-up of recent spanking books. What editor could possibly refuse such an offer?

Meanwhile, we have our sop to the anti-sex faction in our annual Bad Sex Prize of £100 for the reader who sends in an excerpt from any novel published in England this year (since August 1993) which, in the opinion of the judges, provides the worst (most ham-fisted, otiose, coy, mind-blowingly awful) description of the sex act. The prize is presented at a joyous ceremony at the Academy, Beak Street, in December, but it is time people started sending in entries, marked 'Bad Sex', to this address. Preference is given to literary novels, so will all reviewers as well as novel readers everywhere bear in mind that there is £100 to be picked up as they wade their way through the autumn fiction. Our purpose in this enterprise is the salutary one of discouraging novelists from making fools of themselves.

LITERARY REVIEW, AUGUST 1994
A Small Speck in the Ever Widening Atlantic

As the European and American cultures slowly drift apart into a state of mutual and impenetrable incomprehension, perhaps the English are in the best position to understand that what divides us finally is not a matter of taste – as between hamburgers and soft drinks on the other side of the herring pond and hamburgers and soft drinks on this side – but of moral perception. We mock the idea of political correctness and point to its more extreme expressions in order to joke and laugh at them, but what we seem reluctant to accept is that the United States is evolving a system of morality which is completely alien to our own, much stricter in many respects, and uniquely attuned to the exigencies of an unequal, multiracial society struggling to avoid anarchy, riot and terror.

The differences are sharpest among the intelligentsia, or what passes for the intelligentsia, on both sides. Capital punishment, which most intelligent Europeans now find abhorrent, is accepted without question by a majority of intelligent Americans. Murder, which Europeans find deeply shocking, is more or less accepted by Americans as part of the price they have to pay for living in an unequal, not to say multiracial, society. Capital punishment and the ownership of firearms are necessary to defend the extremes of inequality which a classless, incentive-driven economy requires. But there is always the danger of riot, not to say revolution, and it is for this reason that a system of morality must be constructed to sustain the democratic myth; anything that smacks of racial, or class, or sexual, prejudice becomes much more wicked and worrying than an individual act of violence. This last is contained within the system. Riot, revolution or social breakdown can never be.

American television – the truest expression of whatever fantasy survives in that culture – allows violent death, whether falling from a high building, being shot or burning to death in a car crash after a chase, as a normal expression of social disapproval. By the same token, other crimes, financial dishonesty or even corner-cutting, are taken much more seriously, justifying whatever hideous end may be in store for the baddie concerned.

This tendency was particularly noticeable in discussions about the apparent suicide of Vincent Foster, the White House aide, Arkansas attorney and reputed lover of Mrs Clinton. American opinion was resolutely uninterested in the manner of his death, interested only in the light it might throw on Mrs Clinton's commercial activities. No European could give a hoot on this point. We all assume that politicians are in it for the money, and they will all cut corners. What is surprising about the Fiske investigation is not that he should have decided that Foster did, indeed, commit suicide, driven to it by criticism of his job performance in the *Wall Street Journal*, but that Americans should be so little interested in more lurid possibilities.

Even Mr Fiske's explanation, unlikely as it may seem to us, opens up another huge difference between American culture and ours: they take their newspapers with great seriousness and are tremendously sensitive to criticism. Those who followed the brief career of Lynn Barber, this country's foremost practitioner of the journalistic interview, when she was taken on by *Vanity Fair* will have learned how her mildly humorous style was too much for the celebrities to bear. Whether or not there were threats to withdraw advertising, celebrities first demanded total control over the interview, then refused to be interviewed at all. The magazine dropped her.

British journalists, not easily shocked, would be shocked by that story. We do not expect much, but we expect to be free from commercial censorship, whether from advertisers' pressure or vetting by public-relations advisers. American journalism, which takes this like a lamb, is equally shocked by the cliquishness of English journalism, its readiness to accept hospitality, its readiness to bite the hand that feeds it, its readiness to print information as fact without official confirmation...

On the ethics of book-reviewing, I tend to feel that enough newspapers and magazines print reviews for a balance to be achieved. If all reviewers adopted a godlike attitude of fair-mindedness, literary criticism would be unreadable. But then American and British attitudes to the printed word are so different that I fear it may soon be dangerous for us to communicate with each other by this means. Since we are so different, and since both our cultures must be, to some considerable extent, the product of choice and free will, it might seem odious to discuss which is the better approach. Our ethics have practically nothing in common, but if Truth is the guiding principle, we might agree that more Truth is distorted by the European system – for which the British press undoubtedly sets the tone – and more is suppressed by the American system. The bad moment comes with both systems when people cease to care where the Truth really lies.

On Two Immortal Prizes: Bad Sex and Good Poetry

In July I reminded readers of our second Bad Sex Prize for fiction, but rather haphazardly, as if we all knew about it and only needed reminding. The magazine has already received a few entries, but not nearly enough to justify the amount of promotion I propose to give it this year. Other magazines wage great campaigns against massage parlours, or the neglect of pet animals on holiday, or the satanic abuse of children, but this Bad Sex Prize marks our only serious attempt to improve things or make the world a better place. Under the circumstances, I feel I should increase the prize to £250. But first I will spell it out again.

The literary novel is not flourishing, chiefly because not many people want to read it. One reason not many people want to read it is because, in many cases, it isn't much good. One reason why it isn't much good is that the wretched novelist, whether under pressure from his publisher or following some ill thought-out perception of commercial advantage on his own behalf, feels bound to include redundant passages of sexual description in his story. This is thought, quite wrongly, to give it sex appeal.

I use the masculine pronoun advisedly, because men are generally the worst offenders. There are some pretty bad examples of female writers rolling out the purple paint, but at least they seem to be trying to make the sex act an important part of the story. Nothing I have to say about sex in the modern novel should be taken as disparaging the avowedly erotic novel, although even there it is the preamble which creates sexual tension and usually has the most powerful effect. What I am concerned with is the perfunctory, embarrassed description of an act between two people who are almost certainly not much good at it, generally included out of some misguided sense of duty. These passages upset the flow of the narrative, add nothing to the development of character and generally create an awkward atmosphere. At one time beatnik writers would happily describe how they went to the lavatory. While it was a new idea it might have worked, creating a jocular impression of frankness, but there is all the difference in the world between frankness and the sort of pseudo-poetic biology that passes for sex description today.

Our purpose is to shame novelists into dropping this tiresome convention. It is not a particularly ambitious programme, I hope as many readers as possible will join in. What we need are quotable passages, preferably not more than four hundred words, taken from any English novel published this year – that is to say, since the end of August 1993 – which illustrate this Bad Sex tendency. They can be photocopied or copied out, giving the title of the book, the author, publisher and page reference. September is the great month for fiction. I want everyone – novel reviewers as well as ordinary readers – to bear it in mind that there is £250 to be won if your choice is judged the best one. In the event of more than one person sending in the same passage, the money will go to the first opened, and a bottle of champagne to the others...

LITERARY REVIEW, OCTOBER 1994
How the Bad Drives Out the Good

Many writers will have identified with the unfortunate author in Devon, Mr Hinton Sheryn, forty-seven, who, having heard that his book had been accepted by the publishers with an advance of £500, ran out into the road and kissed the first young woman he met. Unfortunately, the young woman concerned, Miss Claire Stacey, twenty-three, unemployed, was not amused. She reported him to the police and he was fined £500 with £45 costs by Bideford magistrates.

History does not relate how long Sheryn had spent on his book, *The Illustrated History of Excavators*, but it sounds the sort of subject which requires extensive research. It is the casual equation, in commercial terms, between perhaps eighteen months' or two years' work on a book and a stolen kiss from a twenty-three-year-old who said she was 'shocked, humiliated and insulted' that many authors will find depressing. Of course, Sheryn might have done worse. If he had kissed the visually challenged forty-year-old Rena Weeks, a former legal secretary, in San Francisco, he might have had to pay $7.1 million, which is the sum Weeks received after alleging that a senior partner in her legal firm had groped her breast. 'I've got my rights, my civil rights,' explained Weeks.

Few British authors could afford Rena Weeks's civil rights. Even Lord Archer might pause. Perhaps the message of the times is that poor authors should kiss no one, not even their wives, since under the new guidelines on marital rape there is no presumption of consent to sexual intercourse in marriage; nor, *mutatis mutandis*, can there be any presumption of consent to being kissed (aka common assault).

None of which should be taken to imply that just because kisses (or gropes) are overvalued, books are undervalued. The sum of £500 seems just about right for an illustrated history of excavators, and rather too much for many of the novels which are still being published, despite a flat refusal by the public to buy them. Nobody who has had to read 130 of this year's novels, as the saintly Professor John Bayley, chairman of this year's Booker Prize jury, has done, can be denied the right to say they are pretty dreadful. They tend to be humourlessly written without any apparent desire to please the readers by telling them a story, by tickling their imagination or generally diverting them from the tedious course of their everyday lives. The only apparent motive among novelists would seem to be a desire to expose themselves.

The novel could nevertheless survive as a minority enthusiasm if literary publishers and the literary-prize industry would allow it to do so. A print run of 1,200 in hardback (for libraries, etc.) and 2,000–3,000 in paperback for novels reviewed and advertised in the intelligent weeklies and literary magazines would keep just as many people employed in the publishing profession as the present mad rush for bestsellers, half of which lose gigantic sums. It would also discourage novelists from this sick desire to be thought important or significant. There are enough intelligent people with a sense of humour and an appetite for diversion to support a fiction industry, and the chances are that it will grow as the universities churn out more English graduates. This market is largely ignored by novelists, publishers and advertisers alike.

Of course, poetry is in a worse state. The saddest aspect of the publishing scene is that there seems to be developing a small but sufficient market of pseuds and halfwits (what the Americans call a campus market) to keep the seventy-year-old Modern Movement on its legs, with generous support from a philistine government. An optimistic poet from Sussex wrote to me recently asking what plans the magazine had to celebrate National Poetry Day on 6 October. This is apparently something funded by the Arts Council in its frenetic struggle to blow on the dead embers of the Modern Movement.

Alas, we have none. The best way for publishers to keep English literature alive is to keep reprinting the masterpieces of the past. Even in this – and even in such excellent publishing houses as Everyman's Library and the Folio Society – they seem bound to spoil the new edition with some redundant introduction by a modem critic or academic, which adds to the cost of the production and can only discourage the potential reader. Recently, the Folio Society sent me the proposed introduction to a new edition of *Brideshead Revisited*, written by a noted critic of the 1960s [the critic and novelist Frederick Raphael]. It was such ignorant, patronizing tripe as would put anyone off the main text. Assuring us in the first sentence that *Brideshead* is Waugh's 'only first-personal novel', it asserted that the book has 'marked affinities with Proust' and went on from there for pages and pages of sneering drivel:

It requires no suggestion that Waugh had read Proust, still less that his novel was derivative from the Frenchman's immeasurably greater achievement, for us to perceive other similarities between the two works...

This poor man has written some sixteen novels, all of them, like mine, more or less forgotten, all of them, also like mine, more or less deservedly so, but we should not encourage the bad to drive out the good in this way.

LITERARY REVIEW, NOVEMBER 1994

Let Us Leave the Teachers Alone

I had proposed to preach a strict and particular sermon this month on the subject of modern English set texts in schools. Under the new plans, English teachers will be required to choose from a list of named authors for all works before 1900, but they have insisted that where the twentieth century is concerned they will have the freedom to choose from any 'critically acclaimed' modern writers. In a newspaper article discussing this development, Jonathan Petre provided two possible lists of twelve authors. One, labelled 'traditionalist', came from Professor Arthur Pollard, formerly of Hull University. It started with Kipling and Conrad, took in Bennett and Lawrence, and ended with Paul Scott and V. S. Naipaul. The second list, compiled by John Haddon, head of English at a Derbyshire comprehensive, also took in Lawrence, but that was all they had in common. Among those on Mr Haddon's list were Berlie Doherty, Rosa Guy, Ursula Le Guin and Jan Mark, to name but four.

Leave anything with English teachers, and in my experience you will end up with Sylvia Plath and *Cider with Rosie*. I was about to take a very strict line with Mr Haddon and his list when it occurred to me that whatever else these authors might have in common, I had actually heard of only three out of the twelve, and read work by only two. How could I possibly say they were the wrong choice, let alone denounce them as rubbish from the Pulpit, if I had never read them? The fact that in a lifetime spent searching for good authors I have never heard anyone mention them may suggest to me that they are not much good, but that is insufficient reason for saying that they are rotten, or forbidding them to be shown to children.

In any case, for anyone who is not a teacher to tell teachers what they should do is an impertinence. The stereotype teacher going the rounds, largely fed by union spokespersons, is a committed, proselytizing socialist determined to stifle any sign of intelligence in the young for fear of encouraging elitism, and consumed by a hatred of the former liberal, humane bourgeois society which produced free education with the welfare state. No doubt such stereotypes are to be found, as they are to be found in nursing and other caring professions, journalism and nearly everywhere else. But it is my experience that many of the noblest and kindest and most idealistic people left in Britain are to be found among the teachers. They are in the front line fighting the good fight against everything that threatens our society, from being overwhelmed by the culture of violence, to being smothered by the trashy products of democratic consumerism, to being left, whingeing piteously, on the rocks of the dependency culture when the tide of state affluence has receded. Teachers and police are all we have. None of us has any business to say they should teach Belloc rather than Robert Cormier (whoever he may be), Burgess rather than Frank O'Connor, William Trevor rather than Robert Westall (who he?).

Even if, as Piers Paul Read surmises, the objection to these good authors is ideological, that they are middle-class, I do not think that matters very much. Children are more likely to discover good authors for themselves, not by having them rammed down their throats. I was taught to take Eliot seriously, and Pound, and Christopher Fry, but I haven't wasted a minute on any of that rubbish since leaving school. Love of Shakespeare came much later and was entirely self-taught. We have no business telling teachers what they should teach because we don't have to put up with frightful classroom smells, resentful parents, the whinnying of child psychologists and the insolence of pupils. We should be endlessly grateful to these martyrs, and if they want to teach their charges about Ursula Le Guin, let us hope that doing so makes the teachers, at least, a little happier.

Which rather destroys my original sermon, as planned, about the riches of English literature being denied to these little darlings ...

LITERARY REVIEW, JANUARY 1995

Towards a Discreet Form of Censorship

It was only two days after the *Literary Review* Bad Sex in Fiction ceremony at Simpson's-in-the-Strand that Mr Newt Gingrich, the new Speaker of the House of Representatives, revealed that he also has written a salacious novel. A couple of fruity extracts were released at the same time to whet our appetites.

Might Gingrich have changed his mind if he had been present to hear extracts from Edwina Currie's novel, *A Parliamentary Affair*, read to great applause by the actress Paula Bingham? Currie was the runner-up for the much-coveted Bad Sex effigy, presented by the lovely Marianne Faithfull to Philip Hook for a passage from *The Stonebreakers*.

This is not the time to rehearse all the reasons for our institution of this Bad Sex in Fiction trophy, but in passing I would like to remind readers to keep their eyes open throughout the year for any suitable passages in novels published between November 1994 and October 1995 inclusive. The prize is now £250, generously supplied by Rowbotham Films.

The question we must ask ourselves when we contemplate Newt Gingrich and Edwina Currie knocking on the door is not so much whether we should let them in – they have no desire, in fact, to join the disreputable company of writers and storytellers – but how we can politely, and without hurting their feelings, discourage them from knocking. Writers essentially belong to the fraternity of poachers rather than the company of gamekeepers. When occasionally a writer is to be seen posing as a gamekeeper – this applies to journalists as much as to novelists – he always makes a fool of himself. People are not interested in our pompous pronouncements. Such things should be left to politicians. Is it too much to suggest that bad descriptions of the sex act should be left to writers? It is not only politicians who are trying to elbow their way into the market. At times it seems that every housewife, out-of-work graduate and redundant executive has something embarrassing to tell us. Nor, of course, is it only bad sex they have to offer. Many wish to publish novels simply to tell us how sensitive they are.

There seems no way we can discourage the publication of all this tosh. Writers, being shifty fellows, know better than to support any suggestion of control. Our automatic response when anybody says that some newspaper article or book should never have been published must be to say, 'Yes it should.' This is not because we necessarily agree with the sentiments expressed, or welcome the information provided, or think it was worth saying, but because as soon as you appeal to an authority with power to determine what should and should not be published, you are in very deep water indeed.

Yet the overproduction of books threatens to become a major problem in countries like Britain where space is restricted. As we know, the average *Literary Review* reader buys nearly thirty-five hardback books a year, thereby accounting for 1,400,000 volumes. How many do they throw away? But the real extent of the problem becomes apparent only when you contemplate the 82,000-odd new titles published in this country every year. Few, I imagine, have a print run smaller than 2,000. At the very least, there are 164,000,000 books, most of them completely worthless, pouring out of the factories into our homes and places of work each year.

It is in this context that we should examine the comic opera of the new British Library, whose additional grant of £46 million in December brings its total cost to £496 million so far. First officially approved in 1978 at a cost of £78 million, it is still at least three years from completion. This is impressive enough. The fact that the building in all its hideousness has been shrunk to half the size originally planned and will be obsolete as soon as it opens, if it ever opens, is something different.

It was intended that the new building would fulfil all requirements of the British Library until 2030. Now that its size has been reduced (the measure of our shrinking prosperity as a nation), there will be only seventy-three more seats than there are currently. This works out at approximately £6,800,000 per extra seat. One could easily decide this magnificent cock-up was the natural result of a meeting between the world of books – the most incompetent business in the country – and the world of politics. By nature, they do not meet, until a politician, in retirement, turns up to collect his cheque from Lord Weidenfeld or Mr Murdoch, as the case may be. By nature, the two worlds are antipathetical, since the politician resents any renown or influence that does not attach to the world of politics. They should be kept apart. Only bad sex can result.

A simple explanation may be that this ugly and unusable building is the architectural expression of the novels of Edwina Currie and Newt Gingrich. But I perceive a destiny at work. The project was doomed from the start by this monstrous tide of new books.

The main lesson must be that where books are not worth preserving it is insane to spend huge sums doing so. The new building should be blown up and the St Pancras site sold. The old Reading Room should be preserved with its present collection of books, and new ones should be admitted only when they have been vetted by a hard-working, underpaid committee of redundant librarians and schoolteachers. Books not accepted should be quietly forgotten, their existence denied.

LITERARY REVIEW, JANUARY 1995

Thou Shalt Not Covet Thy Neighbour's Advances

The United Kingdom publishes more new titles every year than any other country in the world – 86,573 at the last count, against 49,276 in the United States, which has nearly five times the population. We also borrow more books from libraries than any other country – 564,525,000 to be exact, or almost ten library books per year per citizen. This may not be as impressive as Finland, whose five million citizens borrow something nearer seventeen books apiece every year, but it does suggest that the reading habit survives in this country.

It is only the overwhelming incompetence of the publishers which threatens this happy situation. Ninety per cent of books produced are never reviewed, and not even the most desultory effort is put into their marketing. Booksellers despair at the choice available and concentrate on a few they know they can sell – generally down-market biographies and semi-technical, non-literary works offering advice on hobbies and do-it-yourself. Few book buyers will ask for a particular book, and even fewer will find it. If they are lucky enough to have a bookseller prepared to order individual volumes, they will as likely as not have to wait twenty-eight days for delivery.

Various attempts have been made to counter the extraordinary incompetence of the book trade with telephone order systems guaranteeing two-day or even next-day delivery at no extra cost, but they all come to grief against a tradition that seems indifferent to its inefficiency. It is not all that often one needs a book the next day, and telephone numbers are easy to lose. The idleness of booksellers is protected by a sale-or-return system, and that of publishers by a huge mark-up on production costs which makes bestsellers absurdly profitable.

I rejoiced to be told that Alan Bennett's excellent volume of selected diaries, *Writing Home* (Faber & Faber), was selling 6,000 copies a day after its enthusiastic review by Craig Brown in October's *Literary Review*, but I could not help wondering whether it was true. Literary gossip is not always truthful, and gossips are endlessly credulous. I found it hard to believe that Faber & Faber – although undoubtedly one of the most efficient and most agreeable publishers in the business – would have that number of copies to sell, or that booksellers would be prepared to stock so many copies. But whatever the exact figure, the rumour must be based on some sort of truth, and it must prove that there is still a large market for well-written and intelligent work.

It is in this context, I feel, and with the same caveats, that we should approach the great debate about Martin Amis's reported demand for a £500,000 advance against royalties on his latest novel, *The Information* (with a book of short stories thrown in). We do not know if the figure is genuine or the product of Chinese whispers, any more than we know (at the time of going to press) whether he has received the full amount from HarperCollins. If not, he may be left looking rather foolish, but I do not see why. There can be no harm in trying. If there is a publisher prepared to pay that sort of sum, Amis would be foolish to accept less. It would almost certainly be untrue to accuse Amis's fellow writers of envy when they accuse him of greed, but I cannot accept A. S. Byatt's point that what she describes as Amis's male turkey-cocking is 'extremely bad for the industry and makes life hard for young authors'.

On the contrary, it seems to me good for the industry if it can justify these sorts of sums, and it should encourage young writers to know that there is indeed a pot of gold at the end of the rainbow. There is an elementary misunderstanding of publishers' economics behind her cry: 'I always earn out my advances and I don't see why I should subsidize his greed.' Publishers can and do make huge profits from books whose sale does not cover the advance on royalties. The reason for this is that royalties are such a small part of the publishers' budget. If Byatt's publishers try to persuade her otherwise, she should change them, and her agent at the same time. She is not subsidizing Amis, who will pay for himself, if the publishers have done their sums right. She is merely helping to swell her publishers' profits, and encouraging them to short-change their authors.

Publishers have always treated writers with contempt when they could get away with it. A letter from a friend describes how she turned up with a book on which she had been working for four years in a heavy suitcase at 2.30 p.m. to keep a rigorously imposed deadline, only to be told that her publisher was out to lunch. So was his secretary. The three receptionists said they knew nothing about it and refused to accept the manuscript. The publicity girls were all in Morocco. She was told she had to take it to 'package reception' at the back of the building, where they told her to take it to the post room. There she met a nice, older man.

'Please can you sign for the manuscript?' she asked.

'Oh no,' he said.

'Well, they told me at the ground-floor reception to bring it here,' she said.

'Oh, they're always doing that,' he said.

We should wish Martin Amis well. The amount involved – £500,000 – is not so outrageously big when we reflect that it represents no more than £25,000 in 1938–9, when Godfrey Wynn was earning that sum every year from the *Daily Mirror* alone, with a powder-blue Rolls-Royce and a uniformed chauffeur thrown in.

LITERARY REVIEW, APRIL 1995
They Must Learn the Art of Pleasing

Writing books, especially novels, is a lonely business; many writers succumb to various forms of persecution mania, seeing conspiracies against them by the publishing and critical Establishments. Some take it even further, claiming that their books are deliberately ignored by booksellers; when ordered at all, they are hidden underneath other, more favoured books by shop staff...

My first response to the suggestion that English publishers are imposing the same constraints of political correctness on their authors as the Americans was one of profound scepticism. The charge was laid by Jane Gordon, whose first novel, *Hard Pressed*, comes out from Penguin / Signet in August. In the course of heavy editing, she was accused of being lookist, fatist, elitist and insulting to women, of offending gays and upsetting the lesbian readership, she claims. Gordon also made the point that first novelists were particularly vulnerable to editing of this sort, and I am quite prepared to believe that she may have been unlucky.

In fact, I have heard odd reports of Penguin, and am even prepared to believe that the editorial side may have been taken over by ferocious left-wing harpies and their cringing male sycophants. It is a sad truth that if you let one militant anti-smoker or one sexual-harassment freak into an otherwise happy office, she will lose no time in finding sympathizers among the existing staff and reducing the entire office to abject terror and obedience. It is quite possible that one or two publishing offices have been taken over in this way by the PC brigade, but I refuse to believe it is a major feature of the English publishing scene because we do not have the same problems that have produced the PC phenomenon in the United States: the racial tension; the disparities of wealth; and the terror of a violent, drug-crazed criminal underclass.

It is undoubtedly true that in the United States most adult fiction appears to be sanitized, but the same is true of non-fiction. Most of the British writers whom Gordon quoted in her support were complaining about the American practice: Dick Francis was told it was un-American to make jokes about lesbians; Jilly Cooper described how her memorable novel called *Polo*, about macho men, was transformed by its American publishers into a story of beautiful women and sexually ambiguous men – until she sent back the advance and cancelled the contract. As a result, *Polo* has never been published in the United States.

When Alice Thomas Ellis complains of not being allowed to describe a woman as a girl, she puts her finger on a comparatively harmless piece of American rubbish which seems to have made the crossing and settled here. But when Celia Brayfield complains that she has to write popular genre novels because she is frozen out of the literary scene by a prejudiced Establishment, she is speaking of Britain alone:

> I say what hope have I got of writing literary novels? I am not working class. I do not have a regional accent. I'm not a citizen of an oppressive regime nor a member of an ethnic minority. I am not gay, nor am I any kind of addict, and that more or less lets you out of being a literary novelist.

Is Martin Amis working class? Or Julian Barnes? Or A. S. Byatt? Even the eccentric Will Self is middle class, white and heterosexual, for all that he constantly proclaims himself working class. Brayfield is speaking in jest, of course, but the animus behind the jest is immediately recognizable as belonging to a rich seam of English persecution mania that visits middle- and working-class writers alike. One might easily hear working-class novelists make the same charge of rejection by the London literary Establishment.

What all these people must come to accept is that these are bad times for the literary novel and very bad times indeed for first-time novelists. Regardless of whether they are black or white or fat or thin they must cultivate the art of pleasing much more than they have had to do in the past. The first novel can no longer be seen as a useful tool in psychotherapy, like an extended analysis or counselling session for the confused English adolescent. It must justify in terms of the pleasure it will give its readers. This brings us back to the American example, as illustrated by the fate of Jilly Cooper's *Polo*.

Unable to earn a reasonable livelihood editing the *Literary Review* or as an itinerant preacher, I double up with various other occupations, among them being the licensee and wine-buyer for a basement club in Soho. Recently I was visited by an American dealer in Californian wines for the club to taste any that we chose and bottle them under any label we chose. It is inconceivable to think of any European wine merchant offering the same service. It is an extension of the great American principle that the customer is always right.

This principle can be counterproductive and cruel if unintelligently applied. It has produced the tastelessly bland food that disfigures one end of the American culture, and the violent television drama at the other. I have heard it said that no finance is available for any film in Britain that does not include shootings, sex and buckets of blood for the American market. Examples of cruelty are equally easy to find.

Poor Andrew Neil, former editor of the *Sunday Times*, being groomed for the role of presenter on a Murdoch American news programme, was made to shave his hair, take off his tie, put on a lightweight American jacket and grin inanely at the camera. It didn't work. He still wasn't right for the American market, so he crept back to England to write articles in praise of the Fayed brothers for the *Sunday Times*.

Poor Neil, another casualty of the system. But my point is that he was right to try. Jilly Cooper was wrong to send her advance back to the American publishers. If Americans prefer to read about polo being played between castrated men and beautiful, forceful women, let them have their way. Like the wine blender, the television presenter, the prostitute and everyone else, it is the novelist's job to please her customers.

LITERARY REVIEW, JUNE 1995

Don't Let's Be Beastly to the Germans

This sermon is being composed in the middle of all the excesses attendant on our celebration of the fiftieth anniversary of Victory in Europe in May 1945. Did the feeling visit a few, as they listened to the speeches of politicians taking credit for the result, that there might have been some advantages to Britain as well as the obvious disadvantages if Germany had won the war?

On balance, of course, there can be no question where the advantage lay. The unthinkable thought that there might have been some advantage in a military defeat has been prompted, in my own case, by the news that Macmillan, the publisher, has been taken over by a German family firm called Holtzbrinck.

Germany's ascendancy is often produced as a good reason for fighting shy of any European union, as if we had some preferable option of 'going it alone', but it seems to me that a little German leadership – in the sense of the humane, bourgeois liberal democracy that has ruled Germany since the war – is exactly what we need in Britain. National sovereignty means no more than government by whichever gang of opportunists and inadequates is on top in Westminster. They are not really fit to have any say at all, let alone a leading voice, in the development of a free and united Europe.

To explain why we may rejoice to see Macmillan taken over by a German firm, we might first observe how extraordinarily little resentment there has been over a prime minister's family cashing in to the tune of £199.5 million by selling a British asset to the Germans. Nobody has suggested that Harold Macmillan, who fought in the trenches of the Great War, is spinning in his grave. Nobody has suggested that Lord Stockton should give the money to charity or to a cancer hospital, or whatever. All the venom has been reserved for young Winston's decision to sell his family's assets to the Heritage Fund of his own country for £12.5 million derived from the National Lottery. Nobody wanted the Churchill papers, and everybody seemed furious that punters' money should be spent on them. A German offer might have had a clearer run.

Add to this, perhaps, an unspoken feeling of relief that whenever the Germans take on anything, there is a good chance it will be efficiently managed. We read much of the inefficiency and uncompetitiveness of British industry, but the only part of it we ever see in this magazine – the publishing industry – must surely be the least efficient of all. Anything to do with books seems to bring out the worst in the English. My strictures are not confined to the publishing trade. Booksellers are just as idle and inefficient, expecting to be featherbedded with a 'sale or return' system that they interpret as a licence to over-order on anticipated bestsellers, while ignoring nine-tenths of the publishing scene.

Worst of all are the literary agents. There is scarcely an author in the land who has not entertained the thought that his agent and his publisher are in a conspiracy to sabotage his chances of survival. This is generally attributed to the persecution mania of professional writers, but the more stories one hears the more probable it seems that these neuroses are the product of a degree of idleness and incompetence among publishers and agents that seems entirely incredible unless it is also motivated by malice. Time and again literary agents seem to feel they have done all their work when they have agreed an advance and a royalty and put the figures into a standard contract. Subsidiary and foreign rights are pursued listlessly, often only when the agents are approached by a buyer, and the other functions of a literary agent – the soliciting of commissions for books and placing of articles and short stories, the introduction of clients to important contacts – are not even attempted unless someone approaches them first. Time and again when one hears of an author who has had a particular success, he or she will aver that this was despite, rather than because of, the English agent and the English publisher.

So we must rejoice that the Germans are showing an interest. There is money to be made from bestsellers, but there are also huge sums to be made from books that sell 4,000 copies, if they are efficiently produced and well marketed. Our experience of publishers consists largely of trying to get review copies or proofs in time. As a monthly, working in advance, we desperately need the first proofs. Half the time in the office is spent chasing up book proofs from idle publishers. Macmillan is one of the better ones but there is room for improvement, as we have begun to see from Reed International (Methuen, Secker & Warburg, Michael Joseph) as a result of its association with the Dutch.

The worst that can happen is that they should all be taken over by the Americans, as may yet happen with Cape, Hutchinson and Chatto, now under Random House, and the HarperCollins group. American employees are twice as willing, efficient and friendly as their English counterparts, but editorially the American kiss is the kiss of death. Europeans are basically interested in the same things, whereas America is rapidly losing interest in Europe and developing interests of its own. So let us welcome the Germans. If I had been young Winston, I might have sold them my grandfather's papers rather than keep them in a country where tests conducted among 1,600 state-school pupils revealed that 36 per cent of eleven- to fourteen-year-olds could not place Winston Churchill (many of them thought he was an American president), 90 per cent could not name Rommel, 25 per cent could not identify Hitler and more than half thought a doodlebug was a dance.

[Update: Elsevier (the Dutch owners of Reed International) sold its UK publishing to Random House in 1996 – though Methuen bought itself out in 1998. Fifty-three per cent of Random House was bought by Bertelsman, a German megalith, creating 250 'independent imprints', employing 12,000 people around the world.]

LITERARY REVIEW, JULY 1995

From the Pulpit
[The Elusive Nature of Sponsors]

... At one moment in my search for a new sponsor for the Grand Poetry Prize I began to despair for the philanthropic tradition in Britain. In America, private philanthropy claims exemption from income tax to the tune of $160 billion a year. Here, it seems to operate more through a system of eccentric commercial judgement. Thus we read of £500,000 being paid for Martin Amis's last novel [*The Information*]. Somebody must have pretended to think that the figure represented a commercial proposition. Even more strikingly, we read of Martyn Bedford, a mature graduate from Professor Malcolm Bradbury's creative-writing MA course, who came home to Sheffield to learn that a publishing house had bid £100,000 for his first novel, called *Acts of Reason*. [Bron could sometimes get things wrong – the book was *Acts of Revision*.]

Perhaps sales will justify this price, but I prefer to believe the two publishing houses concerned were exercising a suppressed desire to patronize the arts. It appears that the best way to raise money for a good cause is to present a prospectus containing some sort of bogus promise of profitability. Thus when Sir Andrew Lloyd Webber spends £19 million on a hideous Picasso portrait of some long-forgotten Spanish politician, everybody pats him on the back and congratulates him on a sound investment.

How sad, then, that the *Modern Review*, Julie Burchill's brave venture into the inhospitable world of small-circulation arts and literary magazines, should never have found the right sales patter to attract philanthropic investment. The circumstances of its collapse, with the editor, Toby Young, accusing Burchill of undermining his authority through a lesbian relationship with the attractive editorial assistant Charlotte Raven, will be familiar enough to all who have worked on a small magazine, or in any voluntary enterprise. But the occasion of its closing through a cash crisis is infinitely depressing.

I seldom had time to examine the *Modern Review* very closely. It chiefly concerned itself with the dizzier heights of the popular mass culture, which it approached reverentially, with a fixed determination not to be snooty or patronizing. It was inspired, I thought – at any rate so far as its thirty-one-year-old editor was concerned – by the idea of the huge sums of money sloshing around inside this popular mass culture, and by a reckoning that some of it might attach to a 'high-brow' guru in the field. Ah, the optimism of youth! – no less poignant in its cynical manifestations than in its apparent idealism. Even if one does not particularly wish to be better informed about Arnold Schwarzenegger oneself, there must be no rejoicing when a small magazine founders.

Ms Charlotte Raven can join us any time, adding a dash of feminist and Blairite Labour politics to the cocktail, if she wishes. Burchill will be welcome to write a regular column, if she can abide our abysmal rates of pay. As for Toby Young, I feel he should try to join Murdoch. The simple truth is that the popular mass culture which he champions is the enemy of all truth, beauty and wisdom in the modern world. He has no role in the defence of our humane, bourgeois European culture. The collapse of the *Modern Review* suggests that he has no role in the ranks of the barbarians, either. Perhaps it is not too late for him to learn some useful trade, like dentistry.

Literary Review, November 1995
Publishing as a Paradigm of the Nation's Ills

Whatever complaint novelists may have about the modern world, they cannot complain that the novel is ignored by newspapers, radio and television. Recent shenanigans over the Booker Prize came hot on the heels of the great debate about the collapse of the Net Book Agreement, with the usual gloomy predictions that it will sound the death knell for the English literary novel. Next came a sudden outbreak of class war in the Crime Writers' Association, with the contemptuous dismissal of P. D. James by less gifted, younger members of the yobbish tendency. Even before that, acres and acres of newsprint had been taken up with discussing the phenomenon of Nicholas Evans's first novel, *The Horse Whisperer*, sold for £2 million to Hollywood before publication, with another £2 million paid for American publishing rights and £350,000 for British publishing rights ...

We did not review *The Horse Whisperer* in this magazine, but our decision had nothing to do with its qualities. It was simply that the publishers, Bantam, refused to send us a review copy unless we signed an embargo, which would have meant that our review appeared a month after publication. Perhaps Evans will survive the blow, but it was foolish of Bantam, nevertheless, to deny their author access to the *Literary Review*. I would like to think that our early and enthusiastic reviews of Robert Harris's *Fatherland* and Nick Hornby's *High Fidelity* helped to set them on the road to bestsellerdom by bringing them to the attention of the other book pages.

Not having read *The Horse Whisperer*, I have no opinion about its merits, although I observe that the clever young Welsh author has set his story in Montana, rather than in Monmouthshire. In the same way, I would judge (without having read it) that Robert James Wailer's *The Bridges of Madison County*, which is said to have sold ten million copies worldwide, is set in Madison County rather than Middlesex.

Perhaps these figures are correct. There were those prepared to believe that Lord Archer had been paid £32 million pounds by HarperCollins in publishing advances. One wishes these people well. The question is whether all writers should aspire to the same formulae, or whether the market can still sustain novels written for minority tastes, particularly those of the educated English middle class.

At one moment in the Crime Writers' Association imbroglio, P. D. James's challenger, a crime writer called Mark Timlin, who will be remembered for his description of a CWA meeting as being 'like an horrific Hampstead cocktail party', claimed that middle-class crime dominated the genre because 'middle-class people have more money to buy books and they want something which reflects their own tedious lives'.

I do not know what bad experience Timlin will have had at a Hampstead (or should one say 'an Hampstead'?) cocktail party. But he surely has a point when he says that many buyers of crime books prefer to read about their own kind. That was rather the point being made by Lady James.

Is the same no longer true of the literary novel? Perhaps the very expression is seen as a discouragement nowadays, since the word 'literary' has lost its educated, middle-class properties and taken on some of the moronic connotations of 'high-brow' as used by intellectually insecure journalists and academics. Put more simply, the question boils down to this: would the traditional-English-novel readership be happier to read about the lives, loves and problems of the upper middle classes in Hammersmith, Notting Hill and Surrey, or about drug addicts and dropouts in Tower Hamlets, or about a little girl and her horse in Montana? Why should the last choice be the only one available to them?

Those who reckon that the abolition of the Net Book Agreement, whereby publishers undertake to maintain a book's published price, will dig the grave of the traditional English novel, may be disregarding the fact that it has already dug its own grave. The reasons for this are legion: the phenomenon of working wives and the disappearance of a leisured class outside the great areas of unemployment on Tyneside and Merseyside; the malign influence of university English studies and literary prizes, which distract writers from their first task of finding a viable readership; the timidity of our bourgeois cultural elite in the face of proletarian advances; and the American mass culture.

It may be of interest that the French, who removed controls from book prices a few years ago, have now restored them. But the main reason for the disappearance of the traditional English novel as a major part of our national culture is a combination of stupidity, idleness and greed on the part of publishers. Decent profits can be made from selling 2,500 copies of a new novel at £12.99. Respectable profits can be made from selling 4,000 copies at £9.99. By concentrating all their declining energies on a few prospective bestsellers, for which they pay exorbitant advances, they are building on sand. Once the Net Book Agreement has gone by the board,

Bantam will not be able to ask £14.99 for Evans's *The Horse Whisperer*. People will expect to buy it (if that is what they want to do) for £8.99. That advance of £350,000 will begin to look like a loan to Argentina. The fate of the publishing trade is not particular. Like the rest of the country, it has fallen into the hands of stupid people who think they know best.

LITERARY REVIEW, JANUARY 1996

When Public Funding Can Become the Kiss of Death

It is often said that Christopher Wren's designs for St Paul's Cathedral, when first presented, were considered highly controversial, if not actually outrageous. We have been told this so often that a new platitude has been born out of the paradox that by no means all artists achieve recognition in their own lifetime: no truly great work of art is ever identified as such, we are told, except by a highly trained, super-sensitive elite, until many years after its first appearance. The vulgar taste in aesthetics always takes years to catch up. This rhetoric, or a variation on it, has justified the greater part of the government's subsidies to contemporary art, as well as the horrible buildings which philistine departments, local councils and commercial firms have been happy to accept since the war.

In fact it is all based on a fallacy. Wren may not have become as obscenely wealthy as the Richard Rogerses or Norman Fosters of our own time, but he lived with great dignity in elegant quarters in Hampton Court Palace, acquired a tidy fortune and was universally respected. The noises of outrage which greeted his model for St Paul's came from a tiny handful of Protestant fanatics, Europhobes and reactionary boobies whose influence and intellectual standing may, perhaps, be measured beside the small groups which demonstrated outside Westminster Cathedral when the Queen went to Vespers there a few weeks ago.

With the outbreak of democracy in the last century, public debate on aesthetics became intense. People argued in the streets over the rival designs for the Palace of Westminster. It was only after the Modern

Movement became established that public interest receded, an elite of sorts was reinstated, and the masses became as ignorant and resentful as ever. The more amenable of the lumpen proletariat may still be prepared to accept teacher's word for it that even the Lloyd's building, for instance, is somehow progressive, a blow in the class war against bourgeois assumptions of prettiness, a preparation for the glorious ugliness of the workers' paradise. Most timidly accept that they might appreciate it in thirty years, if they are still alive, and it is still standing. Alternatively, they revert to the feudal-peasant mode, and humbly conclude that they are too ignorant to pass judgement on such matters.

All of which must be highly agreeable for the artistic elite, as they dispense public patronage to their friends and those whom they choose to patronize. Just occasionally, however, they go too far and there is a blip. The Turner Prize award of £20,000 to Damien Hirst for his mutilated corpses of a cow and a calf suddenly caught the apathetic multitude on the raw, distressed at the spectacle of a dead calf being exploited so shamelessly. Suddenly, the arty-tarty elite were more unpopular than the bourgeois society they hoped to mock. The *Daily Telegraph* described this Turner Prize as 'an odious and disgusting scandal', and there were few dissenting voices.

By coincidence, I went to two exhibitions on the night of the Turner award. One was in the St Leger Gallery, Old Bond Street, where Julian Barrow was showing his latest collection of reasonably priced oils of domestic and foreign scenes. A friendly gathering of polite, prosperous people bought these agreeable, undemanding pictures entirely for their own pleasure. My second call that evening was at the Dulwich Picture Gallery for the Van Dyck exhibition.

Every other cab driver who has made the journey down to Dulwich will know that the Picture Gallery is one of the greatest delights in London, housing the wonderful collection of 650 oil paintings formed for the last King of Poland in Regency times and never delivered. What both these exhibitions have in common is that neither have received a penny from public funds.

Neither, of course, has the *Literary Review*. Barrow survives commercially by selling his wares, which is surely the best way to survive. The Dulwich Picture Gallery, which has been taken under the wing of Lord Sainsbury, survives by voluntary, charitable donations. We keep going with help from a few friends. Although their motives in helping us can only be charitable, we are not allowed to be treated as a charity, following a decision by the Charity Commissioners.

In paranoid moments, one might see this decision as a last throw by the adherents of the Modern Movement, who control nearly all access to public funding in the arts. Never mind. Time and again it has been proved that public funding is the kiss of death. We have our moments. History is surely on our side. When Mrs Clinton visited this country last month, she sent a request to meet the deputy editor of the *Literary Review*, Lola Bubbosh, explaining that the *Literary Review* is 'a highly respected journal for contemporary creative writing and intellectual trends'. Just so.

Damien Hirst's mutilated cow and calf represent an extreme of the wrong-headedness that has ruled the arts Establishment for fifty years. Their literary equivalents range from monosyllabic obscenities posing as poetry to the gentler quasi-bucolic sillinesses of our nice Poet Laureate, Mr Hughes. What a wonderful thing it would be if the Turner Prize taught them all that the party is over.

LITERARY REVIEW, FEBRUARY 1996

What They Will Do If They Get the Chance

The fourteenth of February, which is traditionally celebrated as St Valentine's Day, will also be remembered this year, wherever literary folk meet, as the twenty-first anniversary of the death of P. G. Wodehouse. Wodehouse's death was rather poignant. On 1 January 1975, it was announced that he had been given a knighthood, after more than thirty years of semi-official disgrace. A month and a half later, he quietly expired at the enormous age of ninety-three.

Most knighthoods and other awards to literary folk are a mistake. We all know that politicians do not like writers, any more than writers like politicians. Each grudges the other's share of the limelight. Fellow writers are automatically suspicious of any colleague who accepts an honour. For what, exactly, is he being paid? Is it for general sycophancy, or some more specific service? But the Wodehouse knighthood is different.

Government papers for 1945 released under the fifty-year rule last month revealed attempts by civil servants to have Wodehouse's books banned in Britain. For those who are not familiar with the story, I will tell it again.

Wodehouse was living in northern France with his wife Ethel at the outbreak of war in 1939. He was interned by the Germans in 1940 and spent the best part of a year behind barbed wire in a concentration camp, along with other Allied civilians. In 1941, at the approach of his sixtieth birthday, he was released – although required to stay under German surveillance – and resumed his business of writing, which was all he knew how to do and his only way of earning a living. In particular, he wrote a humorous account of his capture and his experiences at German hands, which he arranged to broadcast to the United States – from Berlin.

There was nothing remotely improper in anything he wrote or said. His only crime was goofiness in not realizing that the Germans would use his broadcast. Nobody in Britain would have heard of these broadcasts if the Ministry of Information had not decided to make an example of him.

The man chosen to lead the attack with a series of broadcasts portraying Wodehouse as a traitor, a snob, a self-indulgent voluptuary and someone who put class interests before country, was Bill Connor, who wrote a column in the *Daily Mirror* under the name of 'Cassandra'. He told me he had no objection to blackguarding Wodehouse, about whom he knew nothing much, because he believed it to be true at the time. He was not shown the script of Wodehouse's broadcast until after the war when he met him, made his peace and found he liked the old boy. He told me that all animus against Wodehouse came from Cooper, the Tory politician who was Minister for Information at the time. Cooper had his own literary pretensions – his life of Talleyrand, published in 1932, is still readable – and knew Wodehouse as a fellow member of Churchill's 'Other Club'.

This seemed a strange way for one writer to behave towards another, and I put it down as a black mark against Cooper until I happened to befriend A. P. Ryan (1900–72), the historian of *The Times*, who was head of the BBC news service from 1940 to 1947. Ryan told me that instructions to blackguard Wodehouse had indeed come from Cooper, but his colleagues on the BBC were so disgusted that they had sent Ryan to convey their reluctance to touch any of Connor's lies and filth about Wodehouse. By Ryan's account, Cooper received him kindly, accepted all his points but said he would have to clear the matter with the prime minister. Within hours, the message came back. Churchill was adamant. Wodehouse must be attacked with every propaganda weapon available to a country at war.

After Connor's first broadcast, the *Daily Telegraph* opened a correspondence for unpleasant nitwits to show their patriotism by denouncing Wodehouse. Chief among them was the dreadful A. A. Milne. There were calls for Wodehouse to be brought back after the war and tried for treason, and these continued right up to a year or two before his death. If he visited England after retiring to Long Island in 1947, he did so in secrecy.

It is interesting that animus against Wodehouse came from the old brute himself. I have no doubt there was an element of jealousy in it of an inferior writer for a greater one – but what made Wodehouse so particularly detestable to Churchill was something else.

When he died, I wrote an obituary in the *New Statesman*: 'Politicians may be prepared to countenance subversive political jokes, but the deeper subversion of totally non-political jokes is something they can neither comprehend nor forgive. It is no accident that of all twentieth-century writers, Wodehouse is the one they have chosen, in their time, to persecute most bitterly.'

At the time of his ninetieth birthday in October 1971, I was covering a Conservative party conference and spent the whole week trying to organize a telegram from the conference. Various bigwigs were in favour, but Edward Heath, the prime minister, vetoed it.

Three years later, the Tories were thrown out again and it was left to Labour to make an act of reparation by knighting Wodehouse just before he died. I think Roy Jenkins was the person responsible. It seems a shame that the Tories choose to be so vile to writers. As a result, the world is seldom allowed to read about their better side, if they have one.

LITERARY REVIEW, MARCH 1996
On the Gloom of the Intelligentsia

It is the easiest thing in the world to visit one's own anxieties, premonitions, feelings of impending doom on the rest of the world scene. Preachers should be as wary of this temptation as judges must guard against adding a couple of years to a convict's sentence in response to a toothache or some discomfort of the bowel. Civilization has been seen to be collapsing for as long as it has existed. In many, but not all cases, this impending disaster becomes more apparent with old age, in grudging acknowledgement, perhaps, of the prophet's own mortality.

But we would be churlish to apply this explanation to the civilized pessimism of George Steiner in *No Passion Spent* (Faber & Faber) or Harold Bloom in *The Western Canon* (Papermac). It would also be foolish to conclude, just because so many people have announced the collapse of civilization in the past, that it isn't collapsing this time. Obviously, it is changing, and so far as most intelligent and educated people are concerned it is changing for the worse. Are we right to see, with Henry Porter in the *Guardian*, a 'growing anxiety among academics about the sudden descent of Western culture' – and does it matter if academics suffer a growing anxiety in this way?

Bloom writes of English departments where: 'Batman comics, Mormon theme parks, television, movies and rock will replace Chaucer, Shakespeare, Milton, Wordsworth and Wallace Stevens.'

Steiner joins to mourn the neglect of those classical texts which once provided a common language for the educated in every country of the West. More specifically, he regrets that we no longer learn such texts by heart. 'The inner spaces are mute or jammed with raucous trivia.'

How right he is! It is amazing how little even of this raucous trivia seems enough to fill the inner spaces of a typical English teenager. Few of them know more than one or two lines of any pop song. Thereafter they hum or repeat the same lines over again. How much better for them to learn *The Revenge*. At a convivial meeting of writers in Chelsea recently the talk was all of how standards were collapsing, general barbarism threatened, nobody was reading books any more… After many minutes of this, it was agreed that what the company was really complaining about was the collapse of the market for literary novels, although they agreed that the general standard of literary novels was abysmal, and people were quite right not to buy them. In fact, what they were really complaining about was the obstinate refusal of the public to buy their books.

Might one see a similar element of undeclared self-interest in Steiner's regret that nobody is able to recognize the (often obscure) quotations and references with which he presents his arguments? Or in the academics' discovery that since nobody is interested in their subjects, their departments and their jobs are doomed?

Many would see this as a contemptible suggestion beside the immensity of the cultural edifice it seeks to diminish, particularly when relating it to the heroic efforts of people like Peter Jones of Newcastle University to relaunch the Latin language. But the truth of the matter is that academic studies have never formed much more than an irritating appendix to the higher culture, a minor carbuncle if you like. The universities have their own concerns, remote from the daily lives and creative struggles of everybody else, often deeply antagonistic to original thought, and of very limited influence in forming the tastes of the patrons who define a culture.

What has changed (no doubt for the worse) is the nature of the patronage. It is a commonplace that the mass market (where most of the money is) has its own requirements. The higher culture may be studied by anybody with a mind to it, but it no longer controls the public taste. When one thinks of the imbecilities it inflicted on us all throughout the long history of the Modern Movement, even that development may give rise only to qualified regret.

A paradox – not to say a contradiction – in all this is the continuing influence of youth. It is from the young, rather than from a newly enriched uneducated working class, that the real hatred of classical education comes – the repudiation of history, language and literature. In America, of course, the young have masses of money and in time will probably have even more, but in this country, we thought we had fixed the young by ensuring they were not only unemployed, and therefore penniless, but also unemployable, and likely to remain penniless for a long time.

Having no money, youth should be unable to bring its baneful influence to bear on our culture. Why then do car manufacturers, wishing to sell a £20,000 sports car, address their advertisements to some putative teenager, obviously moronic and probably doped? The explanation to this mystery may be found either in the length of time it takes for commerce to follow what may have been apparent to the intelligentsia for years; or in a blind loyalty to things more... American, which will last only as long as the American economy remains predominant; or (as I believe) in an almost religious deference to youth that arises from our growing reluctance to contemplate our own death.

But things are really not so bad as Steiner or Bloom pretend. Even the young still have their inner lives. If they prefer reading from a video screen to reading from a book, that is their choice. Everything's all right, really...

LITERARY REVIEW, JUNE 1997

Who Wants to be a Grand Old Man?

Hot on the heels of Waterstone's survey, when 25,000 people were asked to name the greatest book of the twentieth century and voted overwhelmingly for J. R. R. Tolkien's three-volume *Lord of the Rings*, there came a second survey. On this occasion, the Folio Society asked its 50,000 members to name their ten favourite books of all time. More than 10,000 replied and some of them dutifully mentioned the works of Homer, Chaucer and Dante, as well as Cervantes, Tolstoy and Shakespeare. But the favourite, out of fifty works finally listed, with 3,270 votes, was once again J. R. R. Tolkien's *Lord of the Rings*.

A few commentators sloppily suggested that the voters were giving it as their opinion that Tolkien's whimsical parable was the greatest book ever written. In fact, they were merely recording it as their favourite, which is not quite the same thing. But it is close enough, I would have thought, to be rather depressing for the ambitious contemporary writer who still hopes to achieve lasting fame. Even more depressing must be the thought that of all the authors named on the list of fifty, every single one is dead.

Some, it is true, like the great Tolkien himself, died comparatively recently. *Brideshead Revisited* features in twenty-second place, immediately after Dante's *Inferno* and Gibbon's *Decline and Fall of the Roman Empire*. Steinbeck's *Grapes of Wrath*, in thirty-third place, comes between Pepys's *Diary* and Cervantes' *Don Quixote*. But it is sad to observe that no Amis is mentioned, nor even that doyen of greatest living writers, Anthony Powell, who has given so much pleasure to so many readers of both sexes. Not enough, it would appear, to allow him to feature with Eliot, Kipling, Joyce, Jane Austen, the Brontës, Wodehouse, Dylan Thomas, Homer, Tolkien and Dostoyevsky among the all-time greats.

Powell, as I write, is still alive and living in Somerset at the age of ninety-one. This month he produces the third volume of his *Journals*, covering the three years 1990–92. In an introduction, his wife, Lady Violet, reveals that her husband's last trip to London was to visit the Queen, in 1987, when she invested him as a Companion of Honour. He is already, quite unquestionably, the Grand Old Man of English Letters, if not yet the greatest writer of his generation, although the *Journals* suggest that he may be gaining ground in that direction, too. What they also reveal is that it is hard work establishing yourself as the greatest writer of your generation. There are hostile reviewers to be snubbed, whippersnappers to be kept in place, contemporaries to be denigrated or simply insulted, slights to be recorded, bad reviews to be avenged.

Unfortunately, the publishers did not send the book in time for a proper review, but on a day's leafing through it I seemed to find offence being taken on every page. When Ray Seitz, the most cultivated and beautifully mannered of men, is appointed American ambassador in London, Powell recalls that on a previous occasion he 'said he had never read any of my books, they might sell better if I did not pronounce my name in such a peculiar manner'. Powell's angry riposte is: 'He can hardly fail to have dealings with Sir Charles Powell, Mrs Thatcher's great standby, who pronounces his name in the same way.'

Perhaps Sir Charles was not trying to sell books. A week earlier, we learn of 'a furious letter to the *Spectator* about [Antony] Lambton's comment on my contribution to the David Cecil book, which they have simply not put in. This is the New Journalism, I suppose, which goes out of its way to be insulting, then refuses right of reply. One might have expected something a bit better of the *Spectator*.'

All this in the middle of a monumental row with *The Times* about an unfavourable review that Malcolm Muggeridge had given Powell's *The Valley of Bones* in 1964 – twenty-six years earlier. This runs for thirteen pages over some six weeks. Bernard Levin referred to a row between them, and *The Times* refused to print Powell's letter unaltered: 'On reconsideration, it may be best not to make any public reply to low-grade journalism (all journalism these days).'

In old age, it appears that one spends much time reassessing one's contemporaries and former friends, although of Graham Greene he can say: 'From the word go I had found his books wholly unreadable, long before there could have been any question of jealousy.' Of Henry Green, on his death, he writes: 'My final judgement on Henry, my oldest intimate friend... is that he was really rather a shit... his vanity about his supreme importance as a writer combine no very keen intelligence... In relation to his conceit, Henry once remarked to me in the 1930s, "I suppose I am generally recognized now as being as good as any novelist can be."' On the next page, he discusses his friend Kingsley Amis's *Memoirs*: 'There has been more publicity about the *Memoirs* than I remember for any book of a similar kind. It is not a good book. Kingsley is more spiteful than I thought ...' He complains of Muggeridge's 'unbridled envy', and of Harold Acton he says: 'Harold's supposed wit... could not have been less funny.' Of Waugh, his final judgement is: 'I think Evelyn a shade overrated these days (compared to the big shots).'

Yes, it's tough at the top. Who would want to be a big shot?

LITERARY REVIEW, JULY 1997
Keeping the Show on the Road

At a literary party in London recently I was happy to be approached by a young female novelist who said she wanted to thank the *Literary Review* from the bottom of her heart for instituting the tremendously acclaimed annual Bad Sex Award, celebrating the worst or most redundant passages of sexual description in any of the year's novels. It had saved her from the obligation of including these passages in her novels, as her publishers felt she should, and this was a great relief to her as she was not good at describing sex. That she was an attractive woman is neither here nor there, but it caused a certain glow of happiness in at least one rheumy-eyed old editor's heart.

Then I read Jonathan Coe telling Andrew Biswell in the *Daily Telegraph*: 'I rarely write sex scenes anyway because the spectre of Auberon Waugh's Bad Sex Award is always hanging over me.'

This is most gratifying for all associated with the *Literary Review*, but we must not let it go to our heads, in the way staff on the *Observer* let it go to their heads when they thought they had brought about the defeat of Michael Portillo in the General Election. This is no time to shout 'It was the *Lit Rev* wot dunnit' as we contemplate the chaste pages of Coe's new novel, *The House of Sleep*, which is in part a sensitive study of female homosexuality. It is not given to editors of literary magazines to exert great power. Those who wish to exert power in their society should not become novelists, either. Real power is more likely to be found nowadays in the post of fire-and-safety officer for the local council.

The idea that novelists should be important people addressing themselves to serious subjects, preferably on a global basis, strikes me as an obvious heresy. Its most eloquent and beguiling champion, Lisa Jardine, was to be heard making the point, yet again, when presenting the second Orange Prize for women's fiction last month. English novelists had fallen behind, she said. Only American and Canadian novelists really addressed the important issues nowadays. Among the American writers she cited as carrying the banner of importance and relevance was Thomas Pynchon.

For his interview Jonathan Coe chose to be shown in a large, colour photograph feigning sleep on a bench in Hyde Park. By contrast, Thomas Pynchon has never allowed himself to be photographed at all. As the *Daily Telegraph*'s Washington correspondent reports:

> Since 1963, when Pynchon's dense but brilliant debut novel *V* came out, the writer, widely considered America's most important novelist since the Second World War, has become a figure of myth.

His latest novel, *Mason & Dixon*, about which Professor Malcolm Bradbury gives us what I would like to think is the last word [see below], has been praised ('A book of heart and fire and genius' – *New York Times*) as well as abused ('monster of intrepid tedium' – Ian Hamilton in the *Sunday Telegraph*; 'an over-long, unmodulated, pun-infested, puerile, rambling dud' – Marianne Wiggins in *The Times*).

There are obviously two points of view. Nothing wrong with that. This is the book everyone has been talking about for the last two months. All of which may help to make Lisa Jardine's point, that the American novel occupies a central position in Western culture that has long been vacated by the English novel. I think it makes an entirely different point. Many may decide that the main thing is whether *Mason & Dixon* is an important contribution to Western awareness, a 'book of heart and fire and genius', or whether it is a load of meretricious rubbish. It is not an argument which can reasonably be settled by those like myself who have not read more than twenty pages of it, if that is the issue at stake. But, of course, it isn't. Allan Massie, who makes no bones about the fact that he has not even seen the book, writes:

> There should be no surprise that this sort of book becomes the vogue. There are always books that do, and they are usually meretricious. What they have in common is that they flatter the reader, or at least the purchaser. They make him or her feel cleverer than the common run of folks. The suggestion is plainly that few, if any, of the American purchasers read it. They keep it lying around for a time to impress their friends, and then, no doubt, put it away in the refrigerator in the hope it may come back into fashion.

Is this, in fact, such a contemptible role for the modern novelist, that his work, unreadable and unread, should become the latest American fashion accessory? It could not work without the help of the Lisa Jardines of this world, assuring us that these books are of the greatest significance. An occasional criticism of American culture is that, being attuned to the mass market, it produces nothing but mindless trash, characterized by the three main ingredients of sex, sentimentality and atrocious violence.

Then we have to explain how a dense, virtually incomprehensible book like *Mason & Dixon* can command a first print run of 175,000 copies. However much we sneer, it must provide evidence of a genuine desire among Americans to be thought intellectually respectable. That is something to encourage. As for Pynchon, who is plainly not a stupid man, I have the impression that he is laughing up his sleeve at us all. He, like Lisa Jardine and our own Professor Bradbury, who have taken the trouble to read those 773 pages, are all keeping a worthwhile show on the road.

From Bradbury's review:

'The great "American novel of the century"? Not exactly. The scale is there, the arcane intelligence, the love of mental play, the fascination with an America made out of reason and chaos, freedom and slavery. So is a Melvillelike willingness to break loose from the codes of fictional form, an Eco-like fascination with ancient, obscure conspiracies and conspirators, paranoically presented, never resolved. But Pynchon indulges himself too freely, as one might toward the end of a career of epic inventions which have also been teasing, self-destructing romps. An aptly chosen subject, the Mason–Dixon journey too often becomes a thread on which to hang an excess of set pieces, some too close to repetitious farce. Yet when the prose grows lyrical and poetic, it produces occasions of postmodern textual majesty, reminding us of the distinctive, intelligent pleasure Pynchon can give. It's certainly a book to read, if you are the kind of reader who can thrill to a distinctive, highly American kind of playful intellectual joy. But if, for you, *Gravity's Rainbow* was one of those bestsellers you bought but couldn't finish, *Mason & Dixon* indulgently extends the risk. The fact is that, like his two heroes, Thomas Pynchon never was sure just where to draw the line.'

LITERARY REVIEW, SEPTEMBER 1997

On the Crest of a Great Artistic Revival

It has often been observed that we tend to attribute our own weaknesses to others. Thus, the liar gives himself away by believing nothing he is told, the card or croquet cheat is the first to accuse other players of cheating. My own little weakness – it would be pointless to try and make a secret of it – is that I don't actually read as many new books – especially new novels – as the editor of a literary magazine ought to read. Mercifully there are others in this office who fill this gap. In my time as weekly reviewer for various publications – without a break in twenty-five years – I dare say I read more books than most. Unfortunately, I now find I have forgotten most of them.

However, that is not the point. Possibly because I nowadays read so few, I find it hard to believe that many other people read more. Of course, some people do. Most of them, I should imagine, are also readers of the *Literary Review*. These people form the hard core of those with a genuine interest in the modern novel. To my shame, I no longer belong to it. Others need not feel ashamed in the least. They do not have to pose as editors of literary magazines or pretend to produce lists of the greatest contemporary Merseyside novelists at the drop of a hat.

The English novel, as it has evolved, is a particular taste. What is surprising is that so many people have decided that there is something sacred about it, that it is, or should be, a good cause. Never mind that this remorseless hyping of the novel as an important cultural statement, rather than an idle hour's entertainment, has contributed to its death in either role. That point has been made before. What fascinates me is the number of people who still make the effort to pretend to have read books they have not read.

Perhaps a well-mannered dissimulation of this sort had a useful influence in supporting the liberal, humane, educated bourgeois culture of earlier times. But it is a curious hangover in the age of the Common Man that among 160 MPs who responded to a Dillons survey in answer to a question about which books they had most enjoyed reading in the past year, Irvine Welsh's *Trainspotting* came first, followed by a selection of novels by Trollope. Perhaps it takes a bluffer to spot a bluffer. I always disbelieved Mr Major when he claimed that Trollope was his favourite author.

My guess is that he could not remember the name of a single book he had read. His political brain reminded him that Harold Macmillan had nominated Trollope in this way. Macmillan was undoubtedly a Trollope fan. We should not decide Mr Major was doing anything very wicked if, as I suspect, he was fibbing when he said Trollope was his favourite novelist. He was just reacting as almost any Englishman will react when challenged about his reading. The only surprise is that so many MPs should expect us to believe them when they claim that they too have been reading Trollope throughout the year and put his novels second only to Irvine Welsh's *Trainspotting*.

If we judged by the amount of space given to arts and literature in the daily and Sunday newspapers, news and features, as well as reviews – we might easily decide that Britain was completely obsessed by its artists and on the crest of a great artistic revival. A few fools and crooks are prepared to announce this is the case. We all know it isn't, that editors are desperate to fill the space left empty by the absence of news in our gently disintegrating society.

'Whither the Novel?' we are constantly asked. Various clues are available to the one per cent that cares. Recently the quality press featured a twenty-five-year-old unpublished writer called Keri Beeves who has been offered £750,000 by a sports publisher called Buckley-Bennion for three novels, two of them about serial killers. Buckley-Bennion is now offering the film rights at £1.5 million per book. Keri will get a percentage. Outside such happy little areas of optimism, we read that the new fashion is for novels without sex and without happy endings. This school is apparently influenced by the American TV series.

Beyond that, one observes that the Library Association's Carnegie Medal – a sort of Booker for children – went to Melvin Burgess for his novel *Junk*, which is all about heroin addiction. So was William Burroughs's 1953 first novel called *Junk*, although Burroughs, who died last month at eighty-three, reissued it as *Junkie* eleven years later. Burroughs is chiefly remembered for his *Naked Lunch* on the same subject.

So, of course, is the MPs' favourite reading of last year. The fact that *Trainspotting* is also about heroin addiction may provide the beginnings of an answer to the question *Whither the Novel?* Perhaps Burroughs's importance in the development of the novel will be recognized, closely followed as he has been by Will Self, Martin Amis and now Melvin Burgess. The great prize at the end of the day, if one can establish oneself as the Anthony Trollope *de nos jours*, is that more than a hundred years after your death people pretend to have read your books.

LITERARY REVIEW, OCTOBER 1997

Facing a Common Problem

Many appear to have found something slightly embarrassing in the spectacle of our prime minister returning from his holiday in France and Italy to launch his National Literacy campaign, immediately joined by the *Sun* with £250,000, and an electronics millionaire called Maurice Hatter with £1 million. The government, said Tony Blair, would match any money produced by industry four times over. Perhaps some people think the problem is rather graver than can be solved by these piffling gestures. The virtual collapse of state education at primary level is not something that can be wished away by a few village fêtes and bell-ringing competitions. It is a massive feature of our national condition, even if the *Sun* has now decided to give Tony Blair a helping hand.

The *Observer* columnist Nick Cohen pointed out that he had proposed that the *Sun* should help out the government in its literacy project as long ago as last June, but his suggestion had been made as a joke. Soon afterwards the seriously humourless David Blunkett adopted this suggestion and invited Murdoch executives round. The result, according to Cohen, is that in Rushden School, Northants, children have to wear T-shirts carrying the logos of Murdoch's papers – *Sun* and *News of the World* on one sleeve, *Sunday Times* and *The Times* on the other. But perhaps he is joking when he tells us this. It is not always easy to tell. Even if he is joking, there is a danger that Rushden pupils will now start wearing these garments.

A more serious anxiety is whether the new generation of primary-school teachers has the faintest idea how to cope with the numbers of pupils who go up to secondary school more or less unable to read. Labour puts the figure at 250,000, the Tories (who are scarcely in a position to gloat) at 500,000. How is the money to be spent? Reports of a five-day course set up for primary-school teachers in Islington, one of Britain's most illiterate boroughs, and paid for by the National Lottery project, are not too encouraging.

A recent survey showed that 80 per cent of Islington children in their first year at secondary school were unable to pass a simple reading test. The forty teachers attending the course were told that they could improve this figure if they cultivated calmness:

> Use long, slow, sweeping gazes: e.g. looking out of the window, or looking dreamily at a display, or sweeping your eyes across the children with a gentle smile.

According to a report by Judith O'Reilly, the *Sunday Times*'s education correspondent – I am almost sure she was not joking – the written advice continued:

> Be still and use slow and soft hand signals to hush or calm behaviour that's out of sync with the tone of the moment.

One cannot help groaning a little if this is really how they think they will raise standards of literacy in Islington. More than 40 per cent of Islington parents with children of secondary-school age refuse to educate them in the borough. Tony Blair himself set the example by choosing to send his son, Euan, to a school six miles away.

One further suggestion for improving the literacy of our children may explain the whole mystery. According to O'Reilly, literacy could be improved by sticking stickers on the wall, drawing happy faces on the blackboard or by dropping marbles into a jar. This is how the National Literacy Project spends its money, advising teachers to drop marbles into a jar. The only possible explanation for this must be found in a gigantic misunderstanding. Someone, somewhere, whether in Islington's education department or in the National Literacy Project, or in both, does not know the meaning of the word 'literacy'. Perhaps no one at all in the education department or in the project itself is completely certain what it means. They confuse it with *literature*.

Literature has nothing to do with literacy. Many may feel they are natural enemies. Understanding of literature may well be improved by long, slow, sweeping gazes, looking dreamily at displays or sweeping your eyes across the children with a dreamy smile. There is no knowing what might inspire the muse or produce the first stumbling lines of modern poetry. But it is not the same thing as learning to read and write. Even dropping marbles into a jar is unlikely to teach anyone to spell such tricky words as 'fox', 'rabbit' and 'dinner'.

Tony Blair's first task in launching a National Literacy campaign must be to teach us all what exactly he means by such fancy and elitist words as *Literacy*. Then the nation can pull in its belt and buckle down to face a common problem, as it did in 1939 when all the world was against us.

LITERARY REVIEW, APRIL 1998

The Least We Can Do

When Lord Gowrie unveiled Antony Gormley's sixty-five-foot statue, *The Angel of the North*, near Gateshead, he said it was the proudest moment of his life. Or so a friend told me who claimed to have heard his speech on the radio. I told my friend to wipe the smirk off his face. Those of us who are called upon to make speeches from time to time often say silly things, and Lord Gowrie's motive may have been no more than a desire to be polite to his hosts, Gateshead Council.

One does not need a background in aesthetics to recognize Gormley's statue – with its 175-foot wingspan, like that of a jumbo jet – as a monument to the bureaucratic philistinism of our times. The idea for the statue came from seventy-seven-year-old Councillor Pat Connaty, who describes how the Council struggled to decide what kind of statue would catch the eye of visitors and attract investment: 'I just blurted out, "What we need is a bloody great angel." It had a very quietening effect on people. The sculptor just said: "That's a reasonably good idea."'

We should not forget that the purpose of this ugly and embarrassing thing is to attract investment to Gateshead. There were those

who were tempted to see its title as yet another sneering reference to
the North of England, another insult for them to bear, on top of the
unemployment and the poverty. We hear there are nowadays no jobs
of any description, even as swimming-bath attendants; many families,
who have not worked for three or four generations, have forgotten what
the word means.

So perhaps it was this consideration which persuaded Lord Gowrie
that the unveiling of Gormley's ridiculous statue was his proudest
moment. One forgets that in addition to having been minister for the
arts and chairman of the Arts Council, Gowrie was also minister of
state for employment in the early years of Mrs Thatcher. Perhaps it is
the thought of encouraging investment in Gateshead that makes him
so proud.

I suppose it is possible that one or two of the 32 million people expected
to drive past this ugly and fatuous object every year will be tempted to
invest in Gateshead as a result of the experience. For my own part, I have
no insight into the minds of these people, and always throw away the business section of every newspaper. But I think we must decide that Gowrie
was not asked to unveil Gormley's monstrosity because he was a former
employment minister under Mrs Thatcher, but because he occupies a
certain position in the arts world. What made him proud, I suspect, was
that a dim, northern town, famous for its philistinism even in Tyne and
Wear, had been persuaded to sanction the spending of £800,000 on what
people like Gowrie call the Arts.

Dismal and embarrassing as *The Angel of the North* may be, at least
she does no harm. Her sex is indeterminate as, indeed, is that of the
Millennium Giant, and quite possibly male. But I think it politer to refer
to an anonymous angel as 'she'. I do not know how the bill was divided
between the Lottery Fund (which threatens endless humiliations of this
sort), the local council, and what is left of our national arts sponsorship
scheme, once administered by the Arts Council. But at least foreign visitors
are not expected to pay to visit her. As she stands there, in all her mediocrity, she might even help Britons make up their minds about the general

direction which publicly sponsored art has been taking in the last forty or fifty years. It is tempting to suggest a campaign to have the ridiculous object knocked down again, and the site restored to its earlier role as a pit-head bathhouse, reminding us of the bad old days when there were jobs. People tend to forget, when complaining about unemployment, how much worse things were down the mines, although the memory still rankles. There is a temptation to remind them. But that would be bossy and wrong. The Angel must be left until she is blown down in the ordinary course of events. Gowrie has done nothing really wrong in drawing attention to the philistine gullibility of Gateshead Council; in fact, he has made rather a good joke.

The £775 million Greenwich Dome is entirely different. There, the insult to our national intelligence is more painful, as we have to listen to our Prime Minister describing its contents as 'bold, beautiful and inspiring', the product of our national creativity and talent. Even the marketing operation stinks of everything that is phoney and provincial and second-rate. Blair and Mandelson hope that 12 million people, many of them foreigners, will pay about £30 a head to gawp at this patronizing rubbish. Even if only a quarter as many do so, it will add to our national humiliation.

Perhaps we are wrong to suppose that our qualities of intelligence and native originality might indeed survive, out of sight, in the Tony Blair age. Even if we are wrong, we have a simple human duty to give no encouragement to their replacements. The art critic of the *Daily Telegraph*, Richard Dorment – never mind that he happens to be a brother-in-law – has made a suggestion:

> Right here, right now, put down this newspaper and raise your voice with me to swear a mighty oath: 'Whatever else I do between 31 December 1999 and 31 December 2000, I solemnly swear not to waste my time and money traipsing through that ridiculous tent in Greenwich.'
>
> It may not be a great deal, but I think it is the least we can do.

LITERARY REVIEW, MAY 1998
Does Any Publisher Want to be Rich?

A large volume of valedictory poems to the Princess of Wales, written by members of the public – *Poems for a Princess: In Memory of Diana, Princess of Wales, 1961–97* (Anchor Books) – has excited little but derision in literary and poetic circles. Those few critics who had a kind word to say seemed even more patronizing, and therefore more odious, than those who castigated the would-be poets for their amateurishness, their clumsiness and their inability to handle what may well have been genuine, even passionately felt, emotion. Never mind that granny poems set their own standard. Some of them weren't too bad and one or two were really quite good. The important evidence they afford is that large numbers of people still turn to formal verse when they have a strong emotion to express. In fact, there has always been a preference for formal poetry. Spontaneous reactions of this sort raise the hope that we might yet live to see a revival of the great English poetic tradition.

Some would have been happier if the emotion which inspired *Poems for a Princess* had been more private. Shared public emotion has too many echoes of World Cup hysteria, not to mention the Fascist rallies of the 1930s, to sit comfortably with the idea of a poetic revival. But it was a curious gift of the late Princess that she could inspire intense personal affection in strangers. Those who remember her presenting the *Literary Review*'s Grand Poetry Prize in 1995, sponsored by the *Mail on Sunday* – she even composed a short poem herself for the occasion, although cynics suggested she had been helped by her intelligent and highly educated private secretary, Mr Patrick Jephson – will know that her memory would be an ideal inspiration for the poetic revival which may yet rescue our national pride from two generations of rotten teaching and second-rate opinions.

It would be easy to recommend that the Princess of Wales Memorial Fund should institute a regular national poetry prize for the best verse that rhymes, scans and makes sense, rather like this magazine's monthly poetry prize (at present sponsored by Larkhall Green Farms, makers of the delicious and nourishing vitamin pills), which will soon have been running for twelve years. Our purpose was never more than to keep the flame burning; even a successful and booming literary magazine like the *Literary Review*, which has increased sales with every issue since Nancy Sladek became deputy editor twenty-four months ago, cannot hope to have quite the same instant, mass appeal as the late princess.

The trouble is that whenever there is money available there are hundreds, possibly thousands, of good causes clamouring for it, and we have no reason to suppose that any of the trustees has the slightest interest in the state of English poetry – unlike their beloved sister and daughter. When Aids and landmines have been exhausted, there is always the instant and urgent appeal of sick children, constantly in need of aspirins, glucose, syrup of fig, or whatever.

So I think we should address ourselves instead to the nation's publishers, proposing poetry not as a good cause, but as a neglected approach to the much more important cause of making money. It is true that the Poetry Society and other bodies occasionally announce that there has been an increase in sales of the sort of modern rubbish they purvey. From time to time, its very meaninglessness will appeal to the disaffected young as an appropriate response to the modern world. But they remain a small market. Most people have come to detest poetry even as they detest poets.

At the end of March, when I was applying for a licence to open the new Academy at 46 Lexington Street, next door to the magazine, the magistrate asked me what sort of people we had as members. When I replied that poets were absolutely banned, her whole face lit up, and she signed our licence on the spot, saying she supposed we would wish to start serving alcoholic drinks later that day. The club has been quietly flourishing ever since.

The reason poets were originally banned from the old Academy in Beak Street was partly that they could talk about nothing but themselves, partly that they never paid for their drinks and partly that all the pretty women fell in love with them. But it would be a dreadful shame if general hatred of these mountebanks, clowns and charlatans discouraged publishers from considering the possibilities of a huge revival in formal poetry. This might start from the granny poems of the Princess Diana book to achieve the subtleties of a Blake, the technical expertise of a Tennyson, even the majestic cadences of a Keats.

Some of the serious poetry being written, as I say, is very good, but it is a waste of time sending it to the *Literary Review*. There are a few mainstream publishers who retain a poetry list, such as Faber, Cape and Picador. They are evidently deluged with rubbish and send back unsolicited poetry even by such witty and gifted prizewinning poets as our own Fiona Pitt-Kethley. My point is that if any publishing house announced it was going to publish nothing but formal poetry – which scans, makes sense and (preferably) rhymes – it would immediately corner the market, and become famous on that account. Anybody can see that there is a huge potential demand for reading, as well as writing formal verse which applies itself to the various aspects of modern life. It does not all have to be about Princess Diana. Formal poetry is much easier to judge than the informal variety, and I feel it in my bones that there is a fortune to be made from this neglected market. Is anyone interested?

LITERARY REVIEW, JUNE 1998
Nobody Loves Them ~ Nobody Cares

In the new boastful atmosphere being encouraged by Tony Blair, where Britons are supposed to take pride in the notion that we make the best vacuum cleaners, the best pop music, design the best cushions, nobody has had much to say about the nation's writers. In fact, it was noticeable that once again in this country's richest fiction award, the £30,000 Orange Prize, the shortlist of six this year comprised four American women, one Irish and only one Briton – Pauline Melville, of Guyanese descent, for her novel *The Ventriloquist's Tale*, set in Guyana.

It is true that there is no tradition in Britain for honouring or even acknowledging writers. The feeling among educated folk is that any of us could write if we set our minds to it, and a certain amount of resentment attaches to those who get themselves printed. They seem to lack modesty, the essential British quality of reticence, if they write about themselves. Those who write about the social scene are judged little better than gossip columnists or scandal merchants.

What interest in literary matters is shown by our news media – I am not, of course, talking about the review sections – is always connected to our national obsession with money. When it was claimed that the novelist Robert Mawson had made £2 million overnight from his novel *Lazarus Child* (Bantam Press), about a young girl in a coma after a motor accident, he became a national talking point for that reason. Nobody queried the nation's more interesting, and even less healthy, sentimental obsession with young children, especially girls, which would seem to account for the novel's success. I do not think anyone actually accused Mawson of exploiting this fictional young girl, although it may only be a matter of time before somebody does. But the great Mary Bell debate, which ran for nearly a month when it became known that Gitta Sereny had written a study of the child killer after thirty years, was entirely taken up with the money issue.

Even before it was known that Mary Bell had received £15,000 for her five-month co-operation in the book, we heard cries against Gitta Sereny from June Richardson, the mother of one of the victims. Her suffering face reminded us daily of the thirty-year-old tragedy as she railed against Sereny for making a 'profit' from her loss. At least Richardson was not demanding a share of the money, as we heard of relatives of victims at Dunblane and Hillsborough. But there is a fixed opinion among non-writers that anybody who writes on a subject is exploiting it to his or her own advantage, and making a profit, rather than simply earning a living.

It took the ever-sensible Minette Marrin to point out, in the *Sunday Telegraph*, that anyone even discussing Mary Bell in print was profiting from her crimes. She argued that writers are not usually very pleasant people, in any case:

The English scepticism about writers and artists generally is well founded. It is very often true that artists are dreadful people – vain, self-obsessed, irresponsible and exploitative. They need to be, if only to believe that their perceptions are worth imposing on the rest of the world.

That is exactly what we discovered when the old Academy Club was founded in Beak Street, originally restricted to writers of whose work the Committee approved. They were not very pleasant people, although seldom as dreadful as the poets, about whom I wrote last month [see above] and who remain permanently banned. Of all the writing fraternity, if 'fraternity' can be applied to such a jealous, squabbling group, journalists are generally the most amiable, but some of the nicest people often turn out to be doctors, accountants, funeral directors, even lawyers.

A Waterstone's survey, 'The Cost of Letters: How much do you think a writer needs to live on?', provides an insight into the character of writers and their attitudes to money. It is based on Cyril Connolly's *Horizon* questionnaire of 1946. Under Alain de Botton's direction, forty-two working writers were consulted, nearly all of them familiar names to readers of the *Literary Review*.

Lucy Ellmann: 'I've never been given a fucking penny by the Arts Council, and I'm not happy about it.'

Adrian Mitchell: 'I want to see some bloody enthusiasm for the work of living writers... from those who are meant to help artists.'

Tim Parks: 'Journalism is as antithetical to writing as republicanism is to royalty.'

Michael Ignatieff (quoting Tolstoy): 'Journalism is a brothel which is easy to enter but impossible to escape.'

On the other hand, Bernice Rubens describes self-important writers as a 'pain in the arse', and Will Self says: 'When I hear a writer utter the word "posterity" I reach for my gun.'

When I was a young man, conversation between writers generally consisted of boastful lies about how many copies their books had sold, or how much money they had received from their American publisher. The mood is different now. Writers, by and large, expect to be supported and pampered by the state as revered members of the dependency culture. I doubt that anyone will pay the slightest attention to their moans. You might say that the whole literary climate had changed. Does it matter a fig if it has?

LITERARY REVIEW, JULY 1998

Nobody Loves Them, Nobody Cares 2

I arrived a day late for the Sydney Writers' Festival in New South Wales because it slipped my mind that I had agreed to speak at the Brighton Literary Festival on my day of departure. At certain times of year, those on the fringes of the literary world (as opposed to writers, who might have more important things to do) can happily spend their whole time drifting from conference to conference, patting each other on the back and smiling at each other. It would be absurd to describe such pleasant occasions as a waste of time. Is anything a waste of time, in the perspective of a godless eternity? My own purpose in attending them is always to spread the good news of the *Literary Review* and try to sell a few subscriptions. I managed to shift many subscription cards in Brighton and was full of hope for New South Wales. In Adelaide, South Australia, I once discovered that three quarters of the company at a literary banquet were regular readers, and it was even possible to buy the magazine at a couple of newspaper stalls in the street.

My main problem was an almost complete ignorance of recent Australian literature. This is not something I admit with pride, and perhaps I owned up to it too readily in an interview before I left. It is a sad truth in my life that time spent editing other people's reviews in this magazine and earning a living from columns in the *Telegraph* leaves very little for reading new books. For twenty years I reviewed at least one book a week, but this came to an end in 1990, and since then I have known of the latest books only through other people's opinions of them. In fact, this has always been one of the selling points of the *Literary Review*, that it enables busy people to keep up with the world of letters and inform themselves about what books they should buy and display on their coffee tables without any obligation to read a single book. I am not sure it works, or that it is a very attractive selling point, but at least it provides another possible reason for buying the magazine.

The Australians, however, were hoping for something different. I think they saw me as a violently polemical person who would come and insult their leading writers. They love to see their leaders insulted, and my reputation out there is almost entirely derived from *Private Eye*. It was for this that they had kindly provided a return air ticket and hospitably put me up in the Sydney Inter-Continental. A mildly abusive series of full-page articles in the *Sydney Morning Herald*, the *Melbourne Age* and the *Australian* prepared the ground. One reporter even made the pilgrimage to our offices in Lexington Street to produce two pages of broadsheet abuse in the *Morning Herald* out of a half-hour interview:

> The worn wooden stairs are crooked. They lean and whimper in mild alarm at the tread. The decaying walls seem to sigh with several hundred years of neglect. It is to this exhausted building that you come to the *Literary Review* office. Entering from a dank and teeming Soho afternoon, the narrow, dishevelled hallway could scarcely be less auspicious.

Never mind the hanging participle, anacoluthon or *nominativus pendens* in that last sentence. She had travelled a long way. But worse was to come:

> When you are expecting the fearsomely snobbish satirist, the prolific persecutor, it is something of a surprise to find a dithering scrawny man whose few remaining wisps of hair fly upward like feathers, giving the appearance of a recently plucked chicken.

Oh dear. It is a terrible thing to disappoint people. I could, I suppose, have bluffed my way through with a few rude epithets to describe Patrick White, which would have made everyone happy, but I found I respected my hosts too much. They are altogether too direct, too cheerful, too hospitable and friendly to insult with the tedious English conventions of literary bluff.

Instead we talked about politics. I had been warned to avoid the subject of republicanism. They are all pathetically, childishly keen on the idea of having an Australian president, as a mark of national independence. Impatience with the Royal Family is running high. I started a campaign to convince them that if they abandon the evidence of their historical identity they will soon be swallowed up in an inferior, poorer version of American mass culture.

They looked thoughtful at this. It is true that about three quarters of Australian television comes from America – television and film are now the biggest industry in the richest country in the world, as well as the biggest export. Intelligent Australians resent this state of affairs, and even unintelligent ones often complain about the intellectual standard of the programmes, as well as the moronic sentimentality of the Disneyland ethos which holds Hollywood in its grip of terror.

But I think I was wrong. England will be conquered by Disney long before Australia. There is a scepticism built into the Australian character which shows itself rather well in the desire to see people insulted and preferably in gross language. Far from being the next to succumb to Disney, Australians may prove the salvation of the English-speaking world against the Mickey Mouse invasion. It is true that they are almost insane in their sentimental confusion about the Aborigines, but it is the confusion of decent people faced by an intractable problem. They will put it in its place. I would like to see Australia as the cultural leader of the English-speaking world, rather as England and Scotland seek to lead it at football. But first, perhaps, we should start reading their books.

LITERARY REVIEW, SEPTEMBER 1998

The Good Sex Campaign Comes of Age

British bookselling faces the biggest revolution in its modern history, we are told in *The Bookseller*, organ of the trade, owing to the opening of a superstore by the American chain of Borders ('BOOKS * MUSIC * CAFE') in Oxford Street, of all places. Other Borders superstores will open early next year in Charing Cross Road (on the site of Books Etc.), in Glasgow and in Brighton.

The rhetoric which pours from Borders' chairman, Robert F. DiRomualdo, is exactly the same as justified the disappearance of so many small shops where we once found it easy to buy what we wanted. Why should bookselling be immune to the tough, competitive trends of modern retailing, where twenty-four-hour convenience stores and supermarkets have rendered small grocers and hardware stores redundant, he asks.

Personally, I resent having to spend valuable time searching in a super-market and queuing to pay for a simple loaf of bread or half-pound slab of butter and derive no joy from its being a few pennies cheaper. But the Borders approach also involves efficient and dedicated personal service to help you find the book you want – or so people say – and the creation of a cultural atmosphere, where people can spill coffee and cake-crumbs over books without being required to pay for them. When the multiple grocery chains started selling books – only the trashiest bestsellers, of course – at cut rates, the literary world rallied round to say how unfair this was to the serious, small bookseller, who needed to sell trash at the full rate in order to subsidize the less popular books which might stay in stock for two years before being sold. This was partly true so far as it went, but the sad truth of the matter is that only a few of these small bookshops provide any sort of service worth defending.

Their stock is tiny and only sometimes well chosen. Most of the books are on sale-or-return, so the bookseller risks nothing. Many refuse to consider ordering a book that is not in stock, even with the traditional fifteen-day wait before it arrives, without an order for three copies and/

or a down-payment. A surprising number of booksellers – like sweetshop owners and publicans – always seem to be exceptionally unpleasant people. I do not know why this should be the case, but I have often noticed that many of them refuse to stock the *Literary Review* (also available on sale-or-return), saying they need the shelf-space for more lucrative coffee-table books. Perhaps these people are frightened that the magazine will introduce their customers to exciting new books which the shop will then be unable to supply.

Only the writers – referred to by Mr DiRomualdo as 'content providers' – would appear to make any real effort. They are unlikely to profit by globalization of the book trade, since it threatens to destroy the exclusive territorial rights on which most royalty agreements are based. One may doubt whether the notion of copyright will survive in the written word. This may seem unfortunate for writers, although other satisfactions are available to them, chiefly the mysterious admiration of the opposite sex.

If one accepts that nearly all the books worth writing have already been written, then the arrival on the scene of these efficient, apparently congenial bookstores should be welcomed. In addition to providing cafés, they have an endless succession of in-store events, which may be a Dvořák quartet or a concert by Sting, a reading or an earnest discussion on Virginia Woolf's sex life. Perhaps their most important function will not even be in the field of selling books, but in providing a new social focus on the London scene – something rather like the Academy Club, in its new manifestation at 46 Lexington Street, next door to the *Literary Review* offices, but without the alcohol.

Cynics have suggested that these new bookstores will be nothing more than pick-up joints, although this is not likely to be the case in America, where they have given up that sort of thing. Americans are nowadays expected to be excited that J. D. Salinger had an affair twenty-five years ago. But one could not help noticing that Waterstone's, to meet the new challenge, instituted a 'happy hour' every Thursday throughout August, with 10 per cent off all book prices and free wine for all.

There are worse functions for a bookshop than the encouragement of a certain amount of sexual interaction. The latest fashion in male fiction, we are told, is called *Melancholy for Men*, all written by sad, singleton males. They have been dumped by their girlfriends and spend their time brooding about the loneliness of the single state.

If the new Borders store helps to discourage this new gloomy school, it will have done something useful. In the same way, we hope to discourage bad sexual writing with our annual Bad Sex Prize, sponsored by Hamlet cigars. This goes to the most embarrassing passage of sexual description in any literary novel published during the year. The time is coming round again, and those coveting the magnificent £150 Rowbotham Prize should send in their entries without delay. Send photocopies identifying the book and author responsible by 1 November, with 'Bad Sex' on the envelope.

But perhaps sex has always been a problem for the English writer. When the new Borders store opens in Charing Cross Road, in time for the London Festival of Literature in March, it might alter its sign to read: 'BOOKS * MUSIC * CAFE * GOOD SEX'.

[Borders were to go bankrupt a few years later (2011). The *Literary Review* Bad Sex Prize continues to be awarded each year.]

In the autumn of 1998, Bron was asked if he might want to write an introduction to a collection of 20 postcards called *La Belle Époque*, which Quartet intended to publish for the Christmas market that year. He delivered this the next morning:

La Belle Époque
BY AUBERON WAUGH

The twenty original daguerreotypes which follow may be among the earliest commercial photographic pin-ups ever produced. Posed and taken in the pleasure houses of Paris in the last years of the nineteenth century, they were published in 1900 by Photo-Hall, operating at 5 Rue Scribe in Paris. An early technique of silvered plates and mercury vapour was used, with minimal later colouring by hand, but it is not the photographic technique which makes them of exceptional interest, so much as the subjects.

THE MODELS, we must remember, were working in a profession which was then considered perfectly normal, if not quite respectable. They were certainly not accustomed to posing for nude photographs, and might well have questioned the propriety of such activity in a way they would never have worried about exposing themselves to a customer, or taking his money. One can see the occasional look of hesitation in their eyes as they pose, which is doubly curious nowadays when respectable housewives are happy to pose topless on most beaches, and naked on some.

THE HISTORY of the photographs is that they were found in a Paris antique shop and later sold to Naim Attallah, the publisher and owner of Quartet Books, by an *antiquaire* in Sarlat, a small town in the Dordogne. Nobody who knows Naim Attallah will be surprised to learn that he fell hopelessly in love with them. In an age when nude pin-ups tend to be skeletally thin, and offer nothing by way of intimacy, it is encouraging to see these better covered women who are confident in their attraction to men and obviously sincere in whatever promises they seem to be making.

WE MAY SPEND much time speculating on whether they gave their customers a good time, whether they enjoyed their work or were horrified and ashamed by it, whether they chose the world's oldest profession or had it forced on them. Contemporary English prostitutes, who are rumoured to be the worst in the world, are said to make no pretence of interest in their customers or enjoyment of their work. As in so many service industries in Britain, they appear to hate their customers. The philosophy of political correctness would probably approve of this attitude. While being adamant that women have the right to work as prostitutes if they wish, the new feminist is not quite certain about the male's right to avail himself of her services. Perhaps they will allow it on the grounds that it reduces the risk of rape. But Paris in the Belle Époque was not given to such austere anxieties. There was a robust culture of sybaritism which extended to the pleasure houses or brothels as much as to the restaurants, music halls, theatres and private houses in that happy period which ended so tragically in 1914.

IT WOULD BE nice to think that these pretty, welcoming ladies gave their customers a good time and enjoyed their work, retiring with plenty of money to take a respected place in their families and in society. Of course they are all dead now, but let their memory be honoured. Those who can resist the temptation to send the pictures away as postcards should look at the book of an evening, with a glass of something bubbly to hand and Offenbach's *La Via Parisienne* at full blast on the CD player. If they suffered injustice in their lives, that is the best way to apologize. If they enjoyed their work and looked back on it with pleasure, that is the best way to congratulate them. In any case, it is nice to have them around.

LITERARY REVIEW, FEBRUARY 2000

The Greatest Issue of Our Times

The contents of this magazine have tended to reflect my belief that practically nobody in this country is interested in politics. This is something which politicians can never understand, of course. Possibly their motive is to scatter political advantages of 'full plenty o'er a smiling land, and read their history in a nation's eyes', as Thomas Gray so prettily put it, rather than simply to exercise power and feel important. It would be nice to think so, but this is not the general view, and most of us are happy to leave politics to the tiny minority of social cripples and emotional inadequates who feel the need to join parties, form committees, impose their personal opinions, and change existing arrangements, usually for the worse.

Sadly enough, the better newspapers have a long tradition of taking politics seriously. They think it adds to the power of their editorial presence, and to the influence of their proprietors. In fact, it merely adds to the general disenchantment with the news and gives a voice to every bore and monomaniac in the land. This might not have mattered when newspapers seldom had more than sixteen pages, but the huge increase in available space means that hundreds of pages appear every day, dedicated to schemes for the extension of government in every direction. These suggestions come mostly from special-interest groups and frustrated power maniacs in the various ministries, but it is a frightening aspect of our times that ordinary Britons have grown to accept the idea of more and more government, more and more supervision over all their activities. This is despite our indifference to politicians and lack of enthusiasm for political ideology.

I do not think that the *Literary Review* is a suitable vehicle for addressing this problem, even in the monthly sermon. We avoid politics as much as possible because I do not believe our readers are interested in the subject. This seems good enough reason and is greatly to their credit. In the current issue, some topics may, however, be unavoidable, unless we are to confine ourselves to purely literary subjects. One of them is Britain's participation in Europe… This is because our entire cultural life is bound to be affected if ever we can persuade ourselves that we are Europeans, and part of some dimly discerned European future, rather than an unacknowledged fifty-first state of the USA. It is true that Americans write in the English language, and it would be churlish to ignore their literary efforts. Besides that, American publishers are charming people – so intelligent, well read, well mannered and enthusiastic that it would be easy for literary Britons to decide that this is where their future lies. They would be wrong. Many Americans have never heard of Europe. German publishers pay bigger advances than Americans, and the French actually read books.

But there is no reason why the *Literary Review* should be remotely interested in the economic or political advantages of full membership of the European Union. Other aspects of politics can be quite interesting – studies of foreign statesmen, for instance – but they are few and far between, and I do not see any point in a monthly literary magazine trying to be politically topical. There is only one subject in the current political debate which might be of interest. It concerns the London mayoral elections in two months' time but may be thought to have wider application.

London made a tremendous fool of itself in January with a River of Fire which failed to ignite, a Ferris wheel which did not work, and invited guests even kept waiting four hours for admission to the Dome. This was partly because the tickets had not been sent out, it will be remembered, and partly because the police insisted on searching all the guests for 'security' reasons. The Dome survives as a monument to our national mediocrity, just as the suffering inflicted on guests can be seen as a celebration of our new bossiness and incompetence. But the British genius survives. At last somebody has come up with a good political suggestion. Malcolm McLaren, the musical entertainer, who is standing for Mayor of London, has proposed that alcoholic drinks should be available for purchase and consumption in the public libraries.

His other proposals – to scrap museum charges and legalize brothels – may be thought equally benign, but he should watch his step. The Dutch government has just introduced a law to legalize brothels, which demands that all prostitutes employed must be European. As if that were not contemptible enough, it also insists on endless inspections by health and sanitary services, the registering of employees, etc.

McLaren may already have learned that politics is a tricky business. I do not see any of these proposals in his latest manifesto. Far better concentrate on public libraries. Even then, there will be a scream from the teetotal brigade, demanding that they be allowed to buy soft drinks, then another scream that they are being overcharged for them. He must not waver. People who drink these sweet, fizzy beverages undoubtedly derive as much enjoyment from them as a wine-lover does from a bottle of claret, and there is no reason why they should pay less. McLaren must be bold and strong. He has the massive backing of the *Literary Review*, and no candidate with this magazine behind him has yet failed to be swept to power.

LITERARY REVIEW, APRIL 2000

Another Approach to Criticism

The growing success of Greenwich's infamous Dome – at any rate among schoolchildren at half-term – has led to calls for those who criticized it in the first place to eat their words. My friend and colleague Richard Ingrams has a robust answer to this suggestion. Even if the project can succeed in paying for itself, he wrote,

> It doesn't follow that the Dome is any good. Though I have not been myself, I have closely cross-questioned those who have, and have read innumerable accounts by men and women whose judgement I respect. And there can be no getting away from the fact that the contents of the Dome are thoroughly tacky and second-rate.

This would seem to open a debate on the vulgarity and ghastliness of mass culture, but the most interesting aspect of Ingrams's criticism is that he admits to not having been there or seen any of these tacky and second-rate things himself. He would seem to be basing his judgement on a mixture of intuition and the reported opinions of other people, of whom only a certain number may themselves claim first-hand experience.

> As for the Dome, others may eat their words but I will not be numbered among them. Great is the truth and it will prevail.

In quoting all this, I am not questioning Ingrams's conclusion about the Dome. I am sure he is absolutely right. Without having been there myself, I am convinced it is an embarrassment and a national disgrace. My purpose is to draw attention to a new critical discipline – where the

325

critic cheerfully admits he has not seen, heard or smelled the object he is criticizing. Having had one's attention drawn to it, one realizes it is frequently used in literary conversation if less often in written work. But it exists, and having identified it as a school of criticism, we must surely give it a name.

To call it the Ingramsian School might be thought insulting, although there is no suggestion that it is a less valid form of criticism than any other. The idea no longer holds that ignorance of a subject should prevent anyone from having an opinion on it. Nowadays we must accept that the opinion of those with no knowledge is just as valid as that of an expert, or 'so-called expert' as these people are more rightly dubbed.

Perhaps if we cannot call it the Ingramsian Method we might call it after the Greenwich structure that so few people have actually visited – either 'Domestic', in approval, or 'Domboid', in disparagement. The essence of the new school is that the critic should admit to not having read the book he is discussing or reviewing. One does not need to have great experience of literary criticism, let alone literary conversation or any other aspect of the literary life, to realize that people inside it already spend an enormous amount of time discussing books and authors they have never read.

In many cases they do this very well, and produce amusing, sometimes memorable criticism. They do it, in part, out of politeness, for fear of casting a gloom if they admit ignorance and withhold comment on that score. But of course, most of those present will guess they are bluffing. It does not detract from our enjoyment of the performance, but it adds an unnecessary element of uncertainty if we have not been told. Some may disagree with me, but I should judge it will add a new dimension of enjoyment and insight if we know for certain whether the critic has read the book or not.

A few people to whom I have put this idea have grown quite angry, saying that of course criticism must be properly informed to have any value. If they remain unimpressed by my argument that this weight of knowledge has never stopped critics from drawing all the wrong conclusions or writing gibberish, I have to tell them that I think they are out of date; times have moved on without their noticing. I draw their attention to a book produced in Berlin by five German writers which has taken Germany by storm.

Tristesse Royale, as it is called, is the account of five male German friends staying the weekend in a luxury Berlin hotel, talking about the enjoyment of life. Although the book has none of the ingredients that sometimes cause offence – pornography, violence, obscenity, etc., and does not even commit any of the new crimes of racism, sexism or homophobia – it has been bitterly attacked in every respectable literary quarter.

This is because the five authors are uninterested in history and guilt, unconcerned with social reform, political purpose, literary and artistic theory. They like drinking champagne and enjoy unfashionable rock music. They despise the mass culture of television and down-market films, disdaining it as 'proletarian'. Much of their conversation would be seen in this country as unacceptably snobbish.

Yet *Tristesse Royale*, dismissed by the German president's wife as 'dreadful' and denounced at great length in *Der Spiegel*, continues to sell in its hundreds of thousands in Germany for the simple reason that it describes a new generation of Germans who live for pleasure, and who have never been allowed to read about themselves before. Awareness of this new generation has been suppressed – and not only in Germany. When news of *Tristesse Royale* breaks through to the young people of Britain, France and Italy, I suspect it will be seen as the most important book of the new decade. They will not need to have read it – any more than I have.

LITERARY REVIEW, SEPTEMBER 2000

A Pathetic Nostalgia

The reason why I have never cancelled my subscription to the *Observer* in forty years is partly that it gave an extremely nice review to my first novel, *The Foxglove Saga,* in 1960, and partly that, for all its excitability and occasional silliness, it has a genuine heart of gold. No other newspaper would have been prepared to devote the best part of an entire page to the lament of a minor novelist that he could not find a publisher for his latest novel because he was judged too old.

I hope Nicholas Wollaston does not take offence at being described as a 'minor novelist'. It is a very honourable thing to be. At seventy-four, he has had seven novels published and six non-fiction books. His latest novel, *Man in the Net*, about life at sea during the Second World War, won an award from the Arts Council and extravagant praise from its would-be publisher, before she turned it down on the grounds of the author's age.

Wollaston is understandably peeved. 'I believe that what I write now is better than anything from the days when I had no problem getting a publisher,' he wrote in the *Observer*:

> Well, I would say that, wouldn't I? An old bloke, whingeing with self-pity, who hopes to be judged on words, not wrinkles. On the shelf, it's called. But on the shelf is just where I'd like to be – the one in Waterstone's and the public library. Do people go there for a book or for the author's date of birth? At a pinch, I'd change my name and borrow a photo of the barmaid at my local pub – if that would do the trick.

What makes it so nice of the *Observer* to print Wollaston's lament is that for as long as I can remember, middle-aged male authors have been saying the same thing, mostly complaining about the disadvantage of their sex. Publishers will always go for the attractive young female author. Roger Longrigg, author of *The High-Pitched Buzz*, first produced *The Passionflower Hotel* under the name of Rosalind Erskine, with a ravishing photograph, coinciding with *The Foxglove Saga*. I remember begging my publisher to arrange a tour to coincide with hers, only to hear the bitter truth from the author in person. Longrigg wrote thirty-eight novels under seven assumed names – nearly all of them female – in addition to eighteen or so books under his own name. Only this week I learned of two good and respected American male authors who found they had been dropped by their publishers on reaching fifty. They invented two swinging twenty-something females with voracious sexual appetites and a fondness for smoking marijuana, who were snapped up by their original publishers, with a strict clause in the contract that if anybody discovered the truth about their identity, the contract was null and void.

In the old days, one occasionally wondered whether publishers really thought that a book would sell better if it was written by an attractive young woman, or whether they were simply looking for a lay, as people said in those days. If so, I fear their hopes were likely to be disappointed. These professional enchantresses seldom deliver the goods, and publishers are not very adroit in their seduction techniques.

But the new accent is on youth, rather than on sexual attraction, and this seems more worrying. The young, we are told, especially young women, have largely lost interest in sex. Are we to suppose that they are particularly keen on buying and reading books?

A survey conducted for the *Independent* by Book Marketing Ltd does not suggest this is the case. Although the reading habit still flourishes, particularly among small children, it tails off among the eleven- to twelve-year-olds. Male school-leavers in particular scarcely read at all, although the habit picks up again in middle age, so that the average adult now reads for five hours a week, while 10 per cent read for at least eleven hours. This does not explain the extraordinary emphasis on young writers, whom publishers seem prepared to back beyond any prospect of economic justification.

People may reasonably decide that these are no more than the sour reflections of a sixty-year-old male who gave up writing novels thirty years ago. Nevertheless, it seems to me that there is a lunacy in the air. The young do not write well. In a recent study of teenage literacy from the School Inspectorate, it appears that many English teenagers have more or less abandoned the English language. They communicate through a mixture of gestures and oral shorthand. I see no evidence that they are kinder or less selfish than the rest of us, and no reason at all to hero-worship them.

So long as they are happy with this limited degree of communication, we have no business to worry about them. They do us no harm, and greater subtlety of expression would probably make them no happier. Where profundity of emotion is concerned, they are obviously capable of falling in love. What more can they want? Perhaps publishers' obsessions with finding young writers derives from idealism, a determination to prevent what might be seen as the impending collapse of any understanding between the generations.

But I do not think so. I do not think it derives even from a misunderstanding of their commercial future. Few of these teenagers will ever be employed. It derives from a pathetic nostalgia for lost youth. Perhaps it is time the publishing profession grew up.

LITERARY REVIEW, NOVEMBER 2000
Let Us All Write about Ourselves

In a surprisingly short period of time it has become a cliché to remark that the English novel has had its day. There are wistful noises made about the tiny handful of novels that mysteriously hit the big time and earn hundreds of thousands of pounds for their authors and publishers, but by and large it is generally accepted that the English literary novel, as a way of describing the society in which we live, has disappeared from the scene.

The fault may be with our society, which has no pinnacles above temporary celebrities, and no deprived lower class beyond a few small immigrant areas we do not wish to know about. It certainly does not lie with any shortage of would-be novelists. Practically every teenager in the land will tell anyone prepared to listen that he or she intends to work in some creative field, whether writing novels or making films, and it is hard to meet an insurance broker or property dealer or even an established car salesman who will not confide his intention of writing a novel.

The sad truth would appear to be that this great urge to creativity in our society is not reciprocated by any great demand for its products.

Everybody wants to write novels but does anybody want to read them? It is only when we have tackled this unwelcome question that we can ask ourselves what to do with our creative urges. One reaction to the general disenchantment with other people's fantasies was to turn the novel into mildly fictionalized autobiography. Authors described themselves, their friends and their relations under assumed names, in deeply sensitive character studies. This worked for a time, especially among the lovers, friends, neighbours and relations described, but rather failed to work among the much greater number of people who were none of these things and who might have been expected to buy the books. The general reader did not know who the characters were supposed to be or which of the incidents were true. Once again, boredom set in.

The next step might appear to be for people quite simply to publish their memoirs, unadorned. Two problems arise. In the first place, if the characters are still alive at the time of publication, the laws of libel will require that practically nothing of interest appears. In the second place, few of us have the material inside us for more than one or two volumes, even assuming anybody wants to read them, and that scarcely provides the opportunity for an alternative, creative lifestyle.

The solution, I feel, is for everyone troubled by this creative urge to keep a diary. It should be written without the slightest intention of publication, least of all in the diarist's lifetime. Neither of our first great diarists – the contemporaries Samuel Pepys and John Evelyn – wrote for publication. Pepys even wrote in an impenetrable cipher, which remained untouched at Magdalene College, Cambridge, until 1825, 122 years after his death. John Evelyn's diary was found in an old clothes basket at his family home in Wotton, near Dorking, in 1817 – 111 years after his death. Yet these two men between them have given us a better understanding of late-seventeenth-century England than any novelist, poet or playwright of any period in our history.

When I suggest that diary-writing may prove the great literary art form of the future I do not wish to suggest that its practitioners will be any better than diarists of the past. On page 11 [of this issue], Sebastian

Shakespeare reviews the amazing 704-page anthology of 170 diarists, with 1,800 entries, compiled by Alan and Irene Taylor. But the flood seems to have started. I was interested to read in the course of Hugh Massingberd's review last month of the eighth volume of James Lees-Milne's diaries that 'Lees-Milne's only rivals for the honour of being the Greatest Diarist of the Twentieth Century' are Chips Channon and Harold Nicolson.

Pschaw! Massingberd seems particularly impressed by the fact that all three were married homosexuals, but I do not see what that has to do with it. Upper-class gossip is a tiny part of the pleasures available, which can involve laughing at the diarist as much as laughing with him. Recently we have had the choice between Scott of the Antarctic and Lord Longford, not to mention Woodrow Wyatt and Alan Clark. Perhaps I should declare an interest, deriving some benefit from the publication of Evelyn Waugh's diaries, in the course of which I am described as a fifteen-year-old drunk being taken off a train and put in a police cell.

For my own part, I particularly enjoyed aspects of Alan Clark's *Diaries*. Clark announced it as his belief that you should 'always tell people what you think they want to hear'; about his father, the great Kenneth Clark, he thinks we wish to hear that he was 'such a shit, so sly and weak, without the slightest concept of succession'. By coincidence, I happen to have a large nude drawing of Kenneth Clark by [Ralph] Steadman in my downstairs lavatory.

Diaries may prove to be the last great literary art form to survive, but they must be written for the satisfaction of their authors. The reason for this is that writers are most interested in themselves. The tragedy of Woodrow Wyatt's diaries is that they were written to make money for his widow and children. Woodrow, an old friend, was the kindest, funniest and cleverest of men, but his diaries are a load of rubbish. They might have been written by Nigel Dempster with a toothache. That is because they were written in a good cause. A proper diary is totally consumed by selfishness.

LITERARY REVIEW, DECEMBER 2000/JANUARY 2001

Time to Honour the Booksellers

To judge by its title, one must suppose that the Medical Foundation for the Care of Victims of Torture is a thoroughly admirable charity. A group of authors who have decided to help the foundation hope to raise £70,000 by an auction of character-names, whereby any member of the public can bid to have his or her name used for a character in an author's next novel.

The auction will be held at the British Academy of Film and Television Arts (Bafta) in Piccadilly on 5 December. One hopes the seven popular and successful authors who have already come forward – Nick Hornby, Kathy Lette, Sebastian Faulks, Louis de Bernières, Rose Tremain, Hanif Kureishi and Jim Crace – will be joined by many others. It will be interesting to see how much people are prepared to pay for a measure of immortality, even if cynics will object that the immortality may be limited by the fact that few novels are read more than a year after publication. But at least the books will continue to exist, and entries in them can be shown to generations yet unborn. Alternatively, there may be those who will happily pay not to have their name included in someone else's novel (my wife assures me she belongs to that number), and this might prove another way of raising money for the Medical Foundation for the Care of Victims of Torture, which needs £5 million for a new headquarters in North London.

Never mind that this seems rather a lot of money for such a foundation to need. We must dismiss all such thoughts from our heads. The most interesting aspect of the event is the way it shows that novelists have collectively joined the ranks of celebrities in our Disney culture. Novel-writing has become a respectable profession, even a good cause. I wonder what effect, if any, this development will have on the art form concerned, but I am unlikely to find out because I practically never read a new English novel, unless it is written by a very close friend.

Simon Jenkins, who was chairman of this year's Booker panel and read 120 of last year's novels as part of his duty, believes that 'the novel remains the one serious art form that receives no government subsidy.

This may explain its robustness.' As he points out, books are now sold in supermarkets and petrol stations. 'Last year saw 9,800 works of fiction published in the United Kingdom, an avalanche of literary creativity.'

I happen to believe that Jenkins is a thoroughly good egg, and that the country would be a poorer place without him and am delighted to hear he thinks that last year's novels were particularly robust. The Arts Council, however, would not agree with his statement that the novel receives no public subsidy, and I cannot help wondering about the figure of 9,800 for novels published in 1999. Did he count them? In my experience of the book trade, these statistics are more or less randomly produced. Nor do publishers provide any indication of the type to which the novels now being published in such numbers belong. The survival of publishers is nowadays seen as a noble cause, in which any amount of filth can be justified if they also produce a certain amount of highbrow rubbish that nobody wants to read.

I find myself particularly irritated by publishers' ritual attacks on the rest of the book trade, particularly the booksellers who have to make a living despite carrying enormous stocks of unsold books. This month Mr Chris Rushby, head of Waterstone's supply chain, made the point in a dignified statement about the company's decision to increase profit margins:

> Waterstone's makes a loss from stocking books from quite a large group
> of publishers. There is a lot of risk in stocking what's newly published
> because a lot of bad or unsuccessful books do get published.

The bookseller's dilemma could not be clearer. An enormous number of bad and unsuccessful books are published every year, and it is the book-sellers who are left with them at the end of the day.

The country's 'small publishers' – invariably unnamed – were up in arms on the spot. 'This is outrageous. They gave us virtually only a week's notice. It wasn't even discussed with us.' The truth of the matter is that it is Waterstone's and Dillons – now happily amalgamated – who are fighting the good fight to keep Britain literate and to cater for the intelligent minority, every bit as much as the small publishers, some of whose incompetence is amazing. Let us give credit where credit is due…

*   *   *

That was Bron's last word 'From the Pulpit'. In the March 2001 issue of the *Literary Review* Naim Attallah entered the pulpit for the first and only time himself to write:

I never imagined a time when I would, just for once, be taking Auberon Waugh's place in the pulpit. His death on 17 January is still hard to accept. He leaves a gap on the London literary scene that no one else can fill. At the *Literary Review*, we view his departure with special grief. A unique voice has fallen silent.

I have a clear memory of the day he came with Victoria Glendinning to talk to me about establishing the Academy Club in the basement at 51 Beak Street. A venue was badly needed, he said, where impoverished writers could congregate in relative peace and enjoy a drink and a snack at affordable prices. I also remember his delight when we managed to get a drinks licence, and the celebration that followed. He held impromptu court in the club, surrounded by a cluster of bright young women, and sparkled in response to their undivided attention.

His love of life was contagious. In his company one felt that material things and difficulties scarcely mattered and that the capacity to overcome the elements was the key to leading a full and fruitful existence. His health was precarious, ever since he lost a lung in an accident while doing his national service. Yet he always lived without concern for this hindrance. He drank and smoked and championed the drink and tobacco industries without the least regard for whatever harm their products

335

might inflict on the body. The argument for him was about freedom of personal choice. His old-time philosophy held that hard living enhanced the quality of life and that the desire for longevity could exact a price too high to be acceptable.

To pay proper tribute to Bron is a hard challenge because of his many facets. As a journalist and satirist he was without equal in his generation. His prose was by no means contrived and it had a universal appeal that went across political boundaries. His wit was never-fading in its capacity to amuse, enthral and scandalize. He was an entertainer who used words as an art form and utilized his ingenuity to the full in expressing any opinion. His *Private Eye* diaries remain a testimony to this matchless craftsmanship.

The news of Bron's death rallied both friends and foes to pay him tribute. Past quarrels and rancour were put aside to acknowledge the immense contribution he had made to the literary world. Even the *Sun* newspaper, so often the target of Bron's acerbic pen, was magnanimous in its leader column and showed genuine grief. The solitary exceptions occurred in the obituary notices in the *Guardian*. An unforgiving piece from Polly Toynbee was only to be expected, but it was Geoffrey Wheatcroft who made the unkindest cut of all when he claimed, in a burst of spite and pomposity, that the *Literary Review* 'was not so much bad as pointless' (despite himself being an occasional contributor). In the circumstances, Mr Wheatcroft merely showed himself up as a midget in comparison with the man he was writing about.

No one can talk about Bron today without mentioning the *Literary Review*. It became an integral part of his life. Bron was its inspiration and its driving force. He worked tirelessly to get additional backers for the magazine when my own resources became depleted after supporting it for over twenty years. We were united in our commitment to maintaining the magazine. Occasional tension is not unusual in a relationship between proprietor and editor, but during the years of Bron's editorship there was never a word said in anger on either side. On the contrary, we worked in perfect harmony, each recognizing and respecting the role of the other. Our friendship was the culmination of that relationship.

About three months ago, when a vacancy existed for a business manager, Bron came to me to enquire whether I would agree to having Robert Posner back. Robert had worked at the magazine many years before and had run the Academy Club. He was very popular, but his unorthodox style and free spirit caused ripples in some quarters. Nevertheless, Bron and I retained a soft spot for him and had toyed with the idea of his return. When the day finally came, Bron was so excited he practically skipped with joy as he left my office. Nothing could better describe the spirit of the man I knew.

Only days before he died he telephoned me, frail and depressed in the sense that he was bored. He was quite unused to inactivity. First he asked me how I was. He knew I was battling with some financial problems and endeavouring to marshal them in a positive, constructive way. He wanted reassurance that I was coping. It was typical of him to think first of others when so very ill himself. He ended the conversation by saying I should feel free to dispense with his services if that would help. I almost wept on the phone as I retorted that the suggestion amounted to sacrilege and would never be entertained, that we loved him dearly and awaited his recovery and return to the fold. I had been aware for some time that Bron's health was failing, but refused to accept it, hiding the knowledge deep inside. I went on hoping for some miraculous recovery to set back the clock and reinstate him in all his physical and intellectual vigour.

The *Literary Review* is in good hands under the editorship of Nancy Sladek. Her vast contribution to the magazine over the last few years makes her the obvious choice to continue Bron's legacy. However, given our present circumstances, we need the support and goodwill of all our friends and readers if we are to forge ahead with renewed confidence.

Afterword

MY FRIENDSHIP WITH BRON, DISARMING IN ITS INTENSITY, HAD for me no parallel. Writing about him is a compulsion bordering on an addiction because from it I derive much needed solace. His death at the relatively early age of sixty-one was totally unexpected and left me and his many hundreds of admirers bereft of a man who feared no one, whose wit was uniquely inventive and entertaining and the loss of whose genius is incalculable.

I hope that readers everywhere – past, present and future – will agree with me that Bron was a true master of the written word. With his provocative journalism he aroused the nation like no other. His inimitable style, his contrarian stance on most things and his mischievous humour will for ever be remembered with immeasurable affection. God bless him wherever he may be.

NAIM ATTALLAH

Acknowledgements

I am grateful to all those who have cooperated in helping to compile this book. Victoria Glendinning, Grey Gowrie and Richard Ingrams shared extremely helpful and insightful memories of Bron; Neil Clark and Michael Bywater were delighted to contribute their articles on the formation of the Auberon Waugh Appreciation Society and the demise of the original Academy Club.

Special mention must be made of the invaluable assistance that Nancy Sladek and the staff at the *Literary Review* gave, letting us read through the back copies that Bron had edited, as we transcribed his 'From the Pulpit' editorials. The Arthur Ransome Society has been equally generous in allowing our use of copyright material. The London Library has been as splendid as ever.

Peter Ford has contributed an enormous amount by his careful reading, editing and in selecting material, especially from Bron's *Diaries*. His involvement over so many years with Quartet has always been considerable and was of great use when we selected extracts from my autobiography *Fulfilment & Betrayal*, published in 2007.

Finally I must thank Teresa Waugh, Bron's literary executor, who has been supportive and generous in her reaction to our efforts.

NAIM ATTALLAH